THE PSYCHOLOGY OF THEFT AND LOSS

Why do we steal?

This question has confounded everyone from parents to judges, teachers to psychologists, economists to more than a few moral thinkers. Stealing can be a result of deprivation, of envy or of a desire for power and influence. An act of theft can also bring forth someone's hidden traits—paradoxically proving beneficial to their personal development.

Robert Tyminski explores the many dimensions of stealing, and in particular how they relate to a subtle balance of loss versus gain that operates in all of us. Our natural aversion to loss can lead to extreme actions as a means to acquire what we may not be able to obtain through time, work or money. Tyminski uses the myth of Jason, Medea and the Golden Fleece to explore the dilemmas involved in such situations and to demonstrate the timelessness of theft as fundamentally human. *The Psychology of Theft and Loss* incorporates Jungian and psychoanalytic theories as well as more recent cognitive research findings to deepen our appreciation for the complexity of human motivations when it comes to stealing, culminating in consideration of the idea of a perpetually present "inner thief."

Combining case studies, Jungian theory and analysis of many different types of stealing including robbery, kidnapping, plagiarism and techno-theft, *The Psychology of Theft and Loss* is a fascinating study which will appeal to psychoanalysts, psychologists, psychiatrists, social workers, family therapists and students.

Robert Tyminski is a Clinical Professor in the Department of Psychiatry at the University of California at San Francisco. A Jungian analyst, he teaches in the analytic training program of the C. G. Jung Institute of San Francisco, where he is incoming president. He is a frequent contributor to clinical journals and has a private practice working with children, adolescents and adults.

THE PSYCHOLOGY OF THEFT AND LOSS

Stolen and Fleeced

Robert Tyminski

Routledge
Taylor & Francis Group
LONDON AND NEW YORK

First published 2014
by Routledge
27 Church Road, Hove, East Sussex, BN3 2FA

and by Routledge
711 Third Avenue, New York, NY 10017

Routledge is an imprint of the Taylor & Francis Group, an informa business

British Library Cataloguing in Publication Data
A catalogue record for this book is available from the British Library

Library of Congress Cataloging in Publication Data
Tyminski, Robert.
The psychology of theft and loss : stolen and fleeced / Robert Tyminski.
—First Edition.
pages cm
1. Theft. 2. Psychoanalysis. 3. Motivation (Psychology) I. Title.
BF173.T96 2014
364.16′2019—dc23 2014001040

ISBN: 978-0-415-83088-1 (hbk)
ISBN: 978-0-415-83089-8 (pbk)
ISBN: 978-1-315-77976-8 (ebk)

Typeset in Times New Roman
by Keystroke, Station Road, Codsall, Wolverhampton

CONTENTS

ABOUT THE AUTHOR

Robert Tyminski is a psychologist who practices in San Francisco, where he is an adult and child analyst member of the C. G. Jung Institute. He graduated from the University of California at San Francisco's Doctor of Mental Health program and also has a master's degree in business administration from the University of California at Berkeley, Haas School of Business. Previously, he worked as the executive director of the Oakes Children's Center for 14 years—a therapeutic day school for children and adolescents with emotional and autism spectrum disorders. Dr. Tyminski is currently a Clinical Professor in the Department of Psychiatry at the University of California at San Francisco. He also teaches in the analytic training program of the C. G. Jung Institute of San Francisco. He has published many clinical articles and book and film reviews in various professional journals such as the *Journal of Analytical Psychology*, *Jung Journal: Culture & Psyche*, *International Journal of Group Psychotherapy*, *International Journal of Jungian Studies*, and the *Journal of Child Psychotherapy*. Dr. Tyminski enjoys studying the application of myths to clinical practice as well as how to bridge different theoretical perspectives on clinical work. He grew up in upstate New York and later attended Haverford College in Pennsylvania for his undergraduate degree.

FOREWORD

Getting to Know Robert Tyminski

Mary Brady

Reading a thoughtful book gives one the sense of getting to know its author. Reading a book written by a valued friend and colleague allows the pleasure of revisiting the qualities one already appreciates in the author.

A few words about Robert Tyminski's background might orient the reader in entering this work. He studied Spanish, French, and German at Haverford during his college years, despite an equally strong orientation to science. Upon graduation, he accepted a fellowship to study art history in Germany. He had been reading Freud and Jung during his college and fellowship years and so left his fellowship after a year to attend medical school in Berlin. A valued mentor recommended the Doctor of Mental Health (DMH) program at the University of California at Berkeley and the University of California at San Francisco, and so after almost two years of medical school, he transferred continents to that program. The DMH program was quite psychoanalytic, so a good fit in that way, although Tyminski was also particularly influenced by a Jungian seminar on dream work. After completing his graduate degree, he was offered a position directing Oakes Children's Center in San Francisco. Oakes treats autistic spectrum disorders, early onset severe mental illness, and children suffering the aftereffects of deprivation, neglect, and abuse. While directing Oakes, Tyminski acquired an MBA from UC Berkeley—doubtless contributing to the fiscal solvency and survival of Oakes. Next, he became a Jungian analyst and is currently president-elect of the C. G. Jung Institute here in San Francisco. It would be something of an understatement to say that Tyminski has an unusual breadth of interest and acquired knowledge, from science to the humanities, from psychoanalysis to economics.

Several aspects of Robert Tyminski stood out to me as I read this book. First is his capacity to imaginatively inhabit both ancient and highly contemporary worlds. This strikes me as requiring a strong imagination, coupled with significant empathy. In this book, Tyminski brings to life the myth of Jason and the Golden Fleece and uses it to study stealing in its many forms, including shoplifting, bank robbery, and the theft (kidnapping) of a sibling. I was particularly struck, however, by the chapter titled "Techno-Theft," which includes a fascinating discussion of new realms of stealing related to social media and Internet technology. Tyminski discusses the tragic theft of privacy via webcam of the Rutgers University freshman Tyler Clementi by his roommate Dharun Ravi. He ties this discussion to elements of the myth of the Golden Fleece, including stealing out of the motivation for power, here to share secret knowledge with a group. Tyminski takes pains to acknowledge that his conjecture is just that, conjecture—as the motivations of Ravi are unknown. However, such conjecture strikes me as quite important as we confront the new and vexing problems presented by Internet technology and struggle to weave emotional meaning around this realm.

Tyminski's work with children is connected to his capacity to inhabit ancient and highly contemporary worlds simultaneously. Working with children and adolescents particularly requires one to keep up with the current social moment. Knowing the mores of children and adolescents is essential to speaking their language and Tyminski is an expert at this. While attuned to the "now" of the child or adolescent, an analyst also needs the rich resources of the adult world to have something to offer the young. Tyminski is steeped in myth and fairy tale as well as history and economics. His roots in literature as well as in developmental theory are evident in many places in this book, for instance, in his inclusion of a Winnicottian view of the positive meanings of stealing in his discussion of a severely disturbed child's ("Kyle," see Chapter 5) driven theft of makeup from his teachers. Tyminski views this theft through a Winnicottian lens of a child robbed of the interplay between baby and mother, allowing for the development of transitional phenomena. Tyminski sensitively considers Winnicott's view of thieving as a signal of hope that someone in the environment will respond to the deprivation conveyed in the theft. In this case, experiences Kyle needed had been stolen from him and he was communicating this lack in a symptomatic action. Tyminski contrasts stealing that communicates neglect from sadistic stealing, although noting that deprivation can also be an underlying cause of sadistic stealing.

A third quality that will become evident to the reader is that while Tyminski is a Jungian analyst, he is also conversant with Freud, Klein, Bion, Winnicott, and other theorists of the psychoanalytic tradition. Too often, old and important disputes between Freud and Jung have filtered down to clinicians remaining in our own isolated theoretical corners. Tyminski is the opposite of this, integrating multiple theories in this work.

There are two final qualities I would like to mention. First is Tyminski's very high level of personal integrity with a leavening sympathy for the disturbed and even dishonest. I connect this balance with his many years spent heading a treatment center for disturbed children. Working with severely disturbed children certainly animates a sympathy for the confusions and hungers that lead children to steal. At the same time, these troubled and confused children sorely need the compass of emotional sensitivity and integrity. The second capacity

I was struck by is that of discussing complex cultural and economic issues in plain language.

The breadth of ideas included in this book speaks to the intellectual relevance of analytical ideas to the social discourse, as well as to illuminating our clinical work. Although I have not had as many clinical experiences with stealing as Tyminski has, I was aware throughout reading this book of the close alliance between stealing and lying. When presented in a clinical hour, a lie is a communication, albeit a complex one. In reading Tyminski's chapter "Some Instances of Stealing in the Consulting Room," I was reminded of Alessandra Lemma's[1] discussion of sadistic versus self-preservative lying. In the former the lie is intended to attack and triumph over the duped other, whereas in the latter the lie is used to create an attractive self that will elicit love and admiration from the object or to avoid an overpowering object. Tyminski's discussion of plagiarism in this book in relation to a desire to steal the limelight, demonstrates the coupling of lying and stealing within the adult world. Developmentally, both lying and stealing during adolescence can serve the purpose Winnicott describes of establishing a private area unknown to the former seemingly all-knowing objects. Tyminski discusses the extreme marriage of sadistic lying and stealing here in notorious examples such as Bernard Madoff's Ponzi scheme.

The rich variety of themes and subjects addressed in this book will allow the reader an imaginary excursion with a contemporary writer steeped in the classics and alive to the contemporary moment. Tyminski's view of an archetypal sort of thief alive within all of us, which can even be valued as providing one with "a good dose of shrewd cleverness, a healthy respect for selfishness, and an appreciation that thieving is everywhere" (p. 176, this volume) will also allow the reader an imaginative discourse with his or her self.

Note

1 A. Lemma, "The many faces of lying," *International Journal of Psychoanalysis*, 2005, vol. 86, pp. 737–53.

ACKNOWLEDGEMENTS

Writing this book has been something of a quest for me. Like Jason, I owe a debt of gratitude to my crew, without whose assistance I never would have reached this destination. I would like to thank my colleagues and friends John Beebe, Mary Brady, and Hope Selinger who have each encouraged my writing, generously read many rough drafts over the years, and supportively commented on them. Dyane Sherwood and Elaine Cooper both advised me years ago to keep writing and not get discouraged over dry patches, and I much appreciate that recommendation. Similar encouragement came from Dennis Turner and Philip Moore.

My study group companions Lauren Cunningham, Gordon Murray, and Susan Williams have watched me work with the themes of this myth through many iterations and graciously offered clarifying ideas and guidance when I got confused. LeeAnn Pickrell has been terrific as a copy-editor through multiple revisions. I have been privileged to work with many patients in my practice whose emotional integrity and resilience have been inspiring, and I have appreciated being a partner along their inner explorations. Early in my career, I was fortunate to have worked at the Oakes Children's Center, a special school and treatment program for children with various severe psychological and behavioral challenges; the staff—too numerous in over a decade to begin enumerating—engaged me intellectually and emotionally, and they taught me many treasured lessons about how a therapeutic community heals deep psychological wounds.

Permissions to use material in this book have been granted by Oxford University Press (for Richard Hunter's translation *Apollonius of Rhodes, Jason and the Golden Fleece*, Oxford, Oxford University Press, 1993); Princeton University Press (for the North American rights to *The Collected Works of C. G. Jung*); Routledge (for an article appearing in the *International Journal of Jungian Studies* that is part of Chapter 10, and for the UK rights to *The Collected Works of C. G. Jung*); University of Chicago Press (for Rex Warner's translation of *The Medea* in *Euripides I*, eds D. Grene and R. Lattimore, Chicago, University of Chicago Press, 1955); and the University of California Press (for Peter Green's translation of *The Argonautika: The Story of Jason and the Quest for the Golden Fleece [Apollonios Rhodios]*, Berkeley, University of California Press, 1997).

I am grateful to Routledge, its staff and reviewers for interest in this subject and the opportunity to bring it to a wider audience. All cases in this book have been disguised to protect patient confidentiality.

Many friends warmly supported me through many discussions about myth and psychology, and I have to extend my heartiest gratitude for their tolerance and good humor when I became single-minded. And last but not least—only like Medea in the approximate geography of his homeland—my partner through these years, Gady Heinic, has lifted my spirits countless times, indulged me in a few too many escapades such as trying to slip by Vatican guards to photograph an antique vase not on display, and never once doubted that I'd finish this project: "thank you" doesn't quite capture all of what having you on this journey has meant. But once more, in your language: תודה רבה.

1

ASPECTS OF THEFT

Why do we steal and take what does not belong to us? Theft ranges from a child's pilfering candy all the way to Ponzi schemes in the billions of dollars, such as the recent one associated with Bernie Madoff. The Madoff swindle cost investors over $17 billion in actual losses and ranks as the largest such crime in U.S. history.[1] Retail store theft amounted to almost $40 billion in 2010 or about 1.5 percent of total sales.[2] Two newer forms of stealing are identity theft, in which a person's assets are wiped out and his or her credit record is destroyed, typically as a result of Internet scams such as phishing,[3] and piracy of intellectual property, in which content is stolen for mass distribution at prices far below market value. When such crimes occur, they aggregate into huge financial losses that devour time and work, and lead to drawn-out involvement with the criminal justice system. These costs do not include the psychological pain inflicted on the victims in the form of stress, anxiety, and depression. It might be easy to attribute the bulk of this illegal activity to bad morals and sociopathy, along the lines of "there will always be rotten apples." That attitude clearly indicates that the crime of theft is something we are accustomed to and take for granted, seeing it as part of the human condition and believing it both a bit inevitable and beyond deeper comprehension. Frequently, superficial explanations suffice—for example, calling theft a crime of circumstance, of opportunity, of deprivation, or of greed. But what motivates people to steal, especially considering it is such a widespread activity and one that assumes various guises? Although there are appropriate legal and ethical responses to theft, when viewed psychologically, it is a tricky topic because theft often persists in the face of far better options. How many times do we hear about a theft that appears foolish, self-destructive, and completely unnecessary? How frequently is theft not a question of need?

When I was in training more than 25 years ago in the Department of Psychiatry at the University of California at San Francisco, I met a woman whom I will call Sally. Sally became my patient for a period of time, and she was what we might refer to as "a handful." She phoned me often and in desperately suicidal states of mind. She was single, in her late thirties, overweight, and looked much older than her stated age. She cried easily and was often overwhelmed with emotions. I learned to be careful what I asked her, because even a simple question like "what makes you think that?" could cause her to dissolve into sobbing. I remember telling my supervisor that I felt my well-intended questions hurt Sally as if she were being stung.

Sally came for therapy at the university clinic after being fired from her job when she was caught stealing office supplies. She admitted this was wrong and she deserved to be fired. Telling me about her life, she described making three suicide attempts in her late adolescence and during her early twenties. These involved swallowing sleeping pills on two occasions and slitting her wrists on the third. The oldest of four, Sally's childhood was full of disturbing events such as being flashed by an exhibitionist when she was only 6 years old. Her mother and father had an abusive relationship that Sally thought was caused by their religious differences because her mother was Catholic and her father Protestant. The "religious war," as she called it, played out for years, and the children were forced to attend two Sunday church services, one for each religious denomination.

Sally's father was an alcoholic, and he physically abused Sally and her siblings. He beat Sally, pushed her down stairs, and frequently slapped her face for "speaking out of turn." Sally felt, however, that the physical abuse was actually easier to take than her father's verbal abuse. He would call her "bitch," "lame ass," "dumb fuck," and later, when she started dating in her adolescence, "a whore." Her mother would not intervene and often stood by impassively as Sally's father lambasted her with vulgar insults. And when he hit their children, her mother would merely cry, leave the room, and do nothing to stop it.

During the year that I saw Sally, she often lied to me. At first, these were stories about why she might be late or canceled an appointment. Later, they were fabrications about jobs she had held or was applying for. I noticed her evident anxiety early on—she had a definite "tell," as a poker player might, when trying to deceive me. Her eyes would twitch, and she would rub them harshly, as if she were hoping to blot out that she or I would see through what she was trying to pull over on me. At these times, I just noted her anxiety and reflected to her that she seemed herself unsure about what she was telling me.

Eventually Sally said, "I lie all the time. It's just easier than the truth. Look at how shitty my life has been. Doesn't it make sense that I would lie about it?" I commented that there were various kinds of lies and that she was perhaps most worried about the ways she lied to herself. My unsympathetic remark made her angry (although, as a then relatively inexperienced therapist, I thought this comment reflected how one was supposed to call attention to a borderline patient's manipulations and evasions—Otto Kernberg's work was popular at that time[4]). Sally threatened to quit in reaction to what I had said. I replied that was her choice to make, but I also wondered, now that she had told me about her lying, if there might be an opportunity for us to think about what purposes the lying served.

Over many sessions after this exchange, Sally continued to be angry with me. She listed for me all her complaints about me: I was too young, too remote, too preppy in how I dressed, too soft spoken, and too "hard assed" about her being late, canceling and calling the clinic after hours and on weekends demanding that

I be paged to speak with her. After patiently hearing her out, I commented that she felt badly treated by me, so now she was also dishing out a bit of mistreatment to me. I said that I thought this pattern was a near constant problem for her in her relationships.

Surprisingly, she agreed. She said, "I can be harsh. Everyone tells me that. It's like I only know how to be two ways, either a softy like my mother or a hard ass like my father." It was at this point that Sally told me, "I have a secret to tell you," but she worried about what I might have to report to the police. I said that what she discussed was confidential, the exceptions being if she or someone else were in danger from her actions. She asked, "What if it's about a crime, but a crime that didn't involve anyone getting physically hurt or injured?" This made me feel unsure, and I could not help but wonder what sort of crime she had committed.

She did not immediately tell me. I suspected she noticed my uncertainty and held back as a result. Several weeks passed, and then one day Sally came in late for a session and stated, "The car ran out of gas, and I took the bus because I figured you'd never believe me about the car if I just didn't show up." I mentioned that she was anxious that I harbored doubts about her trustworthiness. She agreed and then said, "I haven't forgot about what I brought up a few weeks back. I'm just not sure I'm ready to tell you." I noted that now she was telling me that perhaps I did not feel trustworthy to her. She actually found this amusing and laughed.

Robbery

Sally soon told me about her crimes. She had worked at a bank for five years, was good with numbers, and eventually was promoted to branch manager. At this time, she was dating a man who belonged to a notorious motorcycle club that was known for criminality, drugs, and brutal tactics. Her boyfriend persuaded her it would be relatively easy in her current position to rob the bank. She realized that he was right because she was in charge of balancing the ledger at the end of the day, which was usually when any shortfalls were caught and reconciled.

On one particular Friday, she forged an entry of $X (a low four-figure amount). She removed an equal amount from one of the cash drawers. The forged entry appeared to be a cash transaction with a customer of the bank. She took the money home, saying she felt "exhilarated and scared shitless at the same time." The ledger report went to the head office of the bank where the discrepancy was discovered only weeks later. A bank officer came to Sally's branch to interview her and the cashier from whose drawer the missing amount apparently came. Sally told me she felt "rotten" watching how nervous her employee became. When she was interviewed, "I was cool and told him that I didn't know of the error until the head office phoned me." This explanation worked, and the bank closed its investigation without anyone being accused of wrongdoing. Sally said that her boyfriend was proud of her. They used the money to go on a trip, where they gambled much of it away.

I asked which bank she had worked at, and she told me it was the XYZ Bank, a bank that I was familiar with. We spent some time discussing her feelings about telling me of the robbery, and she said she was "ashamed" and anxious she could still be turned in. I thought to ask whether this was the only time she had stolen money from the bank. She blushed dramatically and said no.

A year after the first robbery, Sally's boyfriend convinced her that stealing from the bank was far too easy not to try it again. This time, she repeated the same steps as before, only shorting the cash drawer $Y (a low five-figure amount). That the money was missing in exactly the same way aroused much suspicion. The bank's head office called in the police, which they had not done after the earlier episode. The authorities now launched an investigation that included interviews with everyone at the branch. They questioned Sally on several different occasions and also wanted to question her boyfriend, but Sally lied and told them that he was away visiting relatives in Canada, thus providing him with an alibi. She said that her own anxiety grew. "I could really feel the heat," and she feared she would be arrested or lose her job. Neither happened, and the police finished their investigation with a report finding that the incident was unsolved and possibly due to bank error.

This is not yet the end of Sally's story, but before continuing, it might be helpful to look at her pattern of theft. *Diagnostically*, her behaviors fit within the broad category of an impulse disorder and are consistent with a borderline personality disorder. Along these lines, Sally demonstrated great fear of abandonment in her relationships, had significant difficulty in regulating her emotional responses, and was chronically suicidal, which included her history of attempted suicide on three occasions.[5] Less clear is whether she had an antisocial personality disorder because she was able for long periods not only to hold a job, but also to be involved in relationships, although these were often chaotic and abusive. In addition, Sally did show some signs of kleptomania, for example, her exhilaration at stealing and her inability to resist her boyfriend's urging her to steal when she herself did not need the money. The latter, however, could also be seen as her acting to carry out his bidding because she was afraid he would otherwise leave her.

Morally, Sally was aware that what she was doing was wrong. She indicated some regret, although perhaps not exactly guilt, when discussing these incidents. She also worried that the cashier from whose drawer she had stolen the money could be falsely implicated. She argued with her boyfriend that this was a major reason not to repeat the crime after the first theft. In terms of Lawrence Kohlberg's stages of moral development, Sally showed a preconventional level of moral reasoning, which was highly self-centered and based on appeasing her boyfriend.[6] She was not capable of acting in a more sophisticated realm of moral reasoning, which is consistent with the impairment to her psyche caused by her borderline personality structure. Her judgment was compromised by how justified she felt in placing her own needs before anything else when an opportunity arose.

Intrapsychically, Sally was acting out a primitive conflict that she faced within her family, in which the so-called "religious wars" coexisted side by side with her father's repeated abuse, both physical and verbal, and her mother's passivity. Confusingly, their parenting behaviors stood in stark contrast to their professed religious convictions. Sally found a disturbing way to avenge herself against the "authorities" by taking what did not belong to her. We could see this as an act of vengeance at her father's abuse. Donald Winnicott makes the interesting point that the antisocial tendency, which occurs typically among adolescents, is often geared to redressing a felt deprivation.[7] In other words, a person seeks to obtain from the environment something that he or she feels was not provided as a necessary part of his or her earlier development. In fact, Winnicott conceptualizes that there is some hope in this kind of acting out because the person is reaching out to call attention to the deprivation—however, his thinking is primarily about antisocial juvenile acts, not about adult behaviors. I will show in this book how, although the motivations for theft vary considerably, they often are driven by some aspect of snatching to compensate for an inability to tolerate multiple aspects of loss. This can be understood at a *personal*, a *social-economic*, and an *archetypal* or cultural level as well.

Returning to Sally, I asked again if she had anything else to tell me about stealing from the bank. I think, looking back, that intuitively I knew she did. She missed several appointments during this period of her treatment. She began to protest about the fee she was paying, which was quite low, basically nominal at the time. She showed up angry with me and said the hospital where I worked was "in the rip-off business, taking advantage of needy people who can't afford to pay but have to." She burst into tears when I said that she had been telling me a lot about how she felt ripped off and cheated within her family and also how she had later turned to ripping off the bank where she had worked.

Sally then told me that there was a final "heist," as she called it. Several months after the second theft, her boyfriend pleaded for her help, otherwise he would have to leave the country and say goodbye to her. He had amassed a gambling debt to a loan shark for many thousands of dollars. The loan shark had told him he could not carry "dead weight," and the implication was clear to Sally's boyfriend: pay or be killed. She told him she was sure now that she was being watched at the bank. The head office had posted additional security staff at her branch and just installed cameras for video surveillance behind the cashiers—new equipment at that time for her bank. Sally explained to her boyfriend that she could not short the cash drawer again, as she had previously done, without surely being caught.

They consequently hatched a plan to stage an armed robbery when Sally was working at the bank. She knew Thursday afternoon would be the optimal time because that was when excess cash was transported from the safe. The boyfriend recruited two of his shady friends to assist in the staging of the robbery. One was to drive the getaway car, and the other would back him up while he gave the cashier his demand note for money. Because of new surveillance equipment, they knew to wear disguises and chose balaclavas that covered their faces except for their eyes. They set a date for the "heist." They drove to the front of the bank in a stolen car that was missing its license plates. The boyfriend and his accomplice entered the bank, waved a gun, approached a cashier, and demanded all the money. The cashier, a young woman just out of school, got the money from her drawer and asked the other cashiers to do the same. They had been trained to act this way during a robbery.

The boyfriend, having been clued in by Sally, knew this was but a fraction of what would be at the bank that day. He demanded that the cashier remove the money from the vault. Frightened, she told him she did not have access, which was, in fact, true. He asked who did, and she told him only the branch manager did. At this point, Sally stepped forward and announced that the cashier was telling him the truth. They acted out a rehearsed exchange, the result of which was that Sally went to the vault, opened it, and gave him entry to the shelves where the money was waiting. The accomplice patrolled the lobby with a pistol in hand. Sally had intentionally failed to trigger the emergency police alarm at her desk before any of this occurred. She did so only after her boyfriend left the bank with sacks of money. He and his friends made what is known as a clean getaway.

When the police arrived, they took statements from all the employees, including Sally. When the detective pressed her about not using the alarm immediately, she lied that she thought she had, but that in the confusion perhaps she had not. She attempted to mislead them by pretending emotional duress. Needless to say, neither the police nor the bank's head office were convinced by her performance, as this was now the third robbery at Sally's branch. She was subjected to repeated police interviews, suspended from her job in the meantime, and even followed for a period of several weeks by a plainclothes policeman. They were never able to prove her involvement, but the bank terminated her employment under a cloud of suspicion.

Sally told me that they had stolen nearly $Z (a large five-figure amount). Her boyfriend hid the stolen money at a lake house that he shared with one of the accomplices. They put it in a "pickle barrel" because they thought no one would ever think to look there. She realized that any sudden outlays on her part would reignite the investigation, so she had to "lay low" for months until she and her boyfriend moved to another state. Although he paid off his gambling debt, what remained was split between the four of them. As she told me this, she remarked, "Hardly worth it. I lost a good job." She also noted that she experienced no exhilaration following this third robbery. She and her boyfriend eventually separated, and she relocated to the west coast to start over.

After telling me this third tale about theft, Sally became increasingly anxious to the point of panic. She had to visit the emergency department several times for perceived heartbeat irregularities and a fear that she was dying. She wrote me a short letter in which she announced she could not continue in therapy with me. She said this was not because of the cost, as she had earlier told me, but rather she wrote, "I am immobilized by anxiety on the days of our appointments.

I feel nauseous and fearful. Above all, I feel very guilty. I am sorry." She neither returned any of my calls, nor did she reply to two letters I sent her. She had gone into hiding once more.

Sally's last letter to me ended with a message that I think she had not been able to tell anyone, even herself, "I am sorry." Aside from her boyfriend, no one had ever heard her story about the thefts. In telling me about her stealing, I wondered if she had felt more in touch with lifelong losses. Perhaps that awareness panicked her into fearing for her survival. She was sorry she could not escape the lies and live with a truth about herself, a truth that she stole in order to feel loved. I think she might have felt with me that there was another way aside from lying, but it was too frightening to contemplate bearing what that might mean, especially about loss of so much—her family, her boyfriend, her work, her self-respect, and her dignity, which is an odd word to use in a therapeutic context, but which also fit to some degree. *Dignity* connotes both worthiness and standing.[8] I suspect Sally felt that her dignity was gone, not just diminished, but lost forever, which was too much for her to bear.

Anything but Loss: Cognitive and Emotional Subterfuge

My hope is to understand the complex motivations for theft within this context of avoiding loss. Daniel Kahneman and Amos Tversky introduced the idea of loss aversion to the fields of behavioral economics and decision-making.[9] According to their research over many years, people prefer to avoid a loss more than they prefer to make a gain. In other words, a loss of $100 produces more dissatisfaction than a gain of $100 produces satisfaction. This finding significantly impacts how people make choices, and it underscores that people do not consistently behave rationally when making economic decisions. This insight undercuts a fundamental concept of our capitalistic economy, namely that individuals will act rationally in their best interests when making financial choices, and, therefore, a marketplace is simply an aggregate economic entity that includes each of these rational decisions. An example of Kahnemann and Tversky's work might be what I would call the *garage sale dilemma.* The seller prices a used rug for sale at $10. She is perplexed that it does not sell, in part because she sees its value of $10 through a lens distorted by emotional responses she attaches to the rug. Perhaps her son took his first steps on this rug, or her prized cat slept on it.

But if the seller suddenly becomes a buyer and goes to a garage sale where she sees this rug for sale, minus any memories she imbues it with, she is willing to pay only $5 to acquire it. She views this same rug without adding to it a range of emotional implications. In other words, additional factors may be added into a price when selling—this is how a person's loss aversion operates at a feeling level. This phenomenon also explains why owners do not part with favored stocks—or other assets—that are sinking in value. There is an *imagined premium* to account for the experience of loss—in the garage sale example, $5 ($10 price minus the $5 the owner would pay for the rug if she were instead buying and had not already owned it). This personal experience of loss has little or nothing to do with the object's intrinsic "rational" economic value.

Loss aversion provides an interesting cognitive framework to understand why we have difficulty accepting loss emotionally. Freud might have been aware of this split when he wrote "Mourning and Melancholia," one of his seminal essays about the pain of loss that turns into a chronic state of depression or pathological mourning.[10] Freud believed that the loss of a loved one stirs an unconscious ambivalence that creates a conflict because we do not want to accept the darker side of our emotions toward the one who is gone. As a result, we assume many of the unfavorable criticisms ourselves that we might otherwise direct at who we have lost. We become weighted down by the burden of recriminations that we feel unconsciously toward the lost loved one, and bereavement can turn into depression. We have unconsciously identified with our lost one's failures and flaws, and we now upbraid ourselves for the same. Somehow, in this troubled state of mind, this tack seems easier than facing the complex anger and hatred that probably arises in any relationship of depth and long standing. Here, too, there is a similar principle of loss aversion at work: we can only hold onto the positive aspects of the lost one, while repressing the negative qualities that would bring our ambivalence to consciousness. Someone in the midst of this emotional dilemma is averse to recognizing any negative traits in the lost loved one that might then seem to intensify emotional pain. At such a point, we are averse to seeing all the qualities inherent in the loss.

Daniel was a man in his early forties who suddenly lost his partner Frank, who was 20 years older and died one night in bed of a heart attack. Daniel was a successful artist, and Frank had run a thriving antique business. Daniel described Frank as "brilliant—he could just keep it all in his head. He had a fantastic memory." Upon his death, Daniel had to close down Frank's business but could not find any written records of the antiques in the store that were being sold on consignment, a large part of Frank's business. Daniel searched through file cabinets, folders, and boxes, but to no avail. He realized, "Frank just kept it in his head. He knew who each piece belonged to and probably knew their phone number too."

When I pointed out how frustrating this situation was now for Daniel because there apparently were no written records, he rose to Frank's defense. He idealized Frank with a passion that had been absent in his previous descriptions when Frank was still alive. He told me how Frank was "a genius at business" and that Frank "was naturally gifted at keeping it all at the tip of his finger." This finger remark would be salient in our later work. After several months, Daniel was struggling with increased depression. He found fault with himself for not "being better at details. Something's wrong with my memory. Maybe I should get it tested. Could you refer me to a psychiatrist who does neurological assessments?" I mentioned that perhaps this worry had something to do with feelings he had about Frank, whom he had been telling me had such an outstanding memory and never wrote things down. I wondered if Daniel were comparing himself too unfavorably to Frank and maybe even putting Frank on a pedestal. Daniel admitted for the first time that he felt some irritation with Frank. Daniel had recently taken out an advertisement in a local paper that announced Frank's business was closing subsequent to his death. The text of the ad appealed to Frank's customers who might have items on consignment in the store to call in order that their pieces could be returned to them.

Daniel's dilemma in mourning Frank was that he could not yet see his anger at Frank—for leaving him and, importantly, for not paying attention to the details of his health. Frank had been negligent about both his medications for his high blood pressure and timely follow-up visits with his physician. In fact, Daniel discovered that Frank had missed his last scheduled medical appointment two weeks before his death. As we discussed this, I was able to bring Daniel's attention to what he was telling me—that Frank was not always mindful of details and seemed to forget something very important that perhaps could have made a big difference to them both. Daniel cried, saying, "I don't want to be angry at him. But there are moments lately when I am." I think this description of Daniel's struggle gets at the deep conflict that loss can create for any of us—that we do not want to "speak ill" of someone we loved so profoundly. It is as if that admonition "don't speak ill of the dead" is one way to cope with loss by creating a psychological split that imposes what seems like a lesser degree of suffering on the survivor. Yet, at the same time, it demonstrates our loss aversion to what we worry will bring greater emotional pain, namely a fuller emotional recognition of the person who is gone.

Eventually, Daniel came upon a metal box in the basement of the building where Frank had his business. Daniel said, "It was covered with dust, and the lock was rusty. I cut my finger opening it." Inside was a stack of receipts going back three years for various items in the store that Frank had accepted on consignment. Daniel became quite angry when telling me about his cut finger. He protested, "Why did he keep that box in the basement? Here I thought he had all that stuff memorized, and instead, he's got some secret rusty strongbox that . . . well, like he was hiding it in case he did realize he forgot something." Now, Daniel could admit that Frank did not have everything at the tip of a finger as he also took stock of how he had hurt his own finger in discovering the missing receipts.

The example of Daniel and Frank is provided here mainly to discuss how complicated our reactions to loss can be, although it also shows how loss relates to theft. Daniel felt "cheated" by Frank's death. He stated that Frank "was stolen away from me" by the neglectful circumstances related to Frank's health. In that regard, loss and theft can feel connected, although Daniel's situation shows this from the side of the victim, whereas Sally's crimes give us a view into the thieving actor. A premise of this book is that acts of theft frequently occur to forestall a fear of perceived loss. Stealing can be understood as a behavior intended to ward off a conscious sense of loss. In many cases, it appears that stealing is done to rectify a prior loss, but in most of those instances, theft actually serves to obliterate any awareness of that loss. Importantly, people who steal often have a history in which they have felt ripped off themselves—the victim later becomes the thief. The clinical examples in this book like the cases of Sally and Daniel will vary between those who steal and those who are stolen from.

Types of Theft

Variations of what motivates someone to steal are examined in the following chapters. Behind different types of theft we will often find an attempt to avoid consciousness of loss. First is theft that is undertaken purposely to right a wrong, a kind of stealing that aspires to make up for previous occasions of deprivation and can be infused with conscious self-justification. This type of theft ostensibly can assume a reparative, even ethical cloak of taking the high ground, so that the person convinces him- or herself it is not entirely self-serving. The consequences for the victims, however, are far-reaching and even sometimes traumatic because they are left to contend with a problem of stolen resources that have to be replaced. For this thief, most of what constituted the original deprivation remains unconscious and still gnaws away at him or her.

A second type of theft arises out of a desire to maintain a position of power, status, and high social position. Theft of this type is motivated by fear of a loss that would trigger feelings of shame and defeat. Stealing is thus carried out to circumvent any social limitations that the thief finds demeaning or degrading. An omnipotent belief of triumphing over others contributes to this form of theft. Such power-driven theft might re-enact an Oedipal drama, although in fantasy the outcome now results in vanquishing the parent who was once felt to be one's prime competitor. In a more typical Oedipus complex, a child has to recognize the limits of his or her power to influence and possess the desired parent. The rival parent cannot just be gotten rid of, any more than the desired parent can be stolen. This life lesson provides most of us with an introduction to coping with the anxieties of feeling excluded, accepting an inferior position, and respecting someone in greater authority. For some, however, this relational process does not go well, and problematic outcomes can engender a wish to destroy those in power while seizing their position. Limitations around status are frequently difficult to accept and tolerate. When the Oedipal complex goes awry, a child may feel enthralled by a fantasy of victory that would be far beyond his or her means, years, and capabilities—this fantasy then persisting into adolescence and adulthood. Theft can be an all-too-tempting option for achieving a desired end of power and triumph over others.

A third type of theft comes about through a belief in acquiring what one feels entitled to, although fortune might not have cooperated in providing those things. A sense of entitlement grows out of extreme envy of what another has in terms of resources, can do in terms of achievements, or represents in terms of luck and good fortune. Whatever is stolen is believed to be taken as part of a fantasy that the loss, which the victim suffers, will humiliate and weaken him or her. This form of stealing has a primarily destructive motivation that is fueled by feelings of envy and a fantasy of depleting the desired object. Envy is a primitive and potent emotion among people in all societies. When its relevance is denied as though it did not exist, and when the society in question simultaneously prides itself on unbridled social and economic competition, then the practical results can be devastating. Theft in this context can even appear to be socially condoned, especially when those in positions of power turn a blind eye to the wider implications of economic crime, which can include winning by any means and rewarding unethical behaviors. Entitlement thus can migrate from the personal realm into the wider social sphere as a problem for the whole society.

The fourth type of theft arises from a developmental reluctance to grow into adult responsibilities. These people might steal because they are struggling with growing into a more mature posture of adult relationships. Adolescents often steal because they can be impulsive around solving problems that require thought, delay, and planning. Foresight, personal judgment, and self-control are qualities that develop during adolescence. When someone runs into trouble here, difficulties with stealing—as well as substance abuse and other acting-out behaviors—can emerge. Sally's case example, discussed at the beginning of this chapter, most closely fits into this category, although the deprivation and abuse in her history were also factors that likely drove a feeling of self-justification, particularly with the first and second thefts she reported to me. A failure to complete certain adolescent tasks, however, can trap a person into a cycle of impulsive choices and an immature attitude about delaying gratification. Further, there can be a problem of not seeing oneself in the future as someone with independent, productive capabilities. We might speculate that this type of theft reflects an entrenched adolescent mindset that is now evident, for example, in a more openly opportunistic set of social values around piracy of film, music, and video content, identity theft, and plagiarism, all three of which are forms of theft related to—and made easier by—the Internet.

Is stealing sometimes in service of individuation? A fifth type of theft might be what we could call Promethean, in line with the myth about Prometheus who stole fire from the gods and gave it to humankind. At times a theft appears to advance a situation, rather than to derail it, for example, when it creates an opening for the discovery of unconscious feelings and when we are able to learn from an act of restitution. The mythical Promethean theft could also be thought of as a gift of consciousness, the stolen fire kindling a new development for humanity. For most psychotherapists and analysts, symptoms have unconscious meanings that potentially await a process of conscious integration. Sometimes an act of stealing reveals an unconscious dilemma that someone has to face in order to individuate. In a teleological way, perhaps something in a person's unconscious is hiding a vital piece from his or her conscious mind, and this missing piece has to be taken, even stolen, for further development to unfold.

This list is by no means complete. Undoubtedly, there are many other types of theft motivated by psychological and environmental considerations outside of what I have already outlined. For purposes of examining the psychology of stealing, I believe these five categories offer one way to delve into the complexity behind theft, without closing off other possibilities. One pivotal myth about stealing is the story of the Golden Fleece. This tale is at least 3,000 years old and represents a prime illustration of stealing a treasured item. By discussing this myth in some detail, readers will see many of the types of theft mentioned here within both the story of the quest for the Golden Fleece and its subsequent continuation in Euripides's *The Medea*. By studying this myth, we will see that Jason, the compromised hero, acts, in part, as an adolescent who has yet to mature into manhood and, in part, as an entitled young man who cannot recognize his limitations. His future wife, Medea, later murders her own children by Jason to avoid the shame of losing her status and to assert her own idea of justice in the wake of Jason's mistreatment, which she feels as a deprivation. Contained in their long story is another question: When does stealing brutally stop an individuation process?

This myth offers compelling representations for the many facets of theft. In a sense, it is a tale about a problem with treasure—whether gold, tulips, rare earth minerals, oil, high technology companies, or convoluted derivatives—a problem that has potential to shake our economy, underpin inequality, and affect millions of lives dramatically. Treasure creates an allure of easy success, arouses envy, gives its owner an aura of privilege, and makes for collateral suffering that will not rest until given its due. Treasure also can feed an illusion that loss is irrelevant because its possession endows the owner with special qualities that enhance his or her power. As such, treasure is desired in large part because it convincingly can make the reality of loss seem distant, not worthy of attention, and even impossible. We will see how what is treasured oftentimes is illusory, but not recognized as such, a circumstance that adds much to human suffering and anguish.

Organization of the Book

Although the book is not divided into sections, it progresses, each chapter building on the previous one, to provide a detailed examination of the types of theft and their consequences. Chapter 2 tells the story of Jason and the Argonauts as they go on their voyage to retrieve the Golden Fleece, which, in fact, they eventually steal. When they return to Greece, the story continues with the famed dramatic tale of Medea, the mother who kills her own two sons. Over the years, there have been many portrayals of these events, and I discuss some of the major ones to illustrate how the story has evolved and come to exist in its current form. Theft is a principal leitmotif throughout.

Chapter 3 provides an overview of the psychological theory that I rely on to understand the myth and its interpretations, including Jung's concept of archetypes that are universally expressed in myths, fables, folktales, and religious texts. Jung's work on archetypes spanned much of his professional life and reflects his interest in the deeper layers of the human unconscious mind. Freud's insights into power and generational conflict derived from his examination of the myth of King Oedipus. Such unconscious conflicts around power can propel us to steal when we are under their sway for resolution and unable to resist. In addition, Freud's contributions around mourning and the struggle to face (or not) our mortality are theoretically quite useful because they show the difficulties in accepting human loss and, therefore, why we often elect to avoid it. More recent research into cognitive aspects of loss aversion is useful to frame just how persistently we seek to avoid perceptions of loss, and this field provides another perspective on what is also a factor behind a temptation to steal.

I also discuss Winnicott's insights into what he terms "the antisocial tendency," which ties stealing to early emotional deprivation and neglect. Bion's theory, building on Klein, helps us to see envy as a destructive force, especially when someone is driven to steal out of a desire to possess material comforts to make up for missing parts of him- or herself. Envy figures prominently in many of the case examples. An overview of the "Medea complex" will show how stealing can turn lethal. Jung's important ideas about individuation include the necessity of facing one's shadow; these ideas are explored with attention to when stealing might reveal "Promethean" parallels, that is, something positive hiding in the shadow. The myth of Prometheus highlights when stealing can be positive.

Chapter 4 offers some scholarly viewpoints on the myth of the Golden Fleece. These run contrary to many widespread popular interpretations of it, for example, because they document a portrayal of Jason as less than a hero and more of a cad. Much of this same literature also shows Medea as someone who genuinely suffers more heroically than her husband. In general, the opinions of classics' scholars often run more favorably in Medea's direction. Within many of these viewpoints, Medea represents aspects of a degradation of the feminine at the hands of an egocentric masculine.

The clinical chapters (Chapters 5–10) cover a variety of cases that illustrate not only those who steal, but also those who are stolen from. Theft has many consequences, and I hope to show the long-lasting disturbance it can create in the psyche of those who have been taken from because they have to come to terms with the loss, which is often not what they want to do. The thieves, on the other hand, offer us insight into what motivates the types of theft identified here: righting a sense of wrong, taking something for power, feeling envious and entitled, seeking a quick adolescent fix, and trying to take something back from the unconscious. These chapters and their cases thematically address childhood stealing, kidnapping, shoplifting, maternal greediness, and spying. Spying is now made easier by webcams that transmit to a willing, voyeuristic audience scenes not intended to be shared. Stealing another's privacy has become a prevalent problem among adolescents and young adults because of their preoccupation with the Internet and text messaging on cell phones. Text messages are often saved and regarded as potential weapons to unveil secrets not intended for others. In a review of the Rutgers spying case, I discuss the implications for some of these impulsive behaviors in the contemporary age of Internet and cellphone connectivity.

Chapter 10 examines how stealing appears in our consulting rooms. This chapter is relevant for any practicing clinician with a depth-oriented perspective since stealing can imply difficulties in symbolizing, in relating to others with a give-and-take mutuality, and in accepting ambiguous outcomes and our human limitations. All of this is highly significant for understanding transference-countertransference relationships. Chapter 11 looks at how theft has become a major topic socially, culturally, and economically. Tales of theft have circulated in the media and aroused interest from the public and political domains, many because of the recent subprime mortgage debacle, which was associated with underlying economic fraud of mass proportions. Why is inequality tolerated in the face of evidence over decades that shows more unequal societies produce more economic and social disadvantages? Why might one group be permitted to "steal" resources on a societal scale, and what might this have to do with our social attitudes toward loss and decline? While attempting to steer clear of a simplistic explanation on this complicated subject, I hope to show that the myth of the Golden Fleece offers us insights into why theft persists and is more or less accepted throughout human history. In a way, this myth provides an archetypal explanation for the theft of desired treasure within human commerce—in other words, why a treasure problem is enduring and seemingly irresolvable.

As the reader approaches the following chapters, it would be helpful to bear in mind your own reaction to loss as it occurs in life. Personal losses in relationships weigh heavily within this framework. Mourning what one had but is gone—this is easier said than done. Difficulty in bidding someone goodbye is a topic that Shakespeare has made tragic and memorable for generations after him. Loss rests at the heart of our humanity, driving us to feelings of depression, loneliness, abandonment, and, sometimes, even madness. We are wired to attach to others, and when fate compels us to detach, then a momentous challenge arises, one it is natural to wish to avoid. Frequently, theft can seem to help with this. In moving into this material that attempts to link problems of loss with the problems of stealing, perhaps it might be helpful to recall these words from Macbeth, spoken by him after hearing of the queen's death:

> To-morrow, and to-morrow, and to-morrow,
> Creeps in this petty pace from day to day,
> To the last syllable of recorded time,
> And all our yesterdays have lighted fools
> The way to dusty death. Out, out, brief candle!
> Life's but a walking shadow, a poor player
> That struts and frets his hour upon the stage
> And then is heard no more.
> (*Macbeth*, Act V, Scene V, lines 20–27)[11]

Small wonder that the pressing awareness of such human pain—of mortality, loss, and inevitable death—would give pause to anyone with a wish to avoid it at all costs. Is this ultimately part of what brews deep beneath any act of stealing?

Notes

1 P. J. Henning, "A roadblock to recovering money for Madoff's victims," *New York Times*, Dealbook Section, April 10, 2012. Wikipedia notes that the fabricated gains, beyond the actual amount of principal that was lost, would bring the losses to more than $60 billion. Online, available HTTP: <http://en.wikipedia.org/wiki/Madoff_investment_scandal> (accessed April 12, 2012).

2 P. Kavilanz, "Thieves will cost you $423 at the mall this year," CNN Money, October 19, 2010. Online, available HTTP: <http://www.money.cnn.com> (accessed April 4, 2012).

3 Phishing involves the sending of fraudulent email communications in order to induce an unsuspecting recipient to provide bank and credit card account numbers as well as their corresponding passwords.

4 In addition to numerous scholarly articles, four of Kernberg's books from this period include *Borderline Conditions and Pathological Narcissism*, New York, Jason Aronson, 1975; *Object Relations Theory and Clinical Psychoanalysis*, New York, Jason Aronson, 1976; *Severe Personality Disorders: Psychotherapeutic Strategies*, New Haven, Yale University Press, 1984; and with Michael Selzer, Harold W. Koenigsberg, Arthur Carr, and Ann Appelbaum, *Psychodynamic Psychotherapy of Borderline Patients*, New York, Basic Books, 1989. During the 1980s, Kernberg was known for favoring a no-nonsense approach with patients who had a borderline personality disorder. He thought it important to address aggressive acts by the patient, particularly when they occurred in the therapeutic relationship.

5 *Diagnostic and Statistical Manual of Mental Disorders, 4th edition,* Washington, DC, American Psychiatric Association, 1994. Psychodynamically speaking, Sally was prone to splitting, projection, and unstable object relations. She frequently misunderstood others and perceived that they were persecuting her.

6 Lawrence Kohlberg, *Essays on Moral Development, Vol. I: The Philosophy of Moral Development*, San Francisco, Harper & Row, 1981. Kohlberg believed that moral development proceeds through stages: preconventional, conventional, and postconventional. The preconventional stage is governed by rules, their consequences, and who administers them—obedience and punishment being key to how one behaves. The conventional stage encompasses the desire to be seen in the right light by others and an orientation to maintaining social order—awareness of authority, duty, and approval provide an internal framework. The postconventional stage demonstrates self-reflection, critical thinking, and less attention to perceived authority—social values and internalized ideals hold sway over one's choices.

7 D. W. Winnicott, "The antisocial tendency," in C. Winnicott, R. Shepherd, and M. Davis (eds.) *Deprivation and Delinquency*, London and New York, Tavistock Publications, 1984. Originally published in 1956.

8 *Webster's Unabridged Dictionary*, New York, Random House, 1997. The definition includes not only self-respect, but also an appreciation of one's character and intrinsic worthiness. Further, it connotes one's relative standing in the social order. Loss of dignity thus is experienced as dehumanizing, equivalent to being outcast and unworthy of inclusion.

9 See two of Kahneman and Tversky's compilations for further elaboration of prospect theory and the faulty heuristics that distort rational choice: *Choices, Values, and*

Frames, Cambridge, Cambridge University Press, 2000; and with P. Slovic (ed.), *Judgment under Uncertainty: Heuristics and Biases*, Cambridge, Cambridge University Press, 1982. Amos Tversky died in 1996. Kahneman received the 2002 Nobel Prize for economics.

10 S. Freud, "Mourning and melancholia," *The Standard Edition of the Complete Psychological Works of Sigmund Freud, Volume XIV (1914–1916): On the History of the Psycho-Analytic Movement, Papers on Metapsychology and Other Works*, pp. 237–58, London, Hogarth Press, 1917.

11 W. Shakespeare, *Macbeth*, Pelican Shakespeare Edition, A. Harbage (ed.), New York, Penguin Books, 1956.

2

THE TALE OF THE GOLDEN FLEECE AND ITS AFTERMATH

The story of Jason and the Argonauts has been with Western civilization for at least 3,000 years.[1] The epic adventure begins with a voyage by a young man and his crew to obtain the one thing he believes will make his life golden and rich with power, status, wealth, and desire. The *Argonautika*, or more simply *Jason and the Argonauts*, unfolds against a background of treacherous family politics in a Greek kingdom called Iolkos. Its variations include an epic poetic form, chiefly known through Apollonios of Rhodes who wrote it in the third century BCE around the year 270.[2] Two excellent renditions that tell of the long voyage of the Argonauts are Peter Green's translation, *The Argonautika: The Story of Jason and the Quest for the Golden Fleece (Apollonios Rhodios)* and Richard Hunter's *Apollonius of Rhodes, Jason and the Golden Fleece*, the latter being written in prose rather than verse.[3] Rex Warner's translation of Euripides's *The Medea* has stood up quite well over time, and it provides the dramatic story of what happens when Jason and Medea return to the Greek mainland after having stolen the Golden Fleece.[4] In a way, these are companion pieces that complete a cycle about the travels of Jason, his meeting Medea, and their return to Greece.

Medea now lives in contemporary imagination mostly as a witch who murdered her own children, whereas Jason has enjoyed a run of popularity as a daring hero who adventured into dark seas and captured the trophy of a Golden Fleece. Many modern iterations of Jason's side of the myth have appeared in movies, cartoons, and children's books, for example, the illustrated children's book *Jason and the Golden Fleece* and the animated fantasy film *Jason and the Argonauts*.[5] In these, Jason is usually depicted in heroic fashion—strong, courageous, honorable, and loyal, all traits of the classic Greek hero—like Achilles and Odysseus. The original myth, however, casts Jason in a different light, and it is interesting to note how Jason and Medea have been split in the popular imagination.

This story of Jason, Medea, and the Golden Fleece is complicated, to say the least, and it may strike a reader as hard to follow. Epics are spanning tales, weaving in culture, geography, history, myth, and poetic references. Although many of these details might impress us today as tedious, they serve to develop the characters for the audience. A lengthy plot emerges to reveal a character's intentions, weaknesses, and motives in action. In both the *Argonautika* and

The Medea, Jason's foibles are important to understanding him as a flawed and less than traditional hero. He gets bailed out by others time and again. Repeating this pattern, therefore, creates a literary context for seeing him as weakened and dependent.

The Story

Jason's story is presaged by an internecine conflict around who rules the kingdom where the Fleece originated. Two royal children, Phrixos and Hellé, are in grave danger from their mad stepmother Ino, who is plotting to murder them. Their biological mother, Nephele, appeals to the god Hermes, who grants her a magical ram with a Golden Fleece that can both talk and fly. The ram carries the children from the kingdom of Iolkos, located in eastern Greece at the head of the Gulf of Pagasai and below Mount Pelion, far eastward across the Black Sea. Hellé falls off during the flight: The body of water known as the Hellespont is named for her. It is now called the Dardanelles. Her brother Phrixos, luckily, reaches the land of Aia at the easternmost part of the Black Sea, where he is given asylum by the powerful King Aietes. Phrixos then sacrifices the golden ram in tribute to the gods for saving him, hanging its Golden Fleece in a grove sacred to Ares, where it is guarded by a powerful serpent. Aia is believed to be the area at the mouth of the river Phasis where modern day Georgia is found.

Meanwhile, Phrixos's cousin Pelias, a devious schemer in the royal family, becomes king of Phrixos's native Iolkos. Pelias's own mother had tried unsuccessfully to murder him as a child. As a reader might infer, royal politics could be lethal. Later, he murdered his stepmother in the goddess Hera's sanctuary, a crime that crudely violated the goddess's altar. He thereby earned her vengeance, and she comes to figure prominently as Jason's divine supporter when he goes on his quest for the Fleece.

This violent family history highlights both the divisive political struggle for power within the family and the overt cruelty to which children can be exposed because they are perceived to be threats to one or another faction's legacy. These are families beholden to greed and power, families whose members have been profoundly wounded by maternal hatred and abandonment as well as paternal ruthlessness in service of retaining power. This unhappy pattern of abuse continues into the subsequent generation with Jason's behavior toward Medea. In a way, he is a captive of this fate well before his appearance on the dramatic stage.

Pelias is Jason's uncle. Fearing that he might mercilessly eliminate Jason because of his claim to the throne, Jason's parents give him to the centaur Chiron for care and upbringing.[6] As a young man, Jason sets out for his home, and while crossing a stream, he loses one of his sandals. An oracle had proclaimed that a one-sandaled man would one day come to Iolkos and kill Pelias. Someone spots Jason coming into the kingdom wearing one sandal and warns Pelias, who fears that the oracle's prediction has come true. He devises a scheme that will once more effectively exile Jason by sending him on a quest to retrieve the Golden Fleece. The implication is that if Jason succeeds, Pelias will abdicate in his favor. With this maneuver, Pelias believes he is assured of Jason's long, if not permanent, absence.

The Eastward Voyage

To undertake the voyage, a ship is built and named the *Argo* after its builder Argus. Jason assembles a team of heroes, many stronger and more talented than himself. At the outset, Herakles is part of the crew, as are Orpheus, Mopsos (a seer, or prophet, who can interpret the future through sightings of birds), Kastor, and Polydeukes. In all, Apollonios lists more than 50 Argonauts at the beginning of the voyage. Their first stop is the island of Lemnos in the Aegean Sea, which is ruled by a woman named Hypsipyle. The island is inhabited only by women. According to Apollonios, the women all slayed their husbands for infidelity with Thracian women. The sole survivor was Hypsipyle's father Thoas, whom she saved and cast adrift at sea. The Lemnian women do not reveal the truth about their husbands because they hope now to persuade the Argonauts to stay with them, in large part to procreate. Herakles reproachfully scolds the Argonauts for their dalliance on Lemnos and faults Jason for consorting with Hypsipyle. He even suggests they leave without him. Thus, at the very start, Herakles has formed a negative opinion of Jason.

The men leave the island together, although Herakles's judgment points out Jason's relative weakness compared with the others, as though he lacks will and self-control—two necessary heroic virtues. The Argonauts make a short stop on the island of Samothrace to learn "secret rites" that will fortify them for their further journey and perhaps also to atone for their indulgence on Lemnos. They sail through the Hellespont (Dardanelles) and into the Propontis (Sea of Marmara). Here, they make three stops. The first is on an island actually joined to the mainland by an isthmus and inhabited by a people called Doliones, who are ruled by Kyzikos. The Argonauts fight off native monsters, feast in celebration with the Doliones, and then cast off into adverse weather. Under dark of night, however, the wind blows them back into the harbor they had just left. In a case of mistaken identity, the Doliones think they are raiders and attack. During the confusion, the Argonauts kill many of the locals, including the king. At dawn, this awful mistake is revealed and the king's wife kills herself in despair. After 12 days of stormy weather, Mopsos interprets an omen that Jason must make a sacrifice to Rhea, the wife of Cronos and a great earth goddess who bore many of the other gods in the Greek pantheon. Only then do the storms end, permitting them to leave.

They sail next to Kios, where they stop and befriend the Mysians who live there. During a local celebration, Herakles ventures into a forest to find a tree suitable for making himself a new oar. Hylas, Herakles's companion, whom Herakles took when he was but a child, goes in search of a spring to fill a pitcher with water. A water nymph becomes infatuated with Hylas and grabs him as he reaches for water, drawing him into the current where he disappears. Polyphemos, one of the Argonauts, hears Hylas's cry and tells Herakles that his friend is missing. Hearing this news, Herakles, furious, sets out to find Hylas. With favorable winds blowing and no roll call, the Argonauts depart Kios. Only when underway, do they realize they have left Herakles behind. Serving as a dramatic device, this scene allows the voyage to continue without the presence of Herakles overshadowing the plot and, in turn, Jason. Ironically, his loyalty to Hylas affirms him as a hero in action, in contrast to Jason's apparent opportunism.

The remaining crew reaches the land of the Bebrykians, where the ruling king, Amykos, demands, like a bully, that the Argonauts choose someone to box him. Polydeukes consents to the match, with the unfortunate outcome that he kills the king. After yet another melée, the Argonauts leave and sail into the Bosporus where they meet Phineus, a blind prophet who is tormented by the Harpies and can never enjoy a meal without them snatching the food or fouling it.[7] Zeus punished Phineus because he could use his prophetic powers to foretell Zeus's will to men. The Argonauts assist Phineus when Zetes and Calais, the two Boreads who are sons of the North Wind, chase away the Harpies. They stop before killing the Harpies, however, because Iris appears to assure them that they will never bother Phineus again. Because of their help, Phineus foretells the Argonauts how they will know when to pass the Clashing Rocks that block the entrance into the Black Sea. He instructs them to let a dove fly ahead, and if it passes through alive, then this is the moment to push through. He also prophesizes their entire route along the southern shore of the Black Sea.

The Argonauts pass through the Clashing Rocks, called the Symplegades, when a dove flies through safely. (Athena also intervenes to push the ship through the passage.[8]) The crew visits the island of Thynias and then the land of the Mariandyni, where two important crewmembers die, a seer Idmon and the helmsman Tiphys. They finally land at Ares's island, where Phineus earlier advised them to stop. Here, they fend off attacking birds, after which the crew meets the four sons of Phrixos (the same character who flew east on the ram). Phrixos has recently died, but before dying, he asked his sons to return to his homeland so that they could collect his inheritance. They were shipwrecked on the island on their way to Greece.

Instead of continuing their journey, however, Phrixos's sons join purpose with the Argonauts and head to Kolchis. Aietes, king of Kolchis, is descended from Helios, the sun god. One of the sons warns that he is renowned as a ferocious and even sadistic king. The Argonauts' ship enters the estuary of the Phasis River at night, setting anchor, while the crew awaits the following dawn.

Kolchis

Apollonios begins Book 3 with a huddling of three goddesses—Hera, Athena, and Aphrodite. They conspire to enlist Aphrodite's son Eros to shoot an arrow at Medea, an act that Hera claims will bewitch Medea to then become infatuated

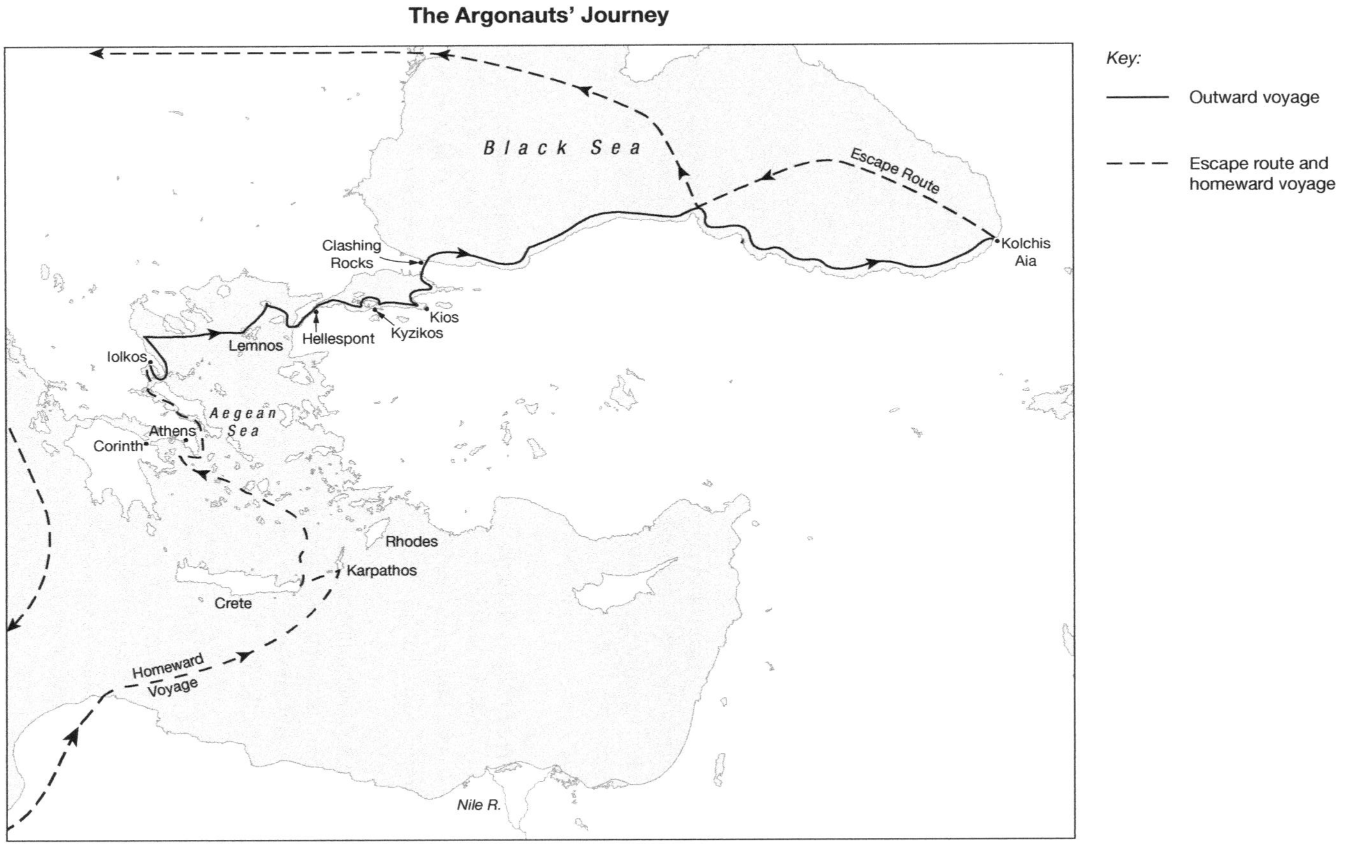

Figure 2.1 Lines show the Argo's departure from Iolkos and travel eastward to Kolchis, as well as the last part of the homeward voyage from Libya to Greece. The cities of Corinth and Athens are indicated because they are important to the subsequent story of Jason and Medea.

with Jason against her own will.[9] Hera supports Jason because he helped her once cross a river when she was disguised as an old woman, and she is Pelias's enemy because he defiled her sanctuary when he murdered his stepmother there. Medea, a priestess of Hekaté,[10] is skilled in the use of drugs and potions, which will later prove helpful to Jason.

Jason meets Aietes, but Argos, one of Phrixos's four sons and Aietes's grandson through his daughter Chalkiope, steps forward to make the Argonauts' case to the king. Aietes does not respond kindly, threatening to commit mayhem. Jason sweet talks him, however, and the king offers what he thinks will be an impossible task for Jason, namely to yoke two fire-breathing bulls and plough Ares's field while scattering serpent's teeth that immediately sprout into spear-wielding earth-warriors. If Jason can complete this contest, then he can claim the Fleece and return with it to Iolkos. Jason accepts the challenge. This interaction shows Jason's gift of persuasion, at least in mollifying Aietes and seeming to obtain a path to the Fleece. Persuasion is not considered a heroic attribute, but it is how Jason achieves so much in this story.

Many of his crew worry whether Jason will survive such a task. Argos suggests that Jason approach Medea, Aietes's daughter and Argos's aunt. "There's a girl . . . skilled in drug-magic . . . If we could but win her, I think there'd be no panic about your defeat in the contest."[11] Recruiting Medea proves easier than they expected because Eros has bewitched her with a love arrow so she is already infatuated with Jason. Chalkiope, Medea's sister and Argos's mother, also implores her to help Jason. Medea has little choice but to consent after a restless night interrupted by a nightmare in which she believes Jason wants to complete her father's challenge, not to obtain the Fleece but because he is in love with her. She, however, is the one who performs the daring tasks, and she then chooses to go away with Jason. Her parents cry out in grief, and she awakens.

> Often her heart fluttered wildly in her breast. As when a sunbeam which is reflected out of water that has just been poured into a bowl or a bucket, dances inside a house and darts this way and that as it is shaken in the rapid swirl, so did the young girl's heart quiver in her breast.[12]

Medea's vulnerability is acute.

Medea makes Jason a special potion, which she gives him to apply to his body to make him invincible for one day. She tells Jason to remember her when he has left, especially that her help was what enabled him to succeed. Jason flatters her by saying she will be treated like a goddess and that the two of them will eventually get married out of their eternal love for each other.

When he appears for the contest after using Medea's potion, Jason is beautiful to behold, resembling both Ares, the god of war, and Apollo, a sun god and the god of music and prophecy. Jason yokes the bulls and slays the earth-warriors thanks to Medea's drugs. Aietes does not relent, however, and he retreats to the palace to plot how to get rid of the foreigners. Stirred by Hera's influence, Medea goes that night to the river where Jason's ship is anchored to warn him and ask for sanctuary because she is frightened. Jason agrees to take her with him, and further promises to make her his bride—but he still needs his real trophy. They go to the grove where the Fleece is guarded by a huge serpent. Medea gives it a sleeping potion so Jason can reach into the oak tree and *steal the Fleece.* They return to the boat and cast off as dawn breaks. Twice already, Medea's ability to concoct drugs has aided Jason.[13]

Back to Iolkos

The fugitives are pursued by Medea's brother Apsyrtos, who commands Aietes's army. He eventually traps Jason's ship. In Apollonios's telling, Medea worries that Jason will turn her over to Apsyrtos, angrily demanding, "Have you no regard for all the speeches you made when necessity pressed you so hard?" (p. 160, lines 357–58). And in a foreshadowing of what awaits them in their future together, she says, "It's not long you'll be mocking me, not long you'll be left in peace, for all your sworn covenants" (p. 161, lines 389–90).[14] Thus, they plan together to lure Apsyrtos to a meeting for their supposed surrender. Jason brutally stabs him, however, and as Apsyrtos lies betrayed and dying, he splatters his blood on Medea's clothes.[15]

Zeus curses them for this crime, proclaims that they must absolve themselves through a cleansing ritual with the sorceress Kirké, Aietes's sister and Medea's aunt, and guarantees that they will endure much hardship before their return to Greece.[16] As a result, Jason and Medea, along with his crew, begin a lengthy, dream-like voyage home. They later encounter Kirké, who leads them through a ceremony to expiate their horrible crime, although she cannot conceal her disgust at what they have done in murdering Medea's brother.

On the island Drépané, known today as Corfu, Aietes's army catches up with them again, and King Alkinoos is inclined to the honorable remedy, which is to return Medea to her father, as she was a maiden. The only exception would be if she became someone's wife. Jason and Medea's wedding then takes place, the marriage bed being made up with the Golden Fleece. The Kolchians abandon their pursuit because now Jason has a claim to Medea. Unfortunately for Jason and Medea, they do not reach the near Greek mainland so easily, because Zeus's wrath is still against them. They are blown off course to North Africa, where they journey into the Libyan Desert for 12 days until they reach Lake Triton, also known as Lake Tritonis.

Once more at sea, the Argonauts steer northward toward the island of Crete. In their final adventure, they confront the bronze man Talos, who throws rocks at approaching strangers to protect the island in his role as its guardian.[17] Medea fells him by bewitching him so he cannot see. When Talos stumbles in confusion, he grazes a sharp rock that cuts him at his vulnerable spot, a vein on his ankle, and he dies. They rest overnight and then sail for an island near Athens. From there, they have an uneventful journey to Iolkos. Apollonios's version of this story ends on the beach from where the *Argo* initially launched. Jason and Medea have finally returned from a long voyage after many harrowing escapes.

In a subsequent tale, Medea deceptively arranges for Pelias's death at the hands of his own daughters. In one commonly accepted version of events, Medea rejuvenates a ram by cutting it up and putting it in a cauldron from which it emerges alive and younger. This demonstration persuades Pelias's naïve daughters to attempt it with him, and, of course, the result is disastrous. Several Attic figure vases depict just these scenes of Pelias's death.[18] Instead of resulting in Jason's elevation to the throne, this act leads to their banishment from the kingdom, at least according to Apollodoros.[19] Destructiveness and betrayal seem to characterize this calamitous couple wherever their fate leads them.

Corinth

There exist differing versions of how Medea came to Corinth and why her children were killed. In one version (1), she accidentally kills her children while trying to immortalize them; in a second (2), she intentionally kills them; and in a third (3), the Corinthians instead kill them.[20] Sarah Johnston believes that Medea was a goddess revered for a time in Corinth but then displaced historically by the goddess Hera. In that process, Medea subsequently took on demonic qualities against which Hera protected her own worshippers. As a result of this mythic and cult evolution, Medea changed from being someone who unsuccessfully sought immortality for her children—but they died, perhaps, before reaching maturity—to someone who deliberately murdered them, becoming, in Johnston's words, a "reproductive demon." This accounts for the shift from version (1) to version (2). In version (3), the Corinthians themselves kill Medea's children, and they seek to cover up their crime by spreading a vicious rumor that Medea did the terrible deed before fleeing their city.[21]

Johnston believes that a primarily negative belief about Medea emerged some time before Euripides wrote his drama, by which today Medea is best known. On the contrary, however, Timothy Gantz, author of *Early Greek Myth*, believes that Euripides invented the plot whereby Medea intentionally kills her two sons.[22] Euripides wrote his play *The Medea* in the fifth century, about 431 BCE. Richard Lattimore calls Euripides "a realist,"[23] who "believed in a world he disliked. His gods represent this world."[24] In the play, Jason and Medea are foreign exiles who bring no particular status or power with them to Corinth, so Jason decides he will marry the king's daughter in order to secure a better position. This, of course, means casting aside Medea, the barbarian princess from the east, who represents a kind of primal otherness to the Greek mind.

Creon is the king of Corinth, and his available daughter Glauce (sometimes called Creusa) is to become Jason's new bride. At the beginning of Euripides's play, Medea's nurse comments, "Love is diseased. / For, deserting his own children and my mistress, / Jason has taken a royal wife to his bed, / the daughter of the ruler of this land, Creon. / And poor Medea is slighted . . . ."[25] Jason acts like a roué, a scoundrel, who abandons an indispensable woman who saved his hide many times. Medea, on the other hand, is something of a victim at the outset of the play. Her demeanor changes over the course of the play, and scholars have debated whether Medea becomes heroic and bears great suffering, although she, in fact, murders her children to avenge herself.

Later, reflecting on her lonely plight, she protests, "I am deserted, a refugee, thought nothing of / By my husband" (p. 67, lines 255–56). Creon informs her that she has to leave his kingdom because he suspects that she will do something dastardly to interrupt the impending wedding. Medea pleads with him to give her but a day to make preparations for her departure, and he relents, "Even now I know I am making a mistake" (p. 71, line 350). He is right to think so, because immediately after he leaves the stage, Medea says, "Do you think that I would ever have fawned on that man / Unless I had some end to gain or profit in it?" (p. 71, lines 368–69). Her initial intention is to kill the king, his daughter, and Jason in revenge for her humiliation. She speaks aloud, "Bitter I will make their marriage for them and mournful / Bitter the alliance and the driving me out of the land" (p. 72, lines 399–400).

Medea faults Jason for his infidelity and for breaking his commitment to her. She rages, "For this is my position—hated by my friends / At home, I have, in kindness to you, made enemies / Of others whom there was no need to have injured" (p. 75, lines 507–9). Medea reminds him of her loyalty and upbraids him for his caddishness. Here, she begins to invoke the heroic code, one central component of which is extreme loyalty to one's friends and allies. Showing poor character, Jason replies insultingly to Medea, "You wouldn't [consider his behavior bad] if the love question hadn't upset you" (p. 77, line 568). In other words, Jason merely believes Medea is creating a fuss because of a broken heart, which, to his mind, is not particularly relevant. But in this, he completely misunderstands her.

Next, Medea meets Aegeus, king of Athens, who appears as a visitor in a dramatic contrivance, because she needs an escape plan, and he will provide it. She describes her misery to him. He is sympathetic and agrees to give her sanctuary in Athens. In return, she promises to cure his childlessness, "The drugs I know can do this" (p. 83, line 718). Medea proposes that they swear an oath of allegiance, which now creates for her an opportunity to wreak havoc in Corinth. She hatches a new plan for revenge, one that does not involve killing Jason.

She will first give Glauce a wedding present of "a finely woven dress and a golden diadem" (p. 86, line 786). When Glauce puts these on, a poison will infect her and "she and all who touch the girl will die in agony" (p. 86, line 788). After this, Medea will kill her own children to "have ruined the whole of Jason's house" (p. 86, line 794). Once she completes this crime, she will escape to Athens, where Aegeus has promised her refuge.

As she ponders this scheme, she reveals her true motivation, which is, "Let no one think me a weak one, feeble-spirited, / A stay-at-home, but rather just the opposite, / One who can hurt my enemies and help my friends; / For the lives of such persons are most remembered" (p. 86, lines 807–10). This complex statement reveals that Medea believes herself to be acting out of her own understanding of heroism: loyalty to friends, revenge on enemies, and no tolerance for public humiliation. One could also add being immortalized through one's deeds. She feigns to Jason that she intends him no harm and has at last come to her senses. He falls for her deception, saying, "It is natural / For a woman to be wild with her husband when he / Goes in for secret love. But now your mind has turned / To better reasoning" (p. 90, lines 909–12). He is gullible to forget all that she has ruthlessly done for him in ways that crossed accepted conventions for behavior and honor—betraying her father, stealing the Fleece, conspiring to murder her brother, and bringing about Pelias's death. At this point in the play, Jason exits with their two sons carrying the poisoned gifts to deliver to Glauce.

Subsequently, Medea's "great monologue" occurs (pp. 94–96, lines 1021–80). It is a dramatic tour de force that classics scholars have analyzed for decades, if not centuries. Medea speaks here in front of her children, who return after having delivered the deadly gifts. Medea laments the pains of child bearing and raising them if she is to leave them, "what was the purpose?" (p. 94, line 1029). Her emotional state swings to empathy when she regards their smiles, "I cannot bear to do it" (p. 95, line 1044). She renounces her plan to murder them but then suddenly resents her softness: "what a weak woman / Even to admit to my mind these soft arguments" (p. 95, lines 1051–52).

She instructs the boys to go into the house (although it is unclear if they actually exit since there is no stage direction to indicate that). In turmoil, she rages toward new resolve, "This shall never be, that I should suffer my children / To be the prey of my enemies' insolence" [meaning if she left them to live with their father in Corinth] (p. 95, lines 1060–61). The children come to her, and she says ominously, "I wish you happiness, but not here in this world" (p. 95, line 1073). The children then exit. A messenger later enters, telling her that the princess and the king are both dead "by your poisons" (p. 97, line 1126). Medea asks to hear the gory details, and the messenger complies:

> The color of her face changed, and she staggered back,
> . . . The white foam breaking through her lips and her rolling
> The pupils of her eyes . . .
> . . . The wreath of gold that was resting around her head
> Let forth a fearful stream of all devouring fire,
> And the finely woven dress your children gave to her,
> Was fastening on the unhappy girl's fine flesh.
> . . . all on fire she ran. . . .
>
> (p. 99, lines 1168–90)

Desperately, Glauce tries to shake loose the diadem, but it adheres painfully to her head. She is at last consumed in fire, and when the king rushes to her, he is consumed as well, because he touches her, and is infected by the poison. No small wonder that Medea is best remembered as a witch.

At this point, Medea concludes that she has no choice but to complete her odious plan because, as she thinks about it, "Force every way will have it that they must die, and since / This must be so, then I, their mother, shall kill them" (p. 101, lines 1240–41). The staging is eerie because Medea goes into the house, and the audience only *hears* the children's cries and pleas from within. One of the brothers says simply, "We are lost" (p. 102, line 1274). Jason appears on stage in search of Medea and his sons, whom he hopes to save from the Corinthians' wrath now that their king is dead. The chorus informs him, "Your children are dead, and by their own mother's hand" (p. 103, line 1309).

Medea is not quite finished exacting her punishment on him. She appears now above the house in a chariot drawn by a dragon.[26] She has with her the bodies of her two dead sons. Jason curses her, "you woman most utterly loathed"; he calls her "an evil thing" and "a monster" (p. 104, lines 1323, 1331, 1342). She points out that he scorned her, mocked her as she sees it, and broke his word to her. She asks, "Is love so small a pain, do you think, for a woman?" (p. 106, line 1368). She implies that she bears great suffering for having killed her own children, whom, she tells him, she loved dearly.

Jason asks for their bodies so he can mourn them, but she refuses his request. She instead tells him that she will establish a "holy feast" in honor of Hera (p. 106, line 1382), a reference to a known cult of Hera.[27] She prophesizes that Jason will die when a piece of wood from his ship hits him on the head.[28] She offers him no shortage of spite. When he laments that he wishes he could kiss the children's lips, she replies, "Now you would speak to them, now you would kiss them. / Then you rejected them" (p. 107, lines 1401–2). In anguish, he cries to God that he will never have the chance to touch his sons' bodies before burying them.[29] The chorus has the last say: "What we thought / Is not confirmed and what we thought not god / Contrives. And so it happens in this story" (p. 108, lines 1417–19).

Gantz notes that in art "there is nothing at all on this story until after the date of Euripides's play, which clearly inspired vase painters."[30] Euripides had a profound, lasting influence on how the fatal love story of Jason and Medea concludes. Others would write about it, including Apuleius, Ovid, and Seneca. But the play by Euripides stands above those, because he describes the complexity of one woman's suffering and her determination to exact vengeance for it. Medea does travel on to Athens, where she stays with Aegeus and attempts to poison his new son Theseus, but that is another story all together.

Modern Interpretations of Medea

Christa Wolf's book *Medea: Stimmen* (1996/2008), translated as *Medea: A Modern Retelling*, presents us with another kind of Medea, one plagued by uncertainty, doubt, and anxiety.[31] In Wolf's telling, Medea is not a child murderer, nor does she come across as witchy. She is a healer, and she helps Creon's daughter Glauce, who appears to suffer from a form of epilepsy. This Medea is an outcast among the Corinthians, exiled from the palace, and even excluded among the Kolchian population that followed her and Jason to Corinth and settled there, albeit in poor circumstances. She helped Jason to steal the Golden Fleece in this story because she was angry that her father had killed her brother Apsyrtos just so he could retain his kingship, which he would have had to abdicate to his son. Other Kolchians then followed her into exile.

What characterizes Wolf's Medea is that she is envied, betrayed, and treated as an outsider. She is not predominantly rebellious, hate-filled, or particularly vengeful in this book. Instead, she becomes privy to Corinth's terrible secret and suffers as a result. Medea stumbles on a discovery that echoes why she came to Corinth—an unjust murder. Here, Medea stands for justice and life, rather than power and revenge. However, the background to her story is colored by deep resentments that develop between the native Corinthians and the refugee Kolchians.

Corinth's secret is the skeleton of the dead princess Iphinoe. The king had his men murder his daughter so he too could retain power. He lied to his people, telling them that his daughter was safely married to a young king far away. A cabal envelops Medea because she has learned the king's secret, and her enemies spread the rumor that she allegedly killed her brother Apsyrtos. When an earthquake occurs, and an outbreak of plague follows, Medea is blamed for these woes, becoming a scapegoat for all of it—a witch who brought misfortune on the kingdom. She is banished, but not before she is also accused of Glauce's death, although the latter commits suicide in Wolf's telling. Still worse comes when the Corinthians stone Medea's children to death. In their subsequent revisionist narrative of this crime, Medea is blamed for her children's deaths, so she will be forever known as a child murderer.

Wolf portrays Medea to a large extent as a victim of circumstances. Medea is helpless once she joins with Jason and flees her own father. The myth is turned on its head as Medea, according to Wolf, is merely scapegoated for the secrets she comes to know: how both Apsyrtos and Iphinoe died, in the name of kings who refused to yield their power. Because of this knowledge, she is falsely accused of the deaths of her own children, her own brother, and the princess Glauce. Medea is victimized and represents the archetypal outsider—foreign, female, and clever or capable—someone who the dominant culture cannot safely take in. As such, she expresses in Wolf's telling both pessimism and hopelessness about humanity's capacity to bridge differences, such as gender and culture, and to accept these more openly. Probably, Wolf's Medea mirrored something of Wolf's own experience as an author and intellectual in East Germany, one who ardently believed in socialism even after the fall of that country. Wolf had to witness the German Democratic Republic being dismantled and absorbed into a capitalist system that she opposed and found largely inhumane. A socialist ideal (i.e., the various murdered children in Wolf's book) died at the hands of a capitalist king, and the voices of opposition were helpless to stop these events.

Pier Paolo Pasolini's film *Medea* (1969) might strike a viewer unfamiliar with the mythical background as esoteric and difficult to comprehend.[32] The film is eerily dreamy and follows a loose plot that is unveiled with arresting imagery. It was shot in locations rich with an aura of ancient civilization—Anatolia in Turkey, in Syria, and Tuscany in Italy. Maria Callas is the star of the film, in the only role in which she does not sing, but she is soulfully beautiful and alluring as Medea.

Pasolini adapts the myth to suit his form of artistic expression that emphasizes the forces of nature, ritual, and sacrifice. The cinematography is nothing but expansive and gorgeous. The movie starts with Chiron, the centaur, speaking to Jason at various ages in his development: 5, about 13, and as a young man. These are significant psychological milestones that mirror the Oedipal period, puberty, and the bridge from late adolescence into early adulthood. Chiron tells Jason, "For an ancient man all myth and rituals are real experiences and part of his daily experience and his body." Thus, Pasolini, who may have identified with Chiron as narrator and shapeshifter, sets a stage in which myth and reality are not at all separate.

The scene shifts to Kolchis, where a young man is being prepared for sacrifice to the gods of the earth, sun, and weather, a harvest sacrifice to insure the next season's bounty. An atonal and jarring musical score conveys otherworldliness. The young man is killed, and his blood is used to wipe leaves, tree trunks, and shafts of wheat. Medea then speaks, "Give life to the seed and be reborn with the seed." This ritual, Pasolini's addition to the myth, incorporates mortal loss as fundamental to an exchange between humankind and nature, symbolizing a greater cycle that cannot be ignored without peril.

In a temple where the Golden Fleece is kept, Medea has a vision of Jason, decides to steal the Fleece, and give it to him; in Pasolini's version, Jason is let off the hook for the actual theft. Medea asks her brother Apsyrtos to help her steal the Fleece, and he actually takes it from its mount on the altar in the temple. They flee, and when Medea recognizes Jason from her vision of him, they join him and his men. The temple's acolytes discover the theft and report it to the king, Medea and Apsyrtos's father. The king and his men pursue the thieves.

Medea kills Apsyrtos, again deviating from the myth, because Pasolini portrays her as the agent driving the story. She scatters the body parts as they flee, and this sacrilege slows down Aietes and his men who stop to gather them. Medea, Jason, and his men reach their raft, barely escaping. Aietes takes Apsyrtos's remains back to his city where everyone is grief stricken. Medea is soon beside herself because nature no longer speaks to her. She wails, "Speak to me, Earth! Speak to me, Sun! I can no longer hear your voices." She represents an alienated soul, cut off from nature and from where she once was at home.

She and Jason make love during the journey back to Iolkos. They are not welcomed there. Pelias intones to Jason, "No king is obliged to keep his promises." Pelias's daughters meanwhile take off Medea's Kolchian garb and dress her in Greek attire, an act that symbolizes her loss of homeland. Chiron appears in a vision to Jason and warns him about Medea's spiritual alienation and that he should not take it lightly, because she is in crisis over all that she has lost.

The scene changes to Corinth, where it is apparent that Jason has now abandoned Medea in order to marry Glauce. In her rage and sorrow, however, Medea once more hears the sun speaking to her. This emboldens her as she proclaims, "The victory I shall have over my enemies will be splendid." It is as if, in being able to recontact her spiritual nature, she discovers a bloodthirsty force that demands satisfaction. She sets her plan in motion, and Pasolini offers a visionary foreshadowing of what will happen, although it plays out quite differently later in the film.

Creon banishes Medea but recognizes her great suffering. She replies, "Only he is guilty, my husband." Callas, in her portrayal of Medea, alternates between a diabolical depiction and a bittersweet victim whom no man could resist. The effect is unsettling to the viewer because these two sides of Medea seem to unite mostly in destruction. She again confronts Jason, who haughtily tells her, "I've given you far more than I've received." This callow response does fit the Jason known to us through Euripides, but here much of that background is missing. He forgives Medea for her having been so smitten with him. There follows a love scene, which again is Pasolini's addition and seems to communicate a supernatural connection between them that defies human understanding.

Medea calls her children, handing them her Kolchian dress to give Glauce as a wedding present. Glauce puts on the dress, and seeing her reflection in the mirror, she intuits Medea's former self and the many losses she has endured, a feeling that, for Glauce, is unbearable. She runs to the palace wall and then jumps to her death. Creon cannot face life without his daughter and so follows her in the act of suicide. Pasolini alters the plot to emphasize themes of loss and death that he seems to consider central to problems of alienation and estrangement from our true nature.

Finally, Medea kills her two sons in the saddest of ways. She bathes them, cuddles them, and puts them to bed before stabbing each of them while their tutor sings a melancholy dirge in the adjacent room. The following morning, Jason arrives enraged, but too late. Medea has set her quarters on fire. As the fire burns, she shouts, "Nothing is possible anymore." Like Wolf, Pasolini borrowed this myth and made it his own, although his focus on Medea is directed toward our loss of a primal connection to nature in its fundamental state as giver and taker. Faced with this dilemma of estrangement, Medea herself becomes a taker, robbing herself and others of any joy in life, because the destructive impulse is not offset by spiritual fulfillment. For Pasolini, the latter would seem to rest in nature and our respect for it.

Regardless of the teller, theft of various kinds permeates this long myth about Jason, Medea, and the Golden Fleece. At first glance, it appears that the major theft is the stealing of the Fleece. But in reviewing different aspects of the myth, many things are stolen both before and after the taking of the Fleece. A throne and birthright are taken. Parents are lost, and although this might not seem like theft, they are taken away from Jason, ostensibly for his protection, and later from Medea, under the spell of Eros. Even Herakles's companion Hylas is stolen from him by a nymph. And, of course, the final crime, although murder, is also theft—of parenthood, of a future generation, and of life.

Exploring this myth will provide a fuller understanding of the four types of stealing: righting a wrong, maintaining or grasping for power, taking something out of a sense of entitlement, and sidestepping the maturational leap from adolescence into adult responsibilities. A temptation to steal exists because we all struggle with experiences of loss and death, as both Wolf's and Pasolini's use of the myth shows. A wish to avoid loss frequently accompanies these four types of stealing, because sometimes the pain of losing something dear, itself all too human, is also all too fragilely borne by us. Theft can then surface as an easy way around that.

Notes

1 Peter Green comments in a footnote that the voyage was previously dated to 1264 BCE. (P. Green, trans., *The Argonautika: The Story of Jason and the Quest for the Golden Fleece [Apollonios Rhodios]*, Berkeley, University of California Press, 1997, p. 14, note 48). The Trojan War is believed to have occurred later than this. Tim Severin writes:

> It [the tale of Jason and the quest for the Fleece] predates even Homer's *Odyssey* and—for reasons I was to learn later—the Argonaut saga describes events that were supposed to have taken place in the later Bronze Age, in the thirteenth century BC.
>
> (T. Severnin, *The Jason Voyage: The Quest for the Golden Fleece*, London, Hutchinson, 1985, p. 21).

Later, Severin comments on evidence from Homer about a King Euneus, who was allegedly the son of Jason and Hypsipyle, that establishes a possible timeline for events:

> [T]his reference to King Euneus enables us to give a date to the quest for the Golden Fleece. If Euneus was king when Troy fell, then his father, Jason, must have visited Lemnos a generation earlier. Archaeologists have dated the fall of Troy variously, mostly between 1250 and 1200 BC, with many authorities preferring c. 1225 BC. Thus Jason's expedition in search of the Golden Fleece would have taken place some twenty to thirty years earlier, in the mid-thirteenth century BC.
>
> (p. 95)

Homer likely wrote the *Iliad* and *Odyssey* before 700 BCE. Michael Schmidt notes that these works survive in their current form from "between 750 and 700 BC" (p. 67). Pindar wrote his fourth *Pythian Ode* about the voyage of Jason and the Argonauts in 462 BCE (p. 323). (M. Schmidt, *The First Poets: Lives of the Ancient Greek Poets,* London, Weidenfeld & Nicolson, 2004). Euripides wrote *The Medea* in 431 BCE, after Pindar's ode but before Apollonios's epic. Timothy Gantz maintains that earliest known art showing the theme of the Argonauts dates from somewhere in the fifth to sixth centuries BCE, including a ship depicted in a carving on a colonnade at Delphi; a cup and a kylix [a shallow bowl] with drawings of the Boreads—the kylix showing them chasing the Harpies away from Phineus; and another kylix with the figure of Jason emerging from the mouth of a large snake with Athena nearby (T. Gantz, *Early Greek Myth*, vol. 1, Baltimore, Johns Hopkins University Press, 1993, especially pp. 344, 354–55, 359). A photograph of the Jason-Athena kylix appears in R. Tyminski, "Fleeced: a perspective from antiquity on contemporary addictions," *Jung Journal: Culture & Psyche*, 2009, vol. 3(3), p. 62.

2 Green notes one scholarly opinion dating the poem to about 270 BCE. Green, *The Argonautika*, p. 12. See Green for a thorough discussion of Apollonios's life and also why the dating of the writing of the *Argonautika* is tricky and uncertain.

3 R. Hunter, trans., *Apollonius of Rhodes, Jason and the Golden Fleece*, Oxford, Oxford University Press, 1993. Cited by permission of Oxford University Press. Others have also written about Jason, Medea, and the Golden Fleece, for instance, Pindar in an ode from the fifth century BCE and Valerius Flaccus in Latin verse from the first century CE. (G. S. Conway and R. Stoneman, trans., *Pindar: The Odes and Selected Fragments*, London, Orion Publishing Group, 1972/1997; and D. R. Slavitt, trans., *The Voyage of the Argo: The Argonautica of Gaius Valerius Flaccus*, Baltimore, MD, The Johns Hopkins University Press, 1999.) Important traces of this story and of Apollonios's interpretation appear in Virgil's *Aeneid*, which was written in the first century BCE (W. F. Jackson Knight, trans., *Virgil: The Aeneid*, London and New York, Penguin Books, 1956.) As a myth that was widely known and taught to the educated within the ancient world that circled the Mediterranean, various forms of this epic tragedy span at least six centuries.

4 R. Warner, trans., *The Medea* in *Euripides I*, eds D. Grene and R. Lattimore, Chicago, University of Chicago Press, 1955. Cited by permission of the University of Chicago Press.

5 J. Riordan (author) and J. Cockcroft (illustrator), *Jason and the Golden Fleece*, London, Frances Lincoln Children's Books, 2005. For a film version, see *Jason and the Argonauts*, screenplay by J. Read and B. Cross, directed by D. Chaffey, Columbia Pictures and Sony Pictures, 1963/1998. There is also another TV movie version released by Hallmark Entertainment in 2000.

6 Chiron also served as a foster parent to the young Achilles.

7 The Harpies were descended from an old sea god named Thaumas. They were bird-like creatures who were forever hungry and gave off a rotting stench. Their sister is Iris, goddess of the rainbow and a messenger of the gods.

8 Athena is an Olympian goddess, daughter of Zeus and Metis. She was born from Zeus's head, which had to be split open since he had swallowed his pregnant wife. Athena, known as the Roman goddess Minerva, is the goddess of wisdom. She was strongly allied with the Argonauts, assisting in the construction of the *Argo*, pushing the ship through the Clashing Rocks, and later persuading Aphrodite to have her son Eros bewitch Medea to fall in love with Jason.

9 Hera is the goddess of marriage and childbirth. In Roman mythology, she is known as Juno. She was born of Cronos and Rhea, Titans who were overthrown by Zeus. Hera is Zeus's sister and wife. She was frequently angry with him because of his numerous affairs and love liaisons.

10 Hekaté is a mystical, ancient goddess of witchcraft, crossroads, and graveyards, and, therefore, associated with the underworld. She has an uncertain origin.

11 Green, *The Argonautika*, p. 125, lines 477–80. Further quotations refer to Green's translation by page and line numbers in parentheses in the main text unless otherwise noted. Cited by permission of the University of California Press.

12 Hunter, *Apollonius of Rhodes*, p. 84. Hunter's translation differs from Green's in that the former is given in prose format, whereas the latter retains the epic poetic style. This metaphor illustrates both Apollonios's literary talent and his deft ability to move into a psychological realm that historically was innovative for his time.

13 Medea is frequently referred to as being skilled and expert with *pharmaka*, the Greek word for drugs.
14 Apollonios wrote after Euripides. Therefore, he would have known of the latter's play in which Medea kills her children by Jason. Apollonios conveys here the seeds of Medea's growing feelings of antagonism and vengeance.
15 Other accounts of his murder include one in which Apsyrtos is a small child, whom Jason and Medea cut into pieces as they flee. The body parts are scattered, an action that forces Aietes and his troops to stop in order to gather them for burial (Gantz, *Early Greek Myth*). The Pasolini film, discussed later in this chapter, shows a variation of this account when the script has Medea kill her adult brother and his body parts are subsequently strewn in order to force their pursuers to stop and retrieve them.
16 Zeus is the god of the sky, ruler and most powerful of the Olympians. He overthrew his father Cronos. The murder of Apsyrtos defiled a temple to Artemis.
17 Hephaestus, god of fire and a blacksmith, created Talos and gave him to Minos, the king of Crete.
18 Gantz, *Early Greek Myth,* pp. 366–67.
19 Ibid., p. 368. Apollodorus was an ancient historian and mythographer of somewhat uncertain lineage. He is not to be confused with Apollonios.
20 S. I. Johnston, 1997, "Corinthian Medea and the cult of Hera Akraia," in J. J. Clauss and S. I. Johnston (eds), *Medea: Essays on Medea in Myth, Literature, Philosophy, and Art,* Princeton, Princeton University Press, 1997, pp. 44–70.
21 Gantz, *Early Greek Myth,* p. 369.
22 Ibid.
23 R. Lattimore, 1955, "Introduction," in D. Grene and R. Lattimore (eds), *Euripides I*, Chicago, University of Chicago Press, 1955, p. v.
24 Ibid., p. 7.
25 Warner, *The Medea*, p. 59, lines 16–20. Hereafter, quotations from *The Medea* appear in parentheses in the text and refer to Warner's translation in *Euripides I.*
26 This dramatic device is a form of *deus ex machina.* It makes possible Medea's escape as well as the play's ending. The flying chariot may have been a gift from her grandfather Helios, the sun god, who was known to fly about the sky in a chariot.
27 Johnston, "Corinthian Medea and the cult of Hera Akraia."
28 Gantz, *Early Greek Myth.* Gantz confirms that two versions of Jason's death involve some part of a ship falling on him. Gantz also mentions another account in which Jason commits suicide.
29 The inference is that God is Zeus.
30 Gantz, *Early Greek Myth*, p. 371. Gantz's reference volumes on Greek myth cover the details of not only the content of various myths, but also their representations in various art forms.
31 C. Wolf, *Medea: Stimmen*, Frankfurt am Main, Suhrkamp Verlag, 1996/2008. Translated as *Medea: A Modern Retelling*, trans. John Cullen, London, Virago, 1998.
32 *Medea*, screenplay by P. P. Pasolini, directed by P. P. Pasolini, produced by San Marco, Rome, Les Films Number One, Paris, and Janus Film und Fernsehen, Frankfurt, 1969.

3

THEORETICAL CONSIDERATIONS

Why bother with a 3,000-year-old myth about stealing the Golden Fleece? In our postmodern era of deconstructing texts and their meanings, perhaps it might strike some as outdated or even quaint to attempt to put a myth at the center of an exploration about theft. We live during a time when technological advances truncate story telling—who writes letters anymore?—when the manic pace of daily existence now regularly twists any continuous narrative we try to formulate in our minds, and when the lust for satisfying material needs routinely thwarts for many, perhaps even for most of us, a longing to connect with deeper meanings inside ourselves. The great depth psychologists—Jung, Freud, Winnicott, Klein, and Bion to name a few of our luminaries—would likely agree that many answers to life's mysteries await discovery inside our psyches. If we, like many before us, reside in a relatively dystopian period when Pandora's box has seemingly opened untold miseries around us, then it is important to recall that on the edge of her box, and last to emerge, was hope.

Myth

Jung strongly believed that access to myths is central to our journeying inside:

> The man who thinks he can live without myth, or outside it, is an exception. He is like one uprooted, having no true link either with the past, or with the ancestral life which continues within him, or yet contemporary human society.[1]

For Jung, the mythic tradition and its reimagined forms continue, whether we choose to perceive them or not. He conceptualized that these myths arise from the collective unconscious, which is like an invisible, emergent, and representational organ of the psyche that houses archetypal processes. These myths are frequently evident in dreams. Jung notes, "The conclusion that the myth-makers thought in much the same way as we still think in dreams is almost self-evident."[2] Thus, dreams often portray archetypal images such as the old man, the shadow, the young girl, the crone, the witch-like woman, the hapless boy, and so forth.

Jung considered myths to be both natural and universal byproducts of the psyche:

> All the mythological processes of nature, such as summer and winter, the phases of the moon, the rainy seasons, and so forth, are in no sense allegories of these objective occurrences; rather they are symbolic expressions of the inner, unconscious drama of the psyche which becomes accessible to man's consciousness by way of projection—that is mirrored in the events of nature.[3]

What might Jung say today about our alienation from nature as well as our greater dependence on technology of all kinds? Would he, for example, hold that our endless preoccupation with the Internet is now fortified in large part because we project these dramatic themes onto it? To the end, Jung believed that myth and its enveloping humanity were inescapable aspects of how our psyche functions, not only internally but also externally, in interaction with our environment.

Jung writes about the Great Mother from many angles, including its destructive and terrorizing perspectives. He associates Medea with Hekaté, for whom Medea is a priestess:

> Hecate is a real spook-goddess of night and phantoms, a nightmare; she is sometimes shown riding a horse, and in Hesiod she is counted the patron goddess of riders. . . . She is the mother of all witchcraft and witches, the patron goddess of Medea, because the power of the Terrible Mother is irresistible, coming as it does from the unconscious.[4]

Jung denotes here that Medea represents a negative side of the maternal and that her darkness resides deep within the unconscious mind. His comment about her being "irresistible" sheds light on the endurance of Euripides's play through the centuries. Medea plumbs the depths of a destructive mother who belongs to a natural cycle of birth, growth, decay, death, and rebirth.

Somewhat later, in his last great opus *Mysterium Coniunctionis* (1963), Jung describes the forms in which the psyche expresses "conjunction," which can mean pairing together or forming a couple in order to create a new thing. This insight was ground-breaking in that he anticipated much of what has come to take a central position in psychoanalysis and psychotherapy—creating an imaginal space for a third possibility to emerge, in other words, the potential for creativity within a relationship. Without this transcending third alternative, we can become somewhat limited by either/or dualities that result in two-dimensional thinking, for instance, me and you, but not us. Short of cloning or parthenogenesis, union with another is how something is born and created. But not all unions are fruitful, and some are, in fact, downright destructive. As Jung comments, "The conjunction can therefore take more gruesome forms. . . ."[5]

This aspect is relevant for understanding the myth of Jason, Medea, and the Golden Fleece, since their union leaves much destruction in its wake.

Jung conceptualizes that often this third possibility can come from a dark, feminine aspect of the unconscious psyche, which he refers to as *prima materia*, an alchemical term meaning first matter. Jung writes about Medea in this regard:

> It is clear from these parallels that Maier was fully justified in giving the name Isis to the prima materia or feminine transformative substance. As Kerényi has brilliantly shown, using the example of Medea, there is in that myth a typical combination of various motifs: love, trickery, cruelty, motherliness, murder of relatives and children, magic, rejuvenation, and—gold. This same combination appears in Isis and in the prima materia and forms the core of the drama instigated by the mother-world, without which no union seems possible.[6]

Jung believed that to understand ourselves and to grow psychologically, we have to plunge to the depths of the unconscious to reach into this matter. The "gold" of this laborious process, the positive outcome, is not available without the pain of delving into this unconscious darkness. Jung thought that many myths illustrate this principle of transformation that happens only after facing the dark matter that we must relate to in order to change.

Mythical themes are typically represented through archetypal images and ideas. Jung describes this as follows:

> The collective unconscious—so far as we can say anything about it at all—appears to consist of mythological motifs or primordial images, for which reason the myths of all nations are its real exponents. In fact, the whole of mythology could be taken as a sort of projection of the collective unconscious. . . . We can therefore study the collective unconscious in two ways, either in mythology or in the analysis of an individual.[7]

Jung believed that archetypes are deeply embedded in the human psyche and function as generative processes in how we make meaning of our place in the world. Archetypes find their homes in the myths that are handed down through the ages. Their influences appear in analytic work through dreams, images, aspects of the transference-countertransference relationship, and fantasies. The myth of Jason, Medea, and the Golden Fleece presents an opportunity to unpack the archetypal dimensions of stealing and to see what commonalities exist between the myth and stealing as we encounter it today.

Jung comments on the Golden Fleece in one of his texts about alchemy. "The Golden Fleece is the coveted goal of the argosy, the perilous quest that is one of the numerous synonyms for attaining the unattainable."[8] He sees the Fleece as representing an archetype of a kind of idealism and even perfection, something that makes the Fleece appear too golden because it contradicts the power of reality on the one hand and of the unconscious on the other. Some archetypal interpretations might view the Fleece as the end of the journey in a positive way—the claiming of the gold as signifying the completion of an arduous process—but this is not always the case. Interpretation depends on how this process is engaged. When stealing corrupts our journey's course, then that metaphorical gold might be won by a reckless impulse from the unconscious that seizes hold of us. In such cases, a claim of having got the gold would, therefore, seem completely at odds with the pursuit of individuation.

It may be helpful to consider briefly the word *archetype* on its own because it can be a term associated with some confusion.[9] Jung considered it variously to apply to primordial images and ideas, but he later grounded it in instinctual actions that shape patterns of behavior.[10] At the end of his life, he remained partial to emphasizing the observable results of archetypes, especially in terms of myths.[11] Jung thought that archetypes are themselves "irrepresentable" and that we only get to see their byproducts in myths, images, stories, and so on.[12] Contemporary Jungian analysts have been trying to clear up the ambiguity with newer conceptions of what archetypes really are, for instance, "minimalist image schemes" and "emergent activity of the brain."[13] The main point is that an archetype is not a concrete thing like a rock. Rather, it is like the natural forces that form and shape the rock we can see and hold.

Loss and Limits

If Jung helps us place the universality of the myth about the Golden Fleece into a psychological context, then Freud helps us comprehend the pain represented through the actions of the myth's characters. Freud and Jung had a professional relationship and friendship that extended for the better part of the years 1906–13.[14] They were certainly familiar with one another's work, both clinically and theoretically. And both were intrigued by classical mythology, especially what it expressed about the human psyche. Freud would find much fertile ground for his thinking within the myth of King Oedipus, from which he derived his now familiar term Oedipal complex.

Freud saw the Oedipal complex as universal and part of every child's development. In the third of his *Three Essays on Sexuality* (1905), he writes:

> It has been justly said that the Oedipus complex is the nuclear complex of neuroses, and constitutes the essential part of their content. It represents the peak of infantile sexuality, which, through its after-effects, exercises a decisive influence on the sexuality of adults. Every new arrival on this planet is faced by the task of mastering the Oedipus complex; anyone who fails to do so falls a victim to neurosis.[15]

Grounded in an awareness of triangular relations, the Oedipal complex generates increased psychological valence for issues of competition, exclusion, and authority.

Freud first writes about the Oedipal complex in his *Interpretation of Dreams* (1900):

> This discovery is confirmed by a legend that has come down to us from classical antiquity: a legend whose profound and universal power to move can only be understood if the hypothesis I have put forward in regard to the psychology of children has an equal universal validity.[16]

In his theory, Freud views the Oedipal complex as a kind of developmental archetype affecting children's sexuality that holds powerfully into adulthood. The Oedipal drama unfolds within a family as a child's loss of innocence of a utopian world where wishes might come true, such as a wish to marry one parent and eliminate the other. Freud writes that the destiny of King Oedipus

> moves us only because it might have been ours—because the oracle laid the same curse upon us before our birth as upon him. It is the fate of all of us to direct our first sexual impulse towards our mother and our first hatred and our first murderous wish against our father. Our dreams convince us that that is so.[17]

Contemporary psychoanalytic understanding of the myth continues in a modified version that now emphasizes the separation of the generations instead of the purely sexual-developmental content. In other words, the child struggles to accept his or her place within the family as a child whose wishes are not routinely granted. Loss and disappointment usually infuse this childhood experience of recognizing limits.[18]

As in many Greek myths, in the myth of the Golden Fleece, an acceptance of limitations is a recurring family problem, and rivals are disposed of cruelly. Jason might be considered a young man who lives out an Oedipal drama when he seeks to defy and depose a cruel father-substitute in the character of Pelias. To do so, he must take something precious guarded by a dragon. Here, we might understand the Fleece to symbolize an aspect of the mother's body, even her forbidden genitals. Jason's desire for the Fleece then represents an incestuous wish toward a mother he barely knows because she abandoned him early in his life. Such lack of family knowledge is almost intrinsic to the Oedipal complex. We might recall that in the story of Oedipus, he too did not know who his mother really was when he took her for his wife. Overstepping and defiance shade an Oedipal drama. Medea also defies her father, and by stealing his treasured object, the Fleece, she tries to satisfy what could be regarded as her own infantile sexual impulses to gain her father's intimate love under the guise of another man. In her case, her actions might indicate a refusal to accept that her father will not yield to her so she resolves her conflict by replacing him with Jason (who now possesses father's "treasure" and is thus identified with him). In one sense, we might view her ensuing wrath toward Jason as deriving from her eventual disappointment over this choice—she gave up her father for him, and he never measured up, even with the treasure.

In the Oedipal drama as discussed here, there are limits to contend with and resolve. Under good enough circumstances, this emotionally painful process ends with a child's hope for the future secured by loving parents, whom he or she internalizes as nurturing and sustaining resources for the next years of development. A child's unfulfilled wishes thus become seeds of imaginative promise for his or her future. Where the sting of this deflation is too great, however, and not captured by parental love and guidance, then a child can feel great loss instead of an acceptable limit. That situation can create a predicament around relationships when winning and dominating might become necessary to circumvent any recognition of loss.[19] Indeed, a child dealing with this particular circumstance frequently resists what is felt to be loss of power, loss of status, loss of influence, and loss of control. In his or her mind, the generational boundary must be overthrown to avoid facing an experience of accepting what it means to be a child and not yet an adult. Although we would view both Jason and Medea as either late adolescents or very young adults, yet we can see their actions as representing some evocation of an earlier unresolved Oedipal drama around these very issues.

Loss Aversion

We all engage in psychological gymnastics to contain and minimize experiences of loss. Freud showed many reasons why we do this, from his theorizing about ambivalence when mourning to his conceptualizing a child's emotional work at accepting limitations. Relatively recently, the cognitive aspect of loss has become a discrete field of study within clinical psychology (for instance, the use of cognitive behavioral therapy to treat depression) and within behavioral economics. A wish to avoid loss permeates our everyday decision making when we face choices about purchases, selling, investments, salaries, and savings. The cognitive acrobatics that we sometimes and even frequently deploy in this endeavor have called into question the idea of rationality in economic decisions. Adam Smith's "invisible hand" of the marketplace is guided by self-interest that is allegedly rational to its core. That this is not so has come as a bit of a surprise to many of those espousing economic theories about individual choice.

Daniel Kahneman and Amos Tversky jointly studied this phenomenon for over 20 years in the late twentieth century. They devised many clever studies that demonstrated over and over that when faced with a possible loss, a person frequently makes an irrational choice that is not in his or her best interests economically. Instead, loss aversion guides how this decision gets made. Kahneman and Tversky came to view this occurrence through the lens of "losses loom larger than gains."[20] They note, "Because losses loom larger than gains, the decision maker will be biased in favor of retaining the status quo."[21] Richard Thaler later called an aspect of this the "endowment effect," in which people tend to not want to give up what they already possess or, as I suggested in Chapter 1, "the garage sale dilemma." This effect distorts market prices because the seller will want to charge more than a buyer is willing to pay, even when the seller and buyer are the same person! Kahneman and Tversky devised a graphic illustration of this problem in what they term *a value function*, which shows that even small losses result in a greater decline in value (or satisfaction) than equal gains.[22]

Two examples show how loss aversion actually works. In the first, years ago, a wine collector bought a bottle of Bordeaux for a price of $10. The wine has appreciated in value to $200 today, but the wine collector prefers to keep it rather than sell it at a wine auction for that current price. Interestingly, he would also not buy the same bottle of wine at its current price. In other words, the wine collector now wants much more (more than $200) to give up what he owns, than he would be willing to pay to acquire it at current market prices.[23] He somehow believes that the pain of losing this bottle of wine is not covered by its new market price. Ironically, the wine collector in this example is actually an economist.

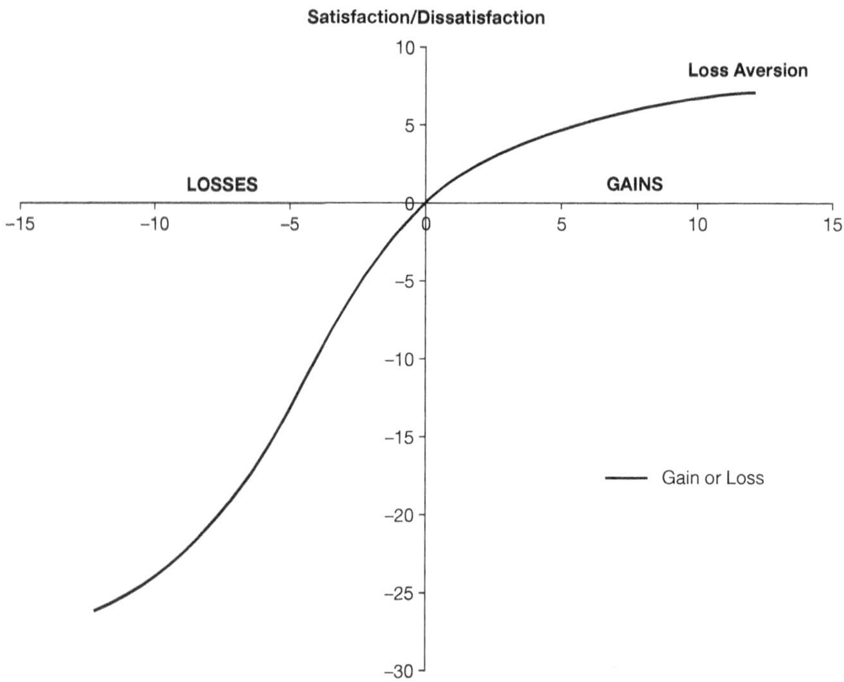

Figure 3.1 A value function looks approximately as shown here. Notice the curve is concave where there are gains (meaning less sensitivity to gains) and convex where there are losses (meaning greater sensitivity to losses). Adapted from D. Kahneman and A. Tversky, *Choices, Values, and Frames*, 2000.

A fair number of the studies on loss aversion involve college students, coffee mugs, pens, and candy bars. Trading and transactions are analyzed to see how prices are determined in ways that contradict a so-called rational model of market clearance. In one of the simplest experiments, a group of students is given a coffee mug that retails for about $5 (its price is known because the mug is sold in the university bookstore). These students have a choice to either keep the mug or sell it. Another group is presented with an option to have either the mug or a sum of money. Essentially, the first group consists of sellers and the second of buyers. In this experiment, the sellers want $7 or more to part with their mug, whereas the buyers would only pay $3 and change to acquire the mug.[24] This study demonstrates that merely owning the mug creates an irrational urge to part with it only for more money than it is even worth. The students in the first group are loss averse because they perceive giving up the mug as a loss. Other studies replicate this phenomenon, showing it to be true across a wide stretch of economic choices, transactions, and trades. Jack L. Knetsch shows that the initial entitlement—or ownership status—is stubbornly held, even in the face of a preference for something else.[25] Repeatedly, these authors demonstrate how losing hurts much more than the pleasure of gaining something of equal value.

How is loss aversion relevant to the myth of Jason, Medea, and the Golden Fleece? Recall that Jason sets out to obtain the Fleece because he seemingly intends to trade it for the kingship of Iolkos, where his uncle Pelias rules. Jason cannot face that he might have permanently lost this opportunity—that his uncle might never abdicate and that the journey for the Fleece is a ruse to send him off for good. He cheats to win the contest that Medea's father sets as a condition for turning over the Fleece, which Aietes clearly never wanted to do, thinking the contest would result in Jason's demise. Even when Jason wins, Aietes refuses to give up the Fleece, showing his own loss aversion. He represents an older generation in the guise of the king who will not go. Jason cannot accept this obstacle, so he transgresses—again with Medea's help—when he steals the Fleece. Yet back in Greece, he is still not able to trade it for what he wants.

I suggest that stealing is one way to irrationally act out loss aversion in a sort of unconscious trade or swap. Taking a desired object then seems to postpone the emotional work of dealing with the pain of loss. Morality aside—which is difficult with this topic because, of course, stealing raises necessary questions of ethics, moral code, and legality—it potentially alleviates recognition of not having what we want. Many times, loss is actually unconsciously displaced onto a stolen object, in other words, from a prior experience when something valued was lost and not emotionally integrated. Thus, the Fleece is polyvalent; it stands for a lost birthright (Jason and Medea), lost parents (Jason and Phrixos), and lost homeland (Phrixos and Medea), to name a few of its lost-related memes. Not coincidentally, Medea's later revenge on Jason seeks to inflict an enduring loss on him that he must live with and can never escape. That is the reason she does not kill him. Loss is salient throughout, as in many myths. The important research from behavioral economics on loss aversion demonstrates how pervasively this paradigm echoes through our psyches in trivial and not-so-trivial ways. Almost as a cognitive default, it appears we prefer to trick ourselves rather than face the true cost of losing or not having what we want.

Deprivation and Envy

To understand stealing, we also have to consider psychological experiences of deprivation and envy. Donald Winnicott writes eloquently about "the antisocial tendency," which he sees as a problem stemming from early deprivation.[26] He relates much of his clinical material to children and adolescents who appear antisocial, that is disruptive, antiauthoritarian, delinquent, thieving, and hostile. His insights are relevant for adults, however, when these behaviors persist, which frequently they do, having had their origins earlier in a person's life course. Winnicott makes clear that he is not speaking diagnostically because "the antisocial tendency may be found in a normal individual, or in one that is neurotic or psychotic."[27]

Key to his understanding of this idea is an assertion that the antisocial act contains an element of hope. Winnicott believed the disruptive behavior is an appeal to the wider environment for some corrective response that would rectify or address an earlier experience of deprivation. He found this act to be hopeful because the child or adolescent has not given up on finding someone to understand. In other words, he or she is still seeking a good enough object to help.

In regard to stealing, which he found central to the antisocial tendency, Winnicott is quite specific about how deprivation triggers later theft. "The child who steals is not looking for the object stolen but seeks the mother over whom he or she has rights."[28] This statement relates to Winnicott's theory that a child has to, in his or her mind and at a very young age, create the mother, who under good enough circumstances makes herself available to find and internalize. I think in our more modern understanding of families we might expand his idea to include the primary caretaker as potentially a father who is capable of deploying maternal care to an infant. This more inclusive approach has an advantage of addressing the many different types of families we work with and also not solely setting up a kind of maternal failure in a reified figure of the mother as a sole explanatory mechanism for when a child's development goes awry.

As so often in reading Winnicott, his meaning is poetic and requires a reader to associate in order to unpack the fullness of what he is saying. The baby's creating a mother is a primal attempt at opening an inner world of object relations and creativity. We might also think that this attempt involves a kind of theft in taking a mother who the baby feels a right to possess. Perhaps this could be conceptualized as the first and most innocent act of stealing. When a mother is missing or not around for this critical activity, however, then a deprivation ensues because the baby is searching for something that is experienced as not there, not to be found, not to be taken, and, therefore, not to be created. Urges to steal much more can become entrenched with the result that this situation later leads to actual thieving behavior.

Winnicott did not view this later behavior as arising from "infantile omnipotence," but rather as a persistence of a "nuisance value" of coping with the demands of rearing a baby and young child:

> The manifestation of the antisocial tendency includes stealing and lying . . . the common factor for my purpose . . . is the nuisance value of the symptoms. This nuisance value is exploited by the child, and is not a chance affair. Much of the motivation is unconscious, but not necessarily all.[29]

By creating a nuisance, a thief potentially draws attention to an early deprivation, hoping someone will notice (this desire to be seen is object seeking and therefore hopeful) and finally do something to rectify it. This kind of early deprivation is, for Winnicott, nothing less than a "disaster" in the baby's environment, because he or she cannot complete the task of creating a mother in his or her mind. Winnicott is open to temperamental conditions that might also cause this disaster. He notes, "But many parents who are well able to bring up normal children are not able to succeed with one of their children who happens to manifest an antisocial tendency."[30] In other words, the disaster can potentially happen in any family regardless of social, economic, and other supportive circumstances.

The myth of the Golden Fleece is rife with child abandonment. Jason's parents turn him over to Chiron. We know nothing about his care under the centaur, but we can suppose that Jason's original mother was someone he could not create in his own mind, and his later theft of the Fleece conjures an image, among many of course, of the Fleece as a mother-substitute: soft, rich, and enveloping. Phrixos, who rode eastward on the ram with its Golden Fleece, was fleeing a murderous stepmother, obviously a disaster in the making. And Medea, too, turns into a murdering mother, invoking the opposite of the creative impulse that Winnicott so tenderly refers to. She becomes a destructive mother, stealing the future from Jason, herself, and her children. She symbolizes at the end a Terrible Mother who can take from any of us life, vitality, and consciousness.

Envy is a part of the myth and certainly a psychic force behind stealing. It is an immensely complicated topic in analysis and psychotherapy, to say the least, and I do not want to treat it in a light manner at all. Envy can be particularly destructive and depleting because it empties not only a person's psyche of positive libido, but also relationships of pleasure and enriching exchange. Melanie Klein outlined many groundbreaking ideas about envy, especially as it pertained to her theories about object relations. She writes, "I consider that envy is an oral-sadistic and anal-sadistic expression of destructive impulses, operative from the beginning of life, and that it has a constitutional basis."[31] She believed that envy operates mostly through projection, and that it results in psychological attacks on an envied object because of what the latter represents. She found "that the anxieties aroused by interpretation of hate and envy toward the primal object, and the feeling of persecution by the analyst whose work stirs up those emotions, are more painful than any other material we interpret."[32] Envy sooner or later presents a nettlesome clinical problem for anyone working in an analytic fashion. Hanna Segal wrote a brilliant guide to Klein's work that provides an excellent understanding of how Klein's ideas shaped her clinical work and how they interrelate with her theory of the paranoid-schizoid and depressive positions.[33]

Wilfred Bion's work on envy, which is an extension of Klein's, shows us how envy destroys a capacity for thinking and dreaming. His contribution to a theory of thinking is grounded in his concepts of alpha elements, beta elements, and alpha function, which transforms beta into alpha elements. *Beta elements* are raw, unprocessed sensory impressions that, according to Bion, must be changed into something else in order to be thought about.[34] They are otherwise simply too disruptive and triggering of unprocessed emotive discharge. Bion thought that *alpha function* is what enables thinking, reasoning, and dreaming because it changes beta elements into more useful alpha elements, which are "digested," available for memories, and like the visual images of dreams. Bion believed that we all struggle to use alpha function because it is frequently under both internal and external (that is, interpersonal or environmental) attacks. In particular, envy can disrupt alpha function. As a result, a person preoccupied with envy cannot make "conscious contact either with himself or another as live objects."[35] In his view, envy incapacitates us significantly by its interference with alpha function.

Bion saw envy as a human impulse that originates in us from infantile experiences when a baby regards the mother's breast (that is, her feeding and care of him or her) as totally good and loving—capable of providing all that the infant cannot. Typically, this one-sided experience is modified over time through the mother's interventions so that babies develop what comes to be their own internal alpha function to handle frustrations, a mother's absences, and other disruptive emotions. For example, a mother notices when her baby is overwhelmed by what Bion calls beta elements. She then steps in to soothe and comfort the baby in a process that repeats thousands of times. Through these interactions of soothing, attentive comfort, and maternal reverie, an infant subsequently develops his or her own internal alpha function that becomes sturdier as he or she grows. Once able to rely on these internal resources, the infant's recourse to envious attacks occurs less frequently.

This complex process is one way to understand why mothering is exhausting. Whenever alpha function seriously degrades, however, Bion hypothesized that, for such a baby, the baby and the mother become dangerously close to lifeless and that they coexist in a sort of primitive dead zone. He believed that a baby repeatedly put in this condition has to turn instead to material comforts because his or her mental functioning is so disturbed. The risk is if a mother (or primary caretaker) does not intervene in this cycle, then a greedy nature can come to predominate the psyche. Someone maturing out of this state will bring along significant troubles in regard to envy and his or her ability to use alpha function.

> This split, enforced by . . . fear of death through starvation on the one hand, and by love and the fear of associated murderous envy and hate on

> the other, produces a mental state in which the patient greedily pursues every form of material comfort; he is at once insatiable and implacable in his pursuit of satiation. Since this state originates in a need to be rid of the emotional complications of awareness of life . . . the patient appears to be incapable of gratitude or concern either for himself or others.[36]

Both Klein and Bion saw gratitude as our saving grace from envy. Gratitude rests on an ability to take in what another offers as good, positive, and enlivening, and to feel thankful in receiving it; an experience of gratitude also means holding onto what has been given as something that enriches one's own inner world. Without gratitude, envy can possess a psyche in an unchecked, blunt way, and it usually produces cravings that cannot be satisfied. For an overly envious person, relationships suffer and are ruined or destroyed, including a person's relationship with him- or herself.

Returning to the myth's characters, Medea openly envies Glauce, Jason's new bride, and this leads to the unhappy outcome in Euripides's play. We could think of her hunger for revenge as being "insatiable," and although not directed at material comforts, it is an urge that Medea acts on because she cannot tolerate her diminished status. In that way, we could further say that she envies the masculine heroic code, which as a woman of her time she stood outside of—her hunger for suitable revenge may have been stimulated even more by her outsider status. Certainly, Jason almost never shows Medea any gratitude, and although not explicit in the texts, his absolute dependence on her and others could have been a source of envy in him.

Medea Complex

Several authors have written about a Medea complex in which children are hurt terribly, even killed, by their parents. In the United States, the total number of those murdered under the age of 18 in 2008 was 1,502, and, of this number, 70 percent were boys. This number represents 11 percent of total murders by age.[37] Marianne Leuzinger-Bohleber's more recent study from 2001 examines the Medea complex from the standpoint of the mother–daughter relationship, with attention to primitive fantasies of feminine destruction as well as psychological difficulties in separating from a depressed mother. In these cases, separation becomes fraught with fears of potential death.[38] According to Leuzinger-Bohleber, the women she describes all demonstrated a problem in claiming their own bodies from the mother and could not become pregnant because of a terror that they would ultimately kill the child or be killed by it. "*Either* the self *or* the object but not both could survive; . . . separation from the primary object signified destruction of *either* the individuating self *or* of the (depressed) primary object."[39]

M. R. Lansky presents a complicated psychoanalytic study of Euripides's *The Medea*, looking at the role of shame in this story. Taking issue with the views of some recent classics scholars, he proposes understanding the play "in terms of shame, vengefulness, and spite."[40] He assesses Medea's psychopathology and does not regard the back-story to Euripides's play, that is, the myth of the *Argonautika*. Lansky views Medea as grandiose, paranoid, and defying social norms.[41] His conclusion omits reference to why Medea acts as she does—that she was betrayed repeatedly and that Jason emotionally abused her over a long period of time.

Lansky disregards the importance of the heroic code for what masculine ideals it represented to Athenian society and the classical world in general up through Roman times.[42] This oversight limits his analysis. His view of how Medea escalates into murdering her children—because of unbearable shame—is also not entirely inaccurate. It links closely to Charles Stewart's theory about lethal actions as outlined in his book *Dire Emotions and Lethal Behaviors*.[43] Medea's crimes result from an intolerable internal state, yet only after a course of events that brought on great suffering: "It is in discussions of unbearable affect that we regularly find a linkage between a state of mind and suicide or homicide."[44]

Barbara Rosenstein and Richard Alperin also view Medea through a pathological lens. They present clinical cases of what they describe as a transgenerational process of maternal acting out, which displaces these mothers' rage from husbands onto children.[45] Similarly, Laura McCloskey presents a statistical analysis of 363 women and children who experienced spousal and paternal abuse.[46] She tries to understand whether domestic abuse by men is related to life-stressors (such as unemployment or alcohol abuse) or committed primarily to retaliate against a wife. She presents evidence that the latter is sometimes true, but acknowledges that families in which violence occurs are also subject to more life stressors.[47]

John Babatzanis and Georgie Babatzanis discuss a documented case of filicide and present clinical material about the mother and a surviving sibling.[48] Their interpretation of the myth, while slightly more sympathetic to Medea, appears to be based on the fact of filicide, rather than on a more in-depth psychological parallel (not all mothers who murder a child would necessarily represent the internal dynamics of a Medea complex). Shelley Orgel and Leonard Shengold hold to a stereotypical split between Jason as hero (good, idealized) and Medea as witch (bad, demonic).[49] They focus on the gifts that she gives others, which can be either helpful (for instance, for Jason) or hurtful (for Pelias, Creon, and Glauce). They view these gifts as representing good and bad magic that depicts her omnipotent wish to control others. Their selective reading of Euripides's *The Medea*, as well as the two cases they describe, rests theoretically on an idea that mothers who use gifts as Medea does desire psychological fusion for narcissistic gratification.

In an article from decades ago, Edward Stern discusses seven cases of mothers with observably hostile feelings toward their children. He defines the Medea complex as arising when "the mother harbours death wishes to her offspring, usually as revenge against the father."[50] Stern reviews extensive anthropological evidence for killing children, including ritual sacrifice and superstitions used to provide protection from wrathful gods and to atone for various calamities. He reminds us that Herakles murdered his children; Agamemnon sacrificed his daughter; and Cronos ate his children. Importantly, he notes, "It is significant that, although infanticide is so common in fact, it is rare in fiction."[51] Stern believes that mythology helps to illuminate this contradiction, especially when "the theme is too repugnant to our sentiments."[52] In other words, this topic of child murder has an archetypal core that we would rather keep in shadow, either unconscious or confined to myth.

In reviewing these writings about the Medea complex, I suggest here that theft is integral to the complex and is often what incites a parent to seek revenge. Bearing in mind the centrality of theft in the myth, we will see, for example, in Chapter 6 how a mother targets her son who represents for her a reminder of a stolen daughter and abandoning husband; likewise, in Chapter 7, we will find a complicated mother–daughter relationship in which the mother's feeling dislodged from "being the center of attention" figures prominently. In such cases, a mother's feeling ripped off—by a husband, a family situation, life circumstances—can evolve into a manic and aggressive impulse for vengeance played out against her offspring.

Promethean Theft

The myth of the Golden Fleece exemplifies much that lies within the shadow of stealing, but there are other myths that sometimes cast stealing in a positive light. One is the kind of stealing Hermes did as a trickster figure, when he took his brother Apollo's cattle. Another is the stealing that Prometheus did for the betterment of humankind. This other mythical tradition offers, then, something of a contrast with the Golden Fleece, and it might also shed light on when stealing advances individuation rather than subverts it.

Briefly, Prometheus is known as a Titan who sides with Zeus in a great war between the Olympian gods and the Titans led by Cronus. Prometheus is thought to have aided Zeus by encouraging him to send out the Cyclops and to take the thunderbolt for himself as a power. Later, though, they become enemies when Prometheus steals fire from the gods on Olympus and gives it to humans so they can advance themselves. Prometheus is also understood to have created these humans out of dirt and clay. Zeus in his rage punishes Prometheus by having him chained to a rock on a mountaintop where each day an eagle devours his liver, which grows back during the night. Much later, Herakles frees Prometheus from his suffering.[53]

What are we to make of Prometheus's stealing in this instance? Clearly, his theft of fire could be viewed symbolically as a creative impulse, a force for good and for growth, because it takes from an unconscious that hoards its powers (that is, Zeus's oppression viewed as an unconscious archetypal force) to the detriment of the conscious part of the self. Prometheus acts here as a thief in service of individuation who takes what cannot be gotten in any other way because there is no bargaining, no negotiation, and no possibility for compromise with a darkness that wants to enslave the rest of the personality. He acts as a rebel who shakes up a rigid, immovable tyranny.[54]

Jung believed that integrating aspects of the shadow held in unconsciousness is a necessary step along the path of individuation. In that sense, sometimes an act of stealing on the outer stage of external life may be a symptom that awaits understanding for whatever turmoil might be occurring internally. Stealing, therefore, can on such occasions point to an unconscious compensation for an imbalance in the personality. Discussing this idea, Jung notes, “Prometheus was the savior who brought light and fire to mankind languishing in darkness.”[55] In other words, Promethean theft rescues valuable energy from the unconscious—literally and metaphorically; it is the light in the shadow.

Prometheus also embodies a primal creativity, and his stealing serves to express an aspect of that, when, for example, an artistic and creative urge might use stealing to achieve its purpose. Jung notes that Goethe’s work on Prometheus portrays him to be self-activating and “exclusively creative, defying the gods out of the strength of his own creative power.”[56] This side of Prometheus may exist in many forms of artistic expression, for example, when artists “steal” or borrow something from other artists, those who often preceded them, and then make it their own, usually in an altered form. Picasso is alleged to have said, “Good artists borrow, great artists steal.”[57] As another example, graffiti artists “steal” open public space to express their ideas and images. Their theft of space on a clean wall actually constitutes a necessary component of this kind of artistic expression. Many extremely important writers have been fascinated by the character of Prometheus, such as Goethe and Mary Shelley. They were especially attracted to the myth’s focus on creativity, which is manifold in terms of Prometheus’s creating humankind, giving it fire, and then later being integral to its survival after the great deluge.[58] The literary tradition that uses this myth frequently centers on the theme of ruthless creativity that steals for its own ends.[59]

Holding in mind this idea of stealing as a positive light within the shadow is important. Some situations like this, when more fully understood, might tell us when stealing supports individuation. This type of stealing is often about obtaining a restricted resource and selfishly making it our own in order to express a creative impulse. Sometimes this occurs externally, as in art and much else that involves intellectual endeavor. But sometimes, it occurs internally when a precious element has to be stolen from the unconscious to bring it into the conscious mind.

In looking at these differing theoretical perspectives, I want to highlight two points. One is that myths about theft are psychologically complex and open to various interpretations about their meanings and their characters’ motivations. The myth of the Golden Fleece is an archetypal tale with deep unconscious resonance even today. It also is a story about our conflicts and frailties in face of loss, abandonment, and deprivation, and the painful emotions these situations arouse such as envy and grief.

Two is to show how, in somewhat summary fashion, these different psychological theories relate to stealing, because each one has something significant to say about what unconsciously motivates theft. Not to be lost in this discussion is that not every act of stealing is negative—sometimes no other alternative exists. Stealing can contain a positive impulse within, for example, in Winnicott's idea of creating the mother by stealing something of her and his notion of hope in the antisocial tendency. That even the worst of what we harbor within us can have, though not always, some aspect of a positive movement in development or individuation is a very Jungian idea. The myth of the Golden Fleece tells us one way of how this goes wrong and no learning occurs. To see how others view Jason and Medea as characters, the next chapter turns to the research and essays of leading classics scholars who have studied this story for a very long time.

Notes

1 C. G. Jung, *Symbols of Transformation*, in H. Read, M. Fordham, and G. Adler (eds), *The Collected Works of C. G. Jung, Volume 5*, Princeton, Princeton University Press, 1912/1956. Hereafter reference to Jung's *Collected Works* will be cited as *CW*, volume number, date of publication (on first mention), paragraph (¶) number, and page (p.) number. This work, originally from 1912, led in part to Jung's break with Freud. It outlined the importance of the mother in the psyche and presented various myths about the Great Mother and our complicated relations with her. This quotation is from p. xxiv of the preface.

2 Jung, *CW* 5, ¶29, p. 24.

3 C. G. Jung, "Archetypes of the collective unconscious," in *The Archetypes and the Collective Unconscious*, pp. 3–41, *CW* 9i, 1959, ¶7, p. 6.

4 Jung, *CW* 5, ¶577, pp. 369–70.

5 C. G. Jung, *Mysterium Coniunctionis*, *CW* 14, 1963, ¶15, p. 21.

6 Ibid., ¶16, pp. 21–22. Kerényi was a twentieth-century scholar of Greek mythology. Maier was an alchemist of the late sixteenth and early seventeenth centuries.

7 C. G. Jung, "The structure of the psyche," in *The Structure and Dynamics of the Psyche*, pp. 139–58, *CW* 8, 1931/1960, ¶325, pp. 152–53.

8 C. G. Jung, "Individual dream symbolism in relation to alchemy," Chapter 3, "The symbolism of the mandala," in *Psychology and Alchemy*, pp. 95–223, *CW* 12, 1953, ¶206, p. 159.

9 Perhaps no other word is more popularly associated with Jung than *archetype*. Yet, the term can be confusing, dense, and saturated with more mystery than meaning. Jung took the step in 1919 of using the neo-Platonic Latin word *Archetypus* when he had previously used the German *Urbild*, which means "primal image." See Jung, "Instinct and the unconscious," *CW* 8, 1919/1928, ¶270, p. 133. Jung may have borrowed the term from Goethe, who used the German *Typus* to suggest scheme, primal image, and natural law to connote the activity of a basic divine order. See D. Miller, ed. and trans., *Goethe Scientific Studies*, Princeton, Princeton University Press, 1995.

10 Jung writes, "Instinct and the archaic mode meet in the biological conception of the 'pattern of behavior.'" See Jung, "On the nature of the psyche," *CW* 8, 1960, ¶398, pp. 200–1.

11 In "Symbols and the interpretation of dreams," Jung writes, "The archetype is . . . an inherited *tendency* of the human mind to form representations of mythological motifs—representations that vary a great deal without losing their basic pattern" (C. G. Jung, *The Symbolic Life*, *CW* 18, 1961, ¶523, p. 228).

12 Jung notes, "The ideas underlying them are . . . distinguished from the organizing archetype, which in itself is irrepresentable because unconscious" (C. G. Jung, "A psychological approach to the dogma of the trinity," in *Psychology and Religion: West and East, CW* 11, 1942/1948, ¶223, p. 151).

13 J. Knox, "Memories, fantasies, archetypes: An exploration of some connections between cognitive science and analytical psychology," *Journal of Analytical Psychology*, 2001, vol. 46, pp. 613–35; and P. Saunders and P. Skar, "Archetypes, complexes and self-organization," *Journal of Analytical Psychology*, 2001, vol. 46, pp. 305–23. See also J. Knox, *Archetype, Attachment, Analysis: Jungian Psychology and the Emergent Mind*, East Sussex and New York, Brunner-Routledge, 2003.

14 See W. McGuire (ed.) *The Freud–Jung Letters*, Princeton, Princeton University Press, 1974.

15 J. Strachey (ed.), *The Standard Edition of the Complete Psychological Works of Sigmund Freud, Volume 7*, London, The Hogarth Press and the Institute of Psycho-analysis, 1905/1955. Hereafter reference to Freud's work in the *Standard Edition* will be cited as *SE*, with chapter and section. The quotation is from a footnote added in 1920 on p. 226 of this volume.

16 *SE* 4, 1900, Chapter 5, section D (β), p. 261. See also Freud's case of the Rat Man (1909), in which he writes of the father as the child's "sexual opponent" who interferes with masturbatory, that is "auto-erotic," activity. (*SE* 10, part I, section G, p. 208.)

17 *SE* 4, 1900, Chapter 5, section D (β), p. 262.

18 Other modern viewpoints on the Oedipus complex have been articulated by H. W. Loewald, "The waning of the Oedipus complex," *Journal of the American Psychoanalytic Association*, 1979, vol. 27, pp. 751–75; R. Britton, M. Feldman, and E. O'Shaugnessy, *The Oedipus Complex Today: Clinical Implications*, London, Karnac Books, 1989; and H. Gee, "The Oedipal complex in adolescence," *Journal of Analytical Psychology*, 1991, vol. 36, pp. 193–210.

19 In Freud's model, the fear of loss in the Oedipal complex was conceived as castration anxiety—that a part of the child's body was threatened with literally being chopped off. This view no longer holds for most contemporary psychoanalytic work. Instead, anxiety at overstepping a generational boundary is emphasized. There are still important bodily fantasies attached to this phase, but these are considered in less formulaic and gender determined ways.

20 D. Kahneman and A. Tversky (eds), *Choices, Values, and Frames,* Cambridge, UK, Cambridge University Press, 2000, p. xiii. This volume is an edited collection of over 40 papers by various contributors. Hereafter, it will be cited as author, paper title, page number, *CVF*, and relevant page numbers for quotations.

21 D. Kahneman and A. Tversky, "Choices, values, and frames," pp. 1–16, *CVF*, p. 13.

22 A. Tversky and D. Kahneman, "Loss aversion in riskless choice: a reference-dependent model," pp. 143–58, *CVF*, p. 144.

23 D. Kahneman, J. L. Knetsch, and R. H. Thaler, "The endowment effect, loss aversion, and status quo bias," pp. 159–70, *CVF*, example taken from p. 159.

24 D. Kahneman and A. Tversky, "Loss aversion in riskless choice," *CVF*, p. 145.

25 J. L. Knetsch, "The endowment effect and evidence of nonreversible indifference curves," *CVF*, pp. 171–79. Students generally would not trade (mugs and candy bars) even when their preferences might have clearly been in another direction.

26 D. W. Winnicott, "The antisocial tendency," in C. Winnicott, R. Shepherd, and M. Davis (eds), *Deprivation and Delinquency*, pp. 120–31, London and New York, Tavistock Publications, 1956/1984.

27 Ibid., p. 122.

28 Ibid., p. 125.

29 Ibid., p. 126.

30 Ibid., p. 130.

31 M. Klein, "Envy and gratitude," in *Envy and Gratitude and Other Works, 1946–1963*, pp. 176–235, New York, The Free Press, 1957/1975, p. 176. See also *The Selected Melanie Klein*, ed. J. Mitchell, New York, The Free Press, 1986.
32 Ibid., p. 232.
33 H. Segal, *Introduction to the Work of Melanie Klein*, New York, Basic Books, 1964.
34 W. R. Bion, *Learning from Experience*, Oxford, UK, Jason Aronson, 1962. See also T. H. Ogden, *This Art of Psychoanalysis: Dreaming Undreamt Dreams and Interrupted Cries*, London and New York, Routledge, 2005; and A. Ferro, *Mind Works: Technique and Creativity in Psychoanalysis*, New York and London, Routledge, 2008.
35 W. R. Bion, *Learning from Experience*, p. 9.
36 Ibid., p. 11.
37 Taken from the US Census Bureau, *Statistical Abstract of the United States*, 2011. Numbers are from 2008.
38 M. Leuzinger-Bohleber, "The 'Medea fantasy': An unconscious determinant of psychogenic sterility," *International Journal of Psychoanalysis*, 2001, vol. 82, pp. 323–45.
39 Ibid., p. 340. Italics in original.
40 M. R. Lansky, "The impossibility of forgiveness: Shame fantasies as instigators of vengefulness in Euripides's *Medea*," *Journal of the American Psychoanalytic Association*, 2005, vol. 53, pp. 437–64, quote from p. 444. He notes, "In the *Medea*, three distinct types of fantasy are operative: anticipatory paranoid shame; shame relocated into the other by projective identification; and shame defended against by omnipotent withdrawal from the social order" (p. 452).
41 Ibid. Lansky writes, "Ultimately, she cannot overcome the powerful shame-evoking forces and assume a degree of cooperation with the social order for her children's sake and her own" (p. 461). As he puts it, "Vengefulness and spite are the cardinal features of the *Medea*" (p. 451).
42 Ibid., p. 442.
43 C. T. Stewart, 2008, *Dire Emotions and Lethal Behaviors: Eclipse of the Life Instinct*, London and New York, Routledge, 2008.
44 Ibid., p. 58.
45 B. L. Rosenstein and R. M. Alperin, "The Medea complex in psychoanalytic thought," *Psychoanalysis and Psychotherapy*, 2001, vol. 18, pp. 261–86.
46 L. A. McCloskey, "The 'Medea Complex' among men: The instrumental abuse of children to injure wives," *Violence and Victims*, 2001, vol. 16, pp. 19–37.
47 She notes that "the only predictor of paternal child abuse to surface was the men's abuse of their wives." Ibid., p. 34.
48 J. Babatzanis and G. Babatzanis, "Fate and the personal myth in Medea's plight: Filicide," in P. Hartocollis and I. Davidson Graham (eds.) *The Personal Myth in Psychoanalytic Theory*, pp. 235–55, Madison, CT, International Universities Press, 1991.
49 S. Orgel and L. Shengold, "The fatal gifts of Medea," *International Journal of Psychoanalysis*, 1968, vol. 49, pp. 379–83.
50 E. S. Stern, "The Medea complex: The mother's homicidal wishes to her child," *The Journal of Mental Science*, 1948, vol. 94, pp. 321–31, quote from p. 330.
51 Ibid., p. 329.
52 Ibid.
53 T. Gantz, *Early Greek Myth, Volume 1*, Baltimore, Johns Hopkins University Press, 1993, pp. 152–66. Gantz notes that some of what we know of Prometheus comes from Hesiod's *Theogony* and *Works & Days*. Prometheus apparently stole fire with a fennel stalk, and Zeus retaliated by creating Pandora who unleashes all kinds of evil on humankind. Gantz also notes the contribution of Aeschylus's drama *Prometheus Bound* from the fifth century BCE.

54 Edith Hamilton remarks about Prometheus, "His name has stood through all the centuries, from the Greek days to our own, as that of the great rebel against injustice and the authority of power" (E. Hamilton, *Mythology: Timeless Tales of Gods and Heroes*, Boston, Little, Brown & Co., 1940, p. 73).
55 Jung, *Psychological Types*, *CW* 6, 1971, ¶314, p. 186.
56 Ibid., ¶292, p. 175.
57 Steve Jobs used this quote "good artists copy, great artists steal" in a well-known YouTube video.
58 Both Gantz and Hamilton note that Prometheus's son Deukalion and niece Pyrrha survive the great flood and go on to populate the race of humans. (Gantz, *Early Greek Myth*, p. 165, and Hamilton, *Mythology*, p. 74).
59 Goethe wrote two pieces about Prometheus, a poem from 1774, and a dramatic fragment from 1773. He was preoccupied at that time with the force of creativity, its spiritual and demonic aspects, and the brute strength of creative urges as natural forces. He chose Prometheus as a figure who rebelled and who also represented characteristics like Christ. Goethe made Prometheus a son of Zeus. Speaking defiantly to Minerva about his own strengths, Prometheus says, "They are mine, and their use is mine alone" (J. W. von Goethe, *Goethe Werke, Band 2*, Frankfurt am Main, Insel Verlag, 1970, p. 104, my translation). In his poem *Prometheus*, the speaker Prometheus warns Zeus, "Leave my earth alone, and my cabin, which you did not build, and my hearth, whose glow makes you envy me." (Ibid., *Band 1*, p. 50, my translation.) This creative impulse belongs to a fierce independence that borders on rebellion. Mary Shelley titled her great work, first published in 1818, *Frankenstein or the Modern Prometheus.* Hindle, in his introduction, notes, "It was, then, the Promethean 'maker', 'artist', 'shaper' of men in a scientist-hero guise that interested Mary Shelley. . . ." (M. Shelley, *Frankenstein or the Modern Prometheus*, ed. M. Hindle, London, Penguin Books, 1818/1991, p. xxx.) Shelley's Frankenstein, modeled after Prometheus, is also a thief, although his stealing occurs in graveyards:

> Who shall conceive the horrors of my secret toil as I dabbled among the unhallowed damps of the grave or tortured the living animal to animate the lifeless clay? . . . I collected bones from charnel-houses and disturbed, with profane fingers, the tremendous secrets of the human frame.
>
> (Ibid., p. 55)

Like Goethe's Prometheus, Shelley's Frankenstein is swept up by his ability to create:

> After so much time spent in painful labour, to arrive at once at the summit of my desires, was the most gratifying consummation of my toils. . . . What had been the study and desire of the wisest men since the creation of the world was now within my grasp.
>
> (Ibid., p.53)

The centrality accorded creativity dominates all other motives, which exist only to enable the production of a creative soul. This includes stealing, which Frankenstein had to do in order to create the monster.

4

HOW CLASSICS SCHOLARS VIEW THE MYTH

It would be monumental to attempt to summarize what classics scholars have written about Medea, Jason, and the Golden Fleece. On Google, a quick search using only the word *Medea* returned more than 15 million hits, and on JSTOR, an academic journal database, over 6,000, while the words *Golden Fleece* resulted in more than 2 million and 2,000 hits on each, respectively.[1] *The Medea* has been studied as exemplifying Euripides's innovations as a writer of great drama. Euripides (ca. 480–6 BCE) was a contemporary of Socrates, Aeschylus, and Sophocles (the latter was the author of *Antigone*, *Oedipus*, and *Electra*). Here I present a selected overview of some recent scholarship on this topic, with additional resources detailed in the notes of this chapter. Focusing on the works of Apollonios (*Argonautika*) and Euripides (*The Medea*), except where otherwise noted, this discussion will show how relevant mythic themes and contents have been elaborated by scholars in ways that relate to many of the complex motivations behind stealing. For example, we find many times in instances of theft an underlying confusion about what the thief regards as heroic, vengeful, victimizing, scandalous, and terrorizing. These scholarly views add another layer of understanding to the types of stealing discussed in the case examples.

Scoundrel and Victim

Opinions of classics scholars have evolved considerably over time in regard to the characters of Jason and Medea. Despite popular appeal, Jason has been described as an antihero, a villain, a schemer, and even stupid. Theodore Klein, in an article about Jason as both hero and scoundrel, writes, "Apollonius' Jason furnishes the paradigm of the compromised hero: it is true that he acquires the Golden Fleece—but only by recourse to a virgin-witch and her drugs."[2] He adds, "Jason is only *amechanos*. Suassez [another classics scholar] defines this word as 'sans resource, sans moyen, sans invention' [without resources, without skill, without inventiveness] and goes on to enumerate Jason's traits as embarrassment and indecision."[3] This characterization of Jason reveals him to be someone of minimal capabilities who is dependent on others to make it through tough situations, and who has to rely on actions such as stealing to achieve what he wants. He is like a thief who needs an accomplice, a situation that we saw in Sally's tale of theft, when she stole at the behest of her boyfriend. Frequently, the accomplice is smarter than the thief.

Richard Hunter notes that Jason "is marked by the absence of extraordinary intelligence and the supernatural skills enjoyed by some of the most prominent Argonauts."[4] Hunter places Jason within the context of someone passing through an initiation. It is doubtful that Jason completes a successful initiation, however, because he is compelled to steal the Fleece out of a naïve assumption that by doing so he will guarantee his destiny. He learns little on his quest. Charles Beye speaks perhaps for a plurality of recent classics scholars when he writes that Jason is "uniformly portrayed as passive" and becomes "the perversion of the hero," although others might not take such a uniformly negative stand about Jason.[5]

Considering Jason's obvious flaws, how does he obtain the Fleece? Only through Medea's assistance. She is a beautiful princess, forced by Eros to fall in love with Jason, owing to the compact between Eros's mother Aphrodite and Hera. Medea is skilled in the use of drugs, or in Greek *pharmaka.* Without Medea's ability, Jason would not have had a chance of getting the Fleece. He begs Medea to give him the drugs: "I beseech you . . . I have come here, both your suppliant and your guest, forced by necessity to clasp your knees."[6] Hunter finds this craving unique: "The subordination of all else in this extremely rich poem to this single obsessive end [the Golden Fleece] is a striking departure from . . . Homeric poems."[7]

Jason is not a classic Greek hero like Achilles or Herakles, who confront fate independently. Early on, Jason is called "helpless and absorbed."[8] After hearing from Phineas the prophet how their journey will go, he asks, "How can I accomplish this? . . . I have no experience."[9] And after passing the Clashing Rocks, he says, "I should have immediately refused this expedition . . . As it is I am in constant terror and my burdens are unendurable; I loathe sailing in our ship . . ., and I loathe our stops on dry land."[10] If anything, Jason is a consummate manager who manipulates others to join him. His leadership cajoles rather than inspires. As James Clauss puts it:

> He does not make things happen but waits for the dust to settle before taking advantage of the opportunities that others—mortal and divine—have provided. Jason's talents include the ability to attract women, to take care of quotidian details of running an expedition, and to make the best of bad situations through skillful crisis management. These are not the qualities one associates with the best of the Greek heroes.[11]

When Jason uses Medea's drug for his contest, its effect is potent: "Then Jason sprinkled the drug over himself: a mighty force entered him, inexpressible, without fear, and his two arms moved freely as they swelled with bursting strength."[12] This description calls to mind what happens in addiction and narcissistic inflation. It also reminds us of how athletes use steroids and other performance-enhancing drugs to steal a victory that they might not fairly obtain;

this form of theft now seems almost commonplace in the world of professional sports. Jason is not a Homeric hero who fights his enemies with respect and honor while abiding a deep love for his allies—the core of the heroic code. Instead, his selfishness contrasts starkly with an older tradition of heroic sacrifice.

Medea knows that she is the one supplying Jason with the means to succeed: "The goddess Hekaté has taught her extraordinary skills in handling all drugs which the dry land and the boundless waters produce."[13] Using those drugs, she assists him by putting the serpent that guards the Fleece to sleep, and only then does Jason steal the Fleece. In their subsequent long escape, Jason nearly abandons Medea on several occasions to what might have been certain death. She conspires to murder her own brother for Jason's sake, although her participation in this deed marks her change into "a murderous witch."[14] At this point in Apollonios's epic, Medea sheds aspects of the victim role. These figures of scoundrel and victim appear in many stories of theft, with the victim sometimes enabling it and, at other times, being helpless against it.

Redefining Heroism

Elizabeth Bongie places Euripides's Medea within a Sophoclean heroic tradition, comparing her to Ajax and to Homer's Achilles. This heroic code differs from what governs the rest of us because a hero sees himself (or herself) as not constrained by the limits of human civil society. This code has a strict rule about taking care of friends (in Greek, *philoi*) and harming enemies (in Greek, *echtroi*). Medea adopts a heroic code of her own, going against a feminine stereotype, which expected women not "to cope with crises, only to survive them. The archetype of this system was, obviously, Penelope."[15] Medea, however, is fixated on her honor, which she feels was spoiled by Jason's broken oaths. Bongie argues, "Here Euripides presents his vision of a woman who, like Antigone, lives in accordance with a male system of values."[16] In this way, Medea aspires to masculine heroic virtue.

Medea is an especially complex character when one tries to fathom her motivations. Patricia Easterling explains Medea's brand of heroism:

> But Medea's appropriation of the code [heroic] seems hideously out of place in a situation where the enemy is her husband and the means of punishing him is to be an act of bloodthirsty treachery followed by the murder of her own children.[17]

Her sacrifice, however, has been too great; she has given "literally everything" for Jason.[18] In transcending the feminine role restrictions of her time, Medea leaves us to question why a divine force does not stop her:

> This is one of the most alarming features of the play, the fact that there is no comparatively distant and objective divine figure to speak with the

> voice of authority . . . restoring a sense of normality after the frightful extremes of action.[19]

To Easterling, the play disturbs us because Medea symbolizes the precarious hold we all have on civilized behavior. She finds Euripides's intent ironic:

> When he [Euripides] makes the insensitive Jason praise Greek society and values and when he gives the barbarian witch the ideals of a traditional Greek hero he is surely suggesting that there is no safe dividing line: civilized life is . . . continually threatened from within.[20]

Medea represents a type of heroic identity that is closer to the classic type than Jason's. She is possessed by righteousness and defiance to achieve her purpose. Thieves too can adopt a righteous attitude that serves to convince them their actions are justified—we might think of Robin Hood. They find excitement in violating social norms, laws, and conventions, especially when, in their own minds, they steal for what can appear to be heroic reasons. Another example of righteous thieving is Aaron Swartz, the computer programmer who stole millions of articles from JSTOR, an academic journal database, because he believed these should be freely available to everyone on the Internet. In 2011, he was indicted for this theft. Swartz, an Internet folk hero, committed suicide in January 2013.[21]

Gender Crossing

Medea's adoption of a traditionally masculine attitude for her time has interested many scholars. Deborah Boedeker, for example, studies the issue of language as Medea uses it in Euripides's play. The Greek *logos* (plural, *logoi*) connotes formal usage of language in rhetoric, logic, law, science, and philosophy—all in the context of reasoned and reasonable discourse. Medea expresses her grievances in terms of violated discourse. Boedeker argues, "The whole tragedy focuses self-consciously on λογοσ [*logos*], both as a medium of communication ('word, discourse, argument'), and as a basis of the way 'reality' is shaped, understood, and remembered ('story, plan')."[22] She continues:

> The *Medea* exemplifies a fascination with language, its dangers and powers, that characterizes many works of the fifth century. This emphasis comes as no surprise, of course, in a democracy where political decisions were conspicuously dependent on rhetorical persuasion, and in a culture where gods were called to witness and defend all sworn transactions.[23]

Medea is expert in using language, rhetoric, and argumentation to achieve her purposes, although this would traditionally have been the purview of male characters.

Medea claims in the play that Jason violated their relationship by breaking his word. Many times she protests that Jason took her words in vain. Boedeker notes, "What is truly 'vain' for Medea, as we have seen, is not her speech but her role as Jason's savior and the expectations, confirmed by oath, that were based on that role."[24] As a result, she and Jason engage in an ongoing argument about their situations, "pitting one narrative against the other."[25] Medea argues that she was instrumental in Jason's success, but Jason counters that it was Aphrodite who saved him, not Medea, and that Medea should be grateful because she benefited from the Argo expedition in many ways. He supposes that his exploits with the Argo match the arc of traditional heroism. When he decides to marry Creon's daughter, he also chooses to revise his history with Medea.

Shirley Barlow addresses Medea's transcendence of feminine stereotype, which ultimately cannot be escaped. When Medea attempts to act heroically, she feels confined by her role as mother. Barlow analyzes these pivotal lines in *The Medea*: "Let no one think me a weak one, feeble-spirited, a stay-at-home, but rather just the opposite, One who can hurt my enemies and help my friends; For the lives of such persons are most remembered."[26] She compares Medea to Herakles, but Herakles is not constrained by any maternal instincts, which do create a bind for Medea:

> What an irony then that Medea who has shown relentless heroic resolve, high courage, and grand rage worthy of any of the great male heroes . . . should in the end be trapped and halted by the very femininity she attempts to discard and professes to despise.[27]

Barlow argues that Euripides was demonstrating to his audience that stereotypes, perhaps like archetypes, are "inadequate," but that they nonetheless serve to reveal "eternal human truths."[28] The psychological problem here is salient—namely, not to demonize Medea, but rather to recognize that human beings are capable of monstrous and immoral acts. Although Medea was bound by her role as mother, she transcended it in a gruesome way, defying the stereotype.

Helene Foley explores the notion of Medea's divided self, asking whether this split can be viewed as just a struggle between reason and passion.[29] She thinks not and, instead, argues that Medea is torn between masculine and feminine aspects of her own identity, and that these, respectively, hinge on her imitation of the heroic code and her maternal instincts. An older understanding of the play would claim it is merely a story about sexual jealousy, which can be accounted for through an overcoming of reason by passion. In analyzing Medea's masculine side, Foley thinks that it originates with an internalized sense of the Greek heroic code, which, above all, is based on doing good for one's friends and harming one's enemies.[30] Therefore, seeing Medea as committing a crime of passion would be a mistake. "To characterize a revenge so carefully motivated throughout the early scenes of the *Medea* as merely the product of irrationality flies in the face of the entire Greek heroic code."[31]

Euripides fashions a stark contrast between what moves Jason and what moves Medea. Foley agrees with many others who see heroic standards as being partially upheld by Medea.[32] Medea's murdering her children signifies, however, a collapse of those heroic standards, and Foley believes that the play is a "tragedy of gender."[33] She proposes that Medea's character reflects the psychology of a victim who then later identifies with her oppressors.[34] This outcome leads to destruction and self-destruction, in so far as the children are killed and their murder also means that Medea harms part of herself. "For a moment in the monologue we hope that her maternal side will successfully contest the masculine heroic logic," but this turns out to not be the case.[35] Instead, Medea loses parts of herself, for example, her maternal identity, and perhaps even some of her feminine identity, when she murders her sons.

Foley is of the opinion that this is the result of "male suppression" that traps women in traditional roles and fails to recognize their independent talents and skills. She thus attempts to make Medea's tragedy of a gender bind relevant for contemporary audiences who continue to be fascinated by the play. But Medea's solution is likewise a doomed one, because it seeks an answer in the masculine alternative:

> Yet in the end her inability to trust her own maternal voice in the monologue destroys our hopes for a more enlightened form of human ethics, for the creation of an authoritative female identity and integrity that could contest masculine ethics, whether archaic or contemporary.[36]

The ending of the play leaves us holding a deep ambiguity, however, since Medea escapes in a heavenly chariot, while Jason pleads for the paternal contact he has lost. He ends up representing the tender aspects of when a parent has to mourn a child. Medea has resolved her gender bind by enacting a criminal abandonment that appears all too typically masculine.

Taking up this gender issue, Bongie finds that Medea acts more manly than womanly.[37] Medea embodies a reversal of gender roles that might have startled an ancient Greek audience. She cannot, however, do battle as a man can and instead achieves her power from magic. Bongie believes that in Euripides's play the heroic code far surpasses in importance the emotional dynamics of the characters:

> And yet too often Medea is seen only as a jealous wife seeking revenge and Jason as the archetype of a hypocritical cad. Jealousy and lust, of course, are universal and tireless emotions, whereas the heroic values that underlie the thinking of Jason and Medea are no longer so easily comprehended.[38]

A modern audience might, therefore, project far more emotionality into the play than was ever intended, whereas for an audience at the time of Euripides, a heroic code of honor would have been accepted as a significant "dimension of motivation."[39] Another view of this gender problem is articulated by Bernard Knox, who regards Medea's status as a woman as fundamental to comprehending Euripides's play, which he regards as "not about woman's rights, it is about woman's wrongs, those done to her and by her."[40]

These scholars take up the topic of gender in the play as something that shows Medea to transgress what is socially and culturally accepted. Medea is a subversive character in this way because she breaks a boundary. Stealing usually includes a subversive dimension when thieves believe they act according to their own code and outside what is otherwise accepted. This belief allows them to take from others and violate their boundaries because they do not feel they have to abide by them. We encounter subversion in many instances of theft that begin through carefully planned deception. In affinity theft, victims are often courted and recruited through social clubs, churches, and civic organizations, and once their trust is gained, they are vulnerable to theft. This kind of thief subverts the norms of the social group by seducing members to invest in scams and Ponzi schemes.

Monster Within

Many describe Medea as monstrous. To us, she could represent a modern-day domestic terrorist. Charles Segal asks, "[W]here is the line where revenge crossed into the zone of the monstrous and inhuman?"[41] He comments that the combination of murder and motherhood unsettles us because it brings creation and destruction into such intimate contact. Likewise, a conceptual violence occurs in Euripides's play, because Medea can be seen as both a defender and destroyer of the institution of marriage. Medea spins jarringly between what seems monstrous and normal and what seems exotic and familiar:

> Yet exactly this interchange between enormity and typicality is the defining quality of the play and its protagonist. Repeatedly the secure ground of domestic realism suddenly seems to give way beneath our feet, and we find ourselves in a nightmarish world of magical powers.[42]

The nightmarish effect leaves the reader or viewer without a safe harbor.

To see her as a terrorist is not farfetched since many understand her to operate as a political being. Segal remarks that Euripides's innovation is to develop Medea "as if she were in the masculine realm of politics rather than the feminine world of domestic life."[43] Medea's monstrosity afflicts us because, although the "immorality" of her action troubles us, Euripides successfully plays on our sympathies to cheer her on when she is most despondent. Yet Medea is an extremist, or archetypal terrorist, who is convinced that the ends, perceived as correct, justify the means, undoubtedly horrific:

> If, however, Medea is not acceptable to our own moral code, she is, in the code of the ancient heroic system, a veritable "saint." She went to the

> outer limits of daring and passion; while other heroes might blind themselves, kill themselves, or wreak terrible vengeances, Medea, to show the mettle of her character, sacrificed what to a Greek would be more precious than life itself—her children, her hope for the future.[44]

At the end of the drama, Medea represents "the unspeakable violence of the repressed and betrayed which, because it has been so long pent up, carries everything before it to destruction, even if it destroys also what it loves most."[45] This finishes a mythical cycle that began with stealing and concludes in brutality.[46] This progression reminds us that theft often ends up as a violent crime.

Others have commented on Medea's monstrousness. Károly Kerényi calls Medea "the murderess" and views her as "a barbaric representation of the Hera world," who leads "the newly born back to death."[47] He infers that Medea originates during a darker, archaic time of pre-Greek culture. Kerényi notes that she is eventually supplanted by Hera, a female goddess, who establishes a more humane order. For Sophie Mills, Medea's monstrousness consists of two threads: a demon-mistress to Jason and child murderer of her own offspring. Mills believes these two aspects of Medea account for her double revenge in the play—that she kills Jason's new Corinthian wife and then hers and Jason's children.[48] The infanticide has other mythological connections, namely with Ino and Procne. Ino was the wicked stepmother who wanted to kill Phrixos and Hellé—and whose actions, therefore, launched the entire myth of the Golden Fleece. Procne killed her son, cut him up, and served him to the king, his father, in revenge for raping her sister. The gods changed "Procne into a nightingale, whose song is a perpetual mourning . . ."[49] As Knox notes, however, Ino was insane and Procne was fated to eternal guilt—neither quite like Medea.[50] An important difference, Knox notes, is that Medea escapes divine punishment at the end.

Medea's terrorism reminds us that we can feel terrorized by thieves. Speak with anyone who has grappled with identity theft, and it is apparent that the effects of this type of theft can invade and take over someone's psyche. It can feel as if not just money, but also time, work, stamina, health, and one's sanity were stolen to some degree in trying to rectify and settle a crime of identity theft. Another terrorizing aspect of thievery appeared in my practice when a 16-year-old boy expressed an obsessive fear of burglars. He suffered from insomnia and was afraid thieves would disable the house's alarm system, gain entry, and then kill family members before making off with loot. He felt these imagined burglars were domestic terrorists with weapons who would destroy him and his family. He had no history of any crime in which he or his family were victims, but that knowledge did little to allay his terror that it could happen.

Stealing

Modern scholars of this myth do not appear to concern themselves too much with the theft of the Fleece. Archeological evidence from the Black Sea area suggests that the Fleece legend originated from the custom of collecting gold from streams with sheepskins that were hung up to dry.[51] These lustrous skins probably called out for mythical explanation. In understanding the myth of the Golden Fleece now, the stealing of it as a protected treasure has come to be seen as a mere dramatic device that sets in motion the more convoluted relationship between Jason and Medea. Viewed psychologically, this is something of an oversight because stealing is an illicit transaction that tells us something about difficulties with limits, boundaries, disturbing emotions, and self-control. Heroes, monsters, scoundrels, terrorists, and subversive characters—they all act out in places where transgression occurs, where something valued is usually seized, and where many others suffer from their actions.

Notes

1 Google, www.google.com, and JSTOR, www.jstor.org (accessed June 12, 2012).
2 T. Klein, "Apollonius' Jason: hero and scoundrel," *Quaderni Urbinati di Cultura Classica*, 1983, vol. 42, pp. 115–26, quote from p. 115.
3 Ibid., p. 116. *Amechanos* is a Greek word for being unresourceful or hapless.
4 R. L. Hunter, "'Short on heroics': Jason in the Argonautica," *The Classical Quarterly*, 1988, vol. 38, pp. 436–53. Quote from p. 441.
5 C. R. Beye, "Jason as love-hero in Apollonios' Argonautica," *Greek, Roman and Byzantine Studies*, 1969, vol. 10, pp. 31–55. Quotes from p. 48 and p. 53.
6 R. Hunter, trans., *Apollonius of Rhodes, Jason and the Golden Fleece*, Oxford, Oxford University Press, 1993, p. 89.
7 Hunter, "'Short on heroics,'" p. 440.
8 Hunter, *Apollonius of Rhodes*, p. 14.
9 Ibid., p. 45.
10 Ibid., p. 50.
11 J. J. Clauss, *The Best of the Argonauts: The Redefinition of the Epic Hero in Book One of Apollonius' Argonautica*, Berkeley, CA, University of California Press, 1993, p. 210.
12 Hunter, *Apollonius of Rhodes, Jason and the Golden Fleece*, p. 95.
13 Ibid., p. 78.
14 C. S. Brye, "The killing of Apsyrtus in Apollonius Rhodius' *Argonautica*," *Phoenix*, 1996, vol. 50, pp. 3–16; L. Schneiderman, "The death of Apsyrtus," *Psychoanalytic Review*, 1967, vol. 54, pp. 159–76.
15 E. B. Bongie, "Heroic elements in the Medea of Euripides," *Transactions of the American Philological Association*, 1977, vol. 107, pp. 27–56. Quote from p. 31.
16 Ibid.
17 P. Easterling, "The infanticide of Euripides' *Medea*," *Yale Classical Studies*, 1977, vol. 25, pp. 177–91. Quote from p. 185.
18 Ibid., p. 180.
19 Ibid., p. 190.
20 Ibid., p. 191.
21 John Schwartz, "Internet activist, a creator of RSS, is dead at 26, apparently a suicide," *The New York Times*, January 12, 2013; and "Obituary: Aaron Swartz," *The Economist*, January 19, 2013, p. 94.
22 D. Boedeker, Euripides' Medea and the vanity of ΛΟΓΟΙ, *Classical Philology*, 1991, vol. 86, pp. 95–112. Quote from p. 97.
23 Ibid.

24 Ibid., p. 103.
25 Ibid., p. 104.
26 R. Warner, trans., *The Medea* in *Euripides I*, eds D. Grene and R. Lattimore, Chicago: University of Chicago Press, 1955, lines 807–10.
27 S. A. Barlow, "Stereotype and reversal in Euripides' 'Medea'," *Greece & Rome*, 1989, vol. 36, pp. 158–71. Quote from p. 163.
28 Ibid., p. 169.
29 H. Foley, "Medea's divided self," *Classical Antiquity*, 1989, vol. 8, pp. 61–85.
30 Ibid., pp. 65–66. This was a "principle of social organization in the archaic and classical periods," and even constituted a Platonic definition of justice.
31 Ibid., p. 66. To bolster her argument, Foley examines in great detail the meanings of the Greek word *thumos* ($\theta\upsilon\mu o\sigma$). She finds that it does not equate with irrationality as many have maintained, but rather that it defines motivation and agency (p. 69). She finds a split within Medea's psyche to be her personal tragedy: "And it is precisely this inseparable combination of rationality and irrationality, passion and intelligence, in Medea's determination for revenge that makes it so very terrifying, and I think, far more tragic than a philosophical defeat of reason by passion" (p. 73). We can, in other words, see how pointedly Medea represents for us a dark dimension of our souls.
32 Ibid., p. 81.
33 Ibid., p. 77.
34 Ibid., p. 79.
35 Ibid.
36 Ibid., p. 83.
37 Bongie, "Heroic elements in the Medea of Euripides," p. 39.
38 Ibid., p. 46.
39 Ibid., p. 51. Bongie frames the central conflict in this light as well. She writes that Medea's "maternal feelings again beg her to spare the children, but once more her fierce honour code prevents her from yielding." This code is what lies behind the ruthless selfhood of a hero that he or she proclaims sometimes violently.

> The heroes of Greek tragedy are not reasonable . . . All reject the "reason" of the Chorus or of other characters, insisting on working out the requirements of their destiny, or the circumstances outside their control, in terms of their own standards and the demands of their own character.
>
> (p. 52)

This motivation is sometimes horrifying, but its unrelenting force fascinates us, draws us to create our own heroes, and ultimately attracts us to their daring and often reckless nature.

40 B. M. W. Knox, "The Medea of Euripides," *Yale Classical Studies*, 1977, vol. 25, pp. 193–225, quote from p. 211. Knox humanizes Medea by asserting that she is not a witch or sorceress because her character predates the origins of that term (p. 213). The concept of witch was not known to fifth-century Greek vocabulary, which instead referred to a woman "who deals with love-charms, drugs and poisons" (p. 214). He also understood Medea to represent an archetype of feminine cleverness—then a novel depiction in Greek drama (p. 222).
41 C. Segal, "Euripides' Medea: Vengeance, reversal and closure," *Pallas*, 1996, vol. 45, pp. 15–44, quote from p. 20.
42 Ibid., p. 27.
43 Ibid., p. 30.
44 Bongie, "Heroic elements in the Medea of Euripides," p. 55.
45 Knox, "The Medea of Euripides," p. 225.

46 Segal, "Euripides' Medea: Vengeance, reversal and closure," p. 42.
47 K. Kerényi, *Goddesses of Sun and Moon*, trans. M. Stein, Irving, TX: Spring Publications, 1979, pp. 21, 32, 37. See also D. Odgen, *Magic, Witchcraft, and Ghosts in the Greek and Roman Worlds*, Oxford, Oxford University Press, 2002.
48 S. P. Mills, "The sorrows of Medea," *Classical Philology*, 1980, vol. 75, pp. 289–96, quote from p. 295. Mills notes that Medea subsequently established a Corinthian cult to atone for her monstrous deed. The practical function of this cult is to serve as a remembrance that Medea is in "perpetual mourning" over her crime.
49 Knox, "The Medea of Euripides," p. 220.
50 Ibid., p. 196.
51 M. L. Ryder, "The last word on the Golden Fleece legend?" *Oxford Journal of Archaeology*, 1991, vol. 10, pp. 57–60.

5

CHILDREN WHO STEAL

I was sitting in my office at the school when a teacher came in and said, "He did it again." I asked who did what again, and she replied, "Kyle. He stole something out of my purse, but one of the other teachers caught him later when he was trying to hide it in his backpack." I asked what had he stolen, and she answered, "My lipstick, same as last time." She continued, "He's a makeup thief. Of all the things to steal, he's just obsessed with makeup. At least we finally know who's been taking it." Kyle at this time was just 5 years old.

Kyle was 2½ years old when I first met him. I was the director of a special school for children with psychological, behavioral, and autistic difficulties, and he had just been placed in this setting because no other preschool would accept him. Oakes Children's Center was a psychodynamically oriented therapeutic school established in San Francisco in 1963 by a group of six parents who each had a child then diagnosed with severe autism, probably of the Kanner type.[1] The center was well regarded for working with a variety of children whose disturbances were rather extreme. Often, but not always, these children had awful family and developmental histories, full of traumatic events, abuse, and neglect. Kyle's young life was unfortunately already true to many of these details.

Kyle behaved primarily in one of two ways: either excessively withdrawn, mute, and unreachable, or driven by manic excitement that included hitting and biting others, speaking incoherently, and acting out completely precocious sexual behaviors such as kissing teachers, touching their breasts, rubbing or thrusting against adults, and groaning in feigned delight. At other times, he would be mute for hours at a time, slumped into a fetal position on a mat, and unresponsive to attempts at interaction. He appeared deep within an autistic shell during these periods, but often would use this withdrawal as a ruse for his other preoccupation—stealing makeup from women staff at the school. Kyle would typically sneak into one of their purses, usually when they had just returned from lunch or a break, and take small items of makeup: lipstick, mascara, nail polish, and cosmetic blush.

Kyle stole from different teachers, so for a period of time, his thefts went mostly unnoticed because the victim generally thought she herself had lost the item or misplaced it. Only later, when we discussed his problem at a case review, did the extent of his stealing become clear—as many as six teachers confirmed missing items, sometimes from their purses, which normally they kept in a separate area from the children, or sometimes when they had just come out of the bathroom and perhaps set a lipstick on a desk before putting it away. Apparently, Kyle could spot an opportunity and move quickly, both of which were seemingly at odds with his more autistic presentation.

Kyle's spoken vocabulary at this point in his life was small, perhaps no more than 100 to 150 words. He could gesture well, used pictograms on flash cards for many basic requests, and knew some basic signs from American Sign Language. Over his first two years at the center, he became more able to communicate his needs and sought more human interactions, both of which spoke well for his development. I supervised Kyle's treatment for over 12 years, and during the times his therapist was away on maternity leave, I substituted for her and saw Kyle for his therapy sessions. He also knew me well because the school was small, with no more than 20 children enrolled, and he often asked his teachers to visit me. These were usually short visits, when he might bring me a drawing (typically a stick figure reaching for something just out of his grasp) or say to me, "You day" meaning "how is your day?" to which I would give him a thumbs up, thumbs down, or thumbs to the side. I would ask about his day, and he would respond in kind and then leave.

Early History

Kyle's early developmental history was nothing short of appalling. His mother, Ms. B., was addicted to heroin and crack cocaine. Prostituting herself to support her addiction, she unwittingly became pregnant. Ms. B. lived in a housing project that was so dangerous and drug-ridden, social workers would not enter it without police escort. (A few years later, the city would completely demolish these apartments in order to build anew.) Ms. B. tried to hide the pregnancy, received no prenatal medical care, and likely persisted in a delusional belief that she was not pregnant. She delivered her baby at home, alone, and did not nurse him. A neighbor, who heard the baby's cries, caught Ms. B. when she was leaving her apartment one day and inquired about the baby. Ms. B. reportedly said, "What baby? Mind your own business!" The neighbor insisted that Kyle's mother show her there was no baby in the apartment; otherwise, she threatened to inform the police. Admitting she had the baby, Ms. B. managed to allay the neighbor for a time by claiming her own mother was going to care for the baby. The neighbor continued to inquire about the baby, however, offering to feed and care for it herself, but Ms. B. put her off. Finally, the neighbor contacted Kyle's grandmother, Mrs. C., through a local church. She told her about the baby, and the grandmother was surprised because she had never even known her daughter had been pregnant.

Mrs. C. went to her daughter's apartment, where she discovered the baby in a dirty closet. By then, Kyle was 3 months old, tiny and malnourished, and had probably spent most of his life in a basket inside that dark closet. He also had burn marks on his arms and legs where his mother had apparently burned him with a cigarette. Mrs. C. took the baby, her grandson, to the neighbor while she went to a nearby police station. She reported her daughter's neglect and abuse of the baby, and the police immediately retrieved Kyle from the neighbor and then took him to the city's public hospital. Kyle remained there for two months, at first in intensive care because of his malnourishment and burns. He also had various medical problems owing to having been born addicted to cocaine and heroin. During this time, Mrs. C. applied to become the baby's guardian, and social services granted her this status. Ms. B. was tried, convicted, and sent to prison for her abuse and neglect of Kyle. The identity of Kyle's father was unknown.

Mrs. C. was a religious and compassionate woman who did her best to care for Kyle. She felt guilty herself for what her daughter had done to him. She took him without fail to all his numerous medical appointments, evaluations, and referrals, and she even took leave from her own job as a bus driver so she could dedicate herself to his recovery. When he was 2 years old and still showing no ability at all to communicate, Mrs. C. took him to a university clinic for a long series of psychological, speech, and cognitive assessments that led to his placement at the center.

Pickpocketing

Kyle's therapist initially uncovered his stealing. She was also pregnant, an event that perhaps precipitated Kyle's rash of thefts. On an especially blustery day, she arrived for their session (they met three times weekly) with her hair in considerable disarray. Kyle gestured that she ought to straighten her hair some as they entered the therapy office. She had a comb in a small case she carried (not her purse), and she looked into the mirror in the therapy office and combed her hair while Kyle watched. He smiled and asked to see the comb. He looked at it like a treasure, and she was reluctant to ask him for it back, but she did. He played in the session as he often did, lining up cars one behind another until he had made a long chain of vehicles. He mumbled, "'room, 'room" over and over (imitating car noise), and she spoke with him about the comfort he got from attaching the cars together like this. Her interpretation about safety matched his relaxed tone and his need to feel attached to her.

As this session ended, he gestured for her to help him put away the cars. They placed them back into the box, and then she lifted the box onto the shelf where the toys were kept, momentarily turning her back to him. When she turned around again, she noticed her case lying on the table with its zipper open. She thought she had closed it before, and when she picked it up, she quickly looked inside and saw her comb was gone. She checked her pockets, looked on the floor, and meanwhile, Kyle began humming, which he often did when anxious. She asked him if he knew where her comb was, but he would not look at her. They returned to his classroom. On just a hunch, his therapist mentioned to his teacher about her missing comb. Later, the teacher spotted Kyle taking the comb from one of his pockets. Perhaps overreacting to her discovery, she then searched his backpack, finding three lipsticks and several other items of women's makeup that he had stolen.

Mother Car

Here, I will comment only on the first phase of a long, complicated treatment that greatly helped to heal many wounds in this boy's traumatized psyche. From the ages of three to six, Kyle created a story in his therapy, through drawings, play, and his fascination with a television show, of what he believed about his mother. In short, he thought she was a robotic car, a character from a television series titled *Knight Rider*. Kyle's grandmother discovered his passion for this show quite accidentally, and she began taping episodes for him that he would watch repeatedly every day. In this series, the hero drives a fantastic talking car that is equipped with advanced weaponry and artificial intelligence. Together, the hero and his super-powered car defeat villains and criminals, including thieves. The car is named Kitt.

One day, Kyle said to his therapist, "My mother." The therapist asked him if he could say something about his mother, and Kyle replied, "My name Kitt." At this point, Kyle could only use the personal pronoun *my* or *mine*, which he used indiscriminately for *your*, *our*, or *her*, and so on. He definitely knew his name was Kyle, so what he meant in this exchange with his therapist was "my mother Kitt." A long story, laboriously told over more than a year, then emerged, and in Kyle's mind, it told about him and his car mother, Kitt.

I can only summarize a few of the details about Kyle's fantasy about his mechanical mother. He showed how he imagined that he was born from her trunk. This occurred in play with a car that had hood and trunk lids that could be opened. For many sessions, Kyle lifted the lids, looked inside, and closed them—time and again, he looked disappointed that the hood and trunk were empty inside. He then found a small toy baby figure that he put into the trunk. When he closed the lid and then opened it again, he laughed gleefully. Although this activity could perhaps convey a primitive notion of an anal birth, it also could allude to his early infancy spent in a dark closet. Later still, he found toy food that he could fit under the hood, thus discovering a way to give Kitt a nourishing breast instead of the empty space suggestive of a dead, vacuous breast.

A recurring story was that Kitt would get captured by an "army." Kyle would have toy soldiers shoot relentlessly at Kitt and then encircle the car. Sometimes he would frown and stop the play suddenly, as if an upsetting image filled him of his mother car, Kitt, possibly being dead. When the therapist mentioned that he looked sad, he would grow angry, throw all the soldiers to the ground, and make the Kitt car attack the therapist while he shouted "'room, 'room." His mother was by now out of prison, yet had had no contact with Kyle since her release.

When his therapist went on maternity leave, I saw Kyle for six months. He was sad and withdrawn and in the first sessions wanted to huddle under the table while insisting that I watch him. I commented on how sad he might be, missing his therapist and feeling left alone to wonder if I might be enough to pull him out for something good to happen between us. I could not help but think of the baby in the closet waiting to be rescued by someone and the despair of this image. Several sessions later, he came out from under the table and picked up with the car play. Pointing to the car, he told me, "Kitt. 'room, 'room, 'room." The car ran over a female doll repeatedly, and thinking of his absent therapist, I commented how mad Kitt was at the doll for not playing with him. He would nod and say "Bad. Bad."

Kyle later attacked me with the Kitt car, and he got quite physical in wanting the car to literally run me over. He tried to get me to lie down on the floor to do this, and when I refused, he instead ran the car over my shoes. I commented, "I'm bad for you and Kitt. I'm not [therapist's name]." He liked this remark and, for a time, would repeat this scene at the start of each session, before changing the play to Kitt and the soldiers who battled one another.

At some point, I thought to say to Kyle that his therapist would remember him. I pointed to my head saying, "Up here, she'll remember you. She has a picture of you right here." He smiled and then pointed at my head and asked, "Radio?" I knew from the television show that Kitt communicated to others through the car radio. I said to Kyle, "Yes, I have a radio, and [therapist's name] does, and Kitt does, and you too." He seemed relieved that our radios could communicate and would not die or go silent. He spontaneously said, "Like radio," which I took to mean that he appreciated my humanizing voice, even if, for now, Kitt still played the fantasy mother and he was disappointed by his therapist's leave.

Early Deprivation and Stealing

Kyle's stealing of cosmetics was linked to his struggle to locate a mother in the real world. In some sense, he felt stolen from: his mother took a precious, vulnerable, even critical time in his infancy and corrupted it. The therapist's maternity leave, likewise, re-created for him a feeling that something trustworthy could be snatched away and put out of reach. He stole conspicuously feminine articles of adornment. Why? Certainly, the car mother, Kitt, was anything but feminine, with its hard surfaces, weapons, robotic voice, and heroic call to duty.

Kyle seemed to be reconstructing a missing first object. His mother had been so unavailable during his early months, that whatever Kyle knew of her was associated with aggression and hardness. A mother who burns her infant behaves with terrible cruelty, and in Kyle's case, this experience left him to take in an abusive object that gave him pain and projected chaos and darkness into him. Kitt's missiles, which we might think of as analogous to his mother's burning cigarettes, probably were not at all a stretch in Kyle's infantile mind for a rudimentary representation of his first object's destructive power over him. Despite what he had been through, he still tried to ascertain some primitive goodness in Kitt, much as any baby wants his or her mother to be good, not bad.

Kyle's stealing of cosmetics seemed to enact his attempt to create a missing piece of his mother puzzle—something softer, more beautiful, and lovely. Winnicott, in his classic paper on transitional objects and phenomena, writes about how a baby's subjectivity arises from the interplay occurring between the baby and its mother.[2] Out of an innate and archetypal experience, an infant looks for his or her mother in the environment because she is needed for nourishment and for nurturance. Kyle's history was one in which he was robbed of this, and this crime affected his development severely.

In a similar way, we could think of Winnicott's ideas about deprivation as it appears through stealing. He understands such thieving as a signal of hope that someone in the environment will respond properly.[3] Such antisocial behavior arises from an early deprivation that has not been addressed or processed psychologically. We might say that Kyle wanted us to know that his mother problem was unsolved and he needed us to pay attention to it—not just his therapist, but all of us—because his own mother had left a gruesome imprint on him. His stealing was a symptom, meaning he wanted us to redress the terrible wrongs done to him by her.

His taking from his female teachers also demonstrated an aspect of the positive side of stealing, or its Promethean dimension, in that Kyle desperately wanted to internalize something more of a caring, attentive feminine object in his psyche. Although his grandmother had helped him along this path, his need was great (as were his past traumas), and he was hungry for more so he could grow. The Promethean aspect of stealing serves to promote growth or to foster development, rather than impede or sidetrack it. There is a popular children's book, *Are You My Mother?*, in which a confused baby bird, lost from its nest, asks this question of cows, planes, and trucks.[4] In this same spirit, Kyle's stealing of lipstick, mascara, and blush imposed on his environment a call for consciousness about what had been stolen from him, namely his chance at bonding with a first maternal object.

Kyle progressed at school, and he acquired good verbal language skills, although with some expressive difficulties. He moved on and eventually finished high school, all the while continuing his psychotherapy at the center. His first job was as an inventory clerk working for an automobile parts supplier. The role that his car mother, Kitt, played in his mind obviously left a lasting impression on him.

We could also interpret from Kyle's story that his mother enacted a type of Medea complex toward him in that she sought his destruction, perhaps even consciously. His story demonstrates an aspect of the archetypal level of the Medea complex because he was forced to internalize his mother's destructiveness, which he later transformed into a compensatory tale about his origins (Kitt, the super-weapon car from *Knight Rider*). His imaginary mother Kitt was hard, powerful, resourceful, destructive, and heroic. In these ways, she resembles Medea in the myth. Thankfully, another type of mother became available to him in the real world through the loving care that his grandmother provided him into his teenage years, and through his many positive attachments to therapists and teachers. The importance of the subjective reality of the car mother never quite disappeared, and even as a 16-year-old, Kyle remarked, "I still never get bored watching that show. And I know I've seen it hundreds and hundreds of times."

Sadistic Stealing

Another example of a child stealing shows some similarity around this theme of deprivation, but also illustrates a very different outcome in terms of what the child's stealing leads to. TJ was a muscular 11-year-old boy when he enrolled at the Oakes Children's Center (the same program as Kyle). He had been expelled from his public school for physically attacking other children as well as teachers. He was the only child of parents who had been locked in a contentious divorce for five years. Both parents worked, and both admitted that their marriage had never been easy, full of intense arguing and failed promises. They each said that they loved TJ, but their actions did not seem to support this claim because he was often left alone after school, on evenings, and on weekends. It was as if he was a burdensome reminder of their failed relationship, and somewhat concretely, they avoided him to keep that thought from awareness. Neither of them understood how seriously disturbed he had become. When he came up as a topic, sooner or later, they would begin to voice mutual recriminations about the other's failures as a father or mother, discussions that often ended in a shouting match. TJ got lost in the process.

Soon after TJ started at the school, he was caught stealing money from a teacher's wallet that he managed to lift from her purse, which was hidden where she thought it would be secure. TJ initially denied he stole the money and lied about what had happened. He blamed another student, who TJ claimed instigated the theft; TJ wanted us to see him as a victimized accomplice. This other student was cognitively quite limited and unlikely to devise or participate in a plan for stealing in a sneaky way because he almost always said what was on his mind without hesitation—he was not someone who could keep a secret. TJ later referred to this boy as "a fucking retard."

When his parents were notified of the theft, they chose to blame one another. Getting them to focus on his needs at a time like this seemed impossible. They were like useless objects, unavailable for any decent parenting because they were too absorbed in their own hatred of one another. In his therapy sessions, TJ would regularly berate his therapist as "a useless piece of shit" and yell at her for being "fat, stupid, and lazy."[5] She felt rejected and helpless in the face of his verbal abuse, a projective identification of his dilemma with his own parents. TJ experienced his parents' overall lack of interest in him as a burning rejection and emotional dismissal. Considering the situation, the school recommended he attend a residential school where he would receive comprehensive care away from his parents. To everyone's surprise, they agreed, although this may have been because social services was then threatening action against them because TJ had been left unattended for such long periods of time.

As is typical in complicated social service systems, nothing happened quickly. While awaiting placement at a residential center, TJ again stole from a staff member, taking more than $100 from her purse during a school assembly. He was caught the next day. He came to school with a new Walkman and tapes, boasting, "I got this because one of you is a sucker." When one of his teachers asked him if he knew anything about the missing money, he became agitated and punched her in the face. She had to be taken to the emergency department of the hospital to be treated for her injury. Meanwhile, he fell into a sullen mood, and wrote a letter admitting that he stole the $100 during the assembly when the teacher was busy coaching a student performance. He scribbled at the end of his letter, "AND I AM NOT SORRY."

Eventually, TJ did leave the center for a residential school where he spent three years. His return home after that did not go well, and he was arrested for bludgeoning someone in a city park. He then entered the juvenile justice system. TJ's acting out of deprivation and emotional neglect escalated into brutality. Even at the school, when he sadistically punched his teacher in her face, there had been signs of this. His antisocial tendency became instead an antisocial personality, and his emotional deprivation did not follow a course like Kyle's, in which stealing showed a symptomatic attempt at restitution for early losses. Rather, TJ identified with his perceived aggressors, his parents, whom he saw battling one another for years in hate and open contempt.

TJ's stealing was likely also motivated by a destructive envy that attacked others for having what he desired and that fed a fantasy of his vanquishing his victims, leaving them, in his mind, depleted and weak. He showed little guilt over his stealing, using a primitive denial and projection to mask whatever anxiety he might have actually felt over being caught. His envy seemed to arise from an omnipotent and infantile part of his mind that could not find a good object anywhere for containment, safety, or replenishment. Instead, his needs, which he likely felt were dangerous, were projected at others, making them contemptible as "suckers" and "fucking retards." In TJ's case, a combination of early deprivation and chronic emotional neglect led to stealing that was infused with pernicious envy.

Variations in Developmental Vulnerability

These two cases show the prominent role of deprivation and neglect as factors in childhood stealing. Each case also illustrates how other developmental effects contribute to what motivates someone to steal. Kyle's case had a Promethean element, positive in many ways, because he was looking for something lovingly maternal to internalize, to take and make his own. In TJ's case, by contrast, destructive envy drove him to spoil, deplete, and destroy many of the objects he took from. TJ seemed compelled to externalize his hate as much as possible.

Winnicott writes, "*Pseudologia and thieving* can be described in terms of an individual's unconscious urge to bridge a gap in continuity of experience in respect of a transitional object."[6] This statement occurs at the end of his paper on transitional objects and phenomena. He outlines in it how transitional space operates to permit a psyche to incorporate illusion and ambiguity. When this fails, a person's subjectivity suffers a kind of collapse into something more two-dimensional that does not work with depth. An object must be presented and understood a certain way, with no exceptions and no amendments. In such a concrete emotional world, lying can assume equal validity with truth, and stealing can become an outlet for gratifying needs. The fix that is sought by stealing (or lying) might seem to someone caught in this predicament to offer relief from memories of emotional deprivation, indifference, and apathy in a caretaker. Unfortunately, such relief never holds.

In both Kyle's and TJ's cases, there were major developmental obstacles to acquiring an internal sense of transitional phenomena. This problem contributed to their stealing. Kyle was able with much intensive therapeutic work from a young age to develop a capacity for listening to the "radio" in other people's minds, as well as in his own. This experience gave him a possibility of psychological depth. TJ, on the other hand, did not fare so well. He continued to relish a sadistic pleasure in his ability to destroy, and sadly, his mind would brook no room for illusion. His ultimate containment ended up being prison.

Notes

1 Kanner's type of autism, no longer diagnosed as such, was characteristic of the nonverbal, withdrawn form of autism in which a child performed repetitive and stereotypic movements and was particularly hard to engage. See L. Kanner, "Autistic disturbance of affective contact," in *The Nervous Child*, 1943, vol. 2, pp. 217–50. Around the same time, Hans Asperger, working in Austria and publishing his findings in German, described another form of autism in which a child was highly verbal, but in peculiar and perseverative ways; these children also had unusual specific interests and frequently scored better on traditional measures of IQ. See H. Asperger, "Die 'Autistischen Psychopathen' im Kindesalter," *Archiv für Psychiatrie und Nervenkrankheiten,* 1944, vol. 117, pp. 76–136.

2 D. W. Winnicott, "Transitional objects and transitional phenomena," *The International Journal of Psychoanalysis*, 1953, vol. 34, pp. 89–97. Winnicott writes, "In another language, the breast is created by the infant over and over again out of the infant's capacity to love or (one can say) out of need. The subjective phenomenon develops in the baby which we call the mother's breast" (p. 95).

3 D. W. Winnicott, *Deprivation and Delinquency*, eds C. Winnicott, R. Shepherd, and M. Davis, London and New York, Tavistock Publications, 1984.

4 P. D. Eastman, *Are You My Mother?* New York, Random House, 1960.

5 Anne Alvarez has written and spoken about "stupid objects." These are usually parents who are unvalued or devalued because they appear to contribute so little to the child's development. The internalized objects of such a child suffer from a kind of atrophy or thinness. A problem then results because the child's self becomes overvalued in omnipotent and inflated ways. See A. Alvarez, "Types of narcissism and apparent narcissism: Some questions concerning the stupid object," paper presented during "A Day with Anne Alvarez," San Francisco Psychoanalytic Institute, San Francisco, California, 2005.

6 Winnicott, "Transitional objects and transitional phenomena," p. 97. Italics in original.

6

KIDNAPPING

Noah was 30 years old when I met him. A handsome man, he had finished his second year of professional education but failed his qualifying exams. As a result, he was on academic probation and could only continue his studies under certain restrictions. Noah came to our first session wearing a tight T-shirt that showed off a well-developed, muscular torso. He smiled nervously throughout this first meeting and looked at me with his head bowed, as if he were a young child formally addressing an adult, even though we were roughly the same age.

Noah told me that he was depressed and worried about finishing his professional studies. "I screwed up bad by failing the exams. I knew I should have studied, but I just didn't. I blew it off like something in me wanted me to fail. I guess it's my low self-esteem." I wondered with him if it might be something more complicated than just that, and he agreed this might be possible and seemed interested in trying to understand what that might be. Noah was gay and told me he had recently broken off a relationship of six months. He said he missed his former boyfriend but added, "He was a handful. He has a temper and was always going off on me. I couldn't take it anymore."

Encouraged to speak more about his depression, Noah added that he had seen the foster family he had lived with for about year when he was 15. He said, "Actually, I call them my almost foster family. They were great. They tried to adopt me, but because they moved, it would have meant an out-of-state adoption, and for some reason, the two states wouldn't allow it." I asked why he was in foster care at age 15.

"That's when my mother got arrested. They found one of her patients drowned in a bathtub. There were signs that she did it." He said all this too indifferently, like trauma victims who recount horrors with an absence of emotion that is dissociated from the actual events and without any sense of how it might sound to the person listening to them. This latter circumstance, of course, evokes a projective identification in the listener around the victim's shock, helplessness, and terror. I soon realized that Noah spent much of his waking life in a dissociated state of mind.

Noah told me that his mother was in a state prison for the criminally insane where she was serving a life sentence for murdering at least five elderly women who had been in her care when she worked as a home health aide. Noah's father lived in Europe, where he fled when Noah was 6 years old. At that time, his father took Noah's younger sister, who was just 3, and left the country. Although there were court orders for him to return, his father somehow managed to evade them, essentially kidnapping Noah's sister to begin a new life apart from Noah and his mother. Noah said he remembered his sister as "a little princess; she even had a glittery tiara she wore around the house." He said his father was very close to her and not so close to him. Only later would I learn more about the details of his father's abandonment of Noah and how he took his sister away.

Several sessions later, Noah reported this initial dream:

> *I am taking the anatomy course again, but the cadaver is only half there. The top of the body above the waist is missing. I couldn't find the vagina because it is so small. I realize that this corpse is a former instructor. Someone tells a joke, and I get indignant and say, "This is no place to joke!" I keep wondering what her life had been like, but other students keep joking about her body. I thought it odd that she left her body to students she once instructed. Then I'm alone with the corpse, now whole, in a school classroom. The corpse speaks and moves. I ask her, "Why did you donate your body?" She answers, "I thought it was important to donate." There's a pause; then the corpse says to me, "You have to leave." It pushes me out the back door. I run around to the front of the school where one of my friends is dressed like a corpse. He wants my green shirt. We run to the second floor of the school. I try to jump off the roof, but a vine catches my foot. I loosen it and jump. Then I woke up.*

Noah told me he believed he was all right at the end of the dream "because it was just a jump from the second floor. I probably landed on my feet." I was not so sure and found myself alarmed by the dream's seeming message about Noah's relating too closely to the dead and his apparent self-destruction. I did not say any of this, however, as it would have been too early for any such interpretation. I did tell him that I was concerned and would like to meet with him as often as possible.

Initial dreams often convey much about the state of the psyche when a patient enters treatment.[1] Noah's first dream told of dead and dissociated objects that were not even whole, perhaps alluding to his parents—his murderous mother and his father who abandoned him and stole the princess sister and went far away. The small vagina might also indicate how problematic it is to get inside another because Noah was fearful he might find another dead or deadly person. This seemed to be a dilemma for him in relationships. The joking in the dream might have represented the perverse reality that Noah was forced to grow up in, when it was no joking matter that he was left in the care of a criminally disturbed mother. This sense of a perverse, topsy-turvy world pervaded our work together, as Noah found it hard to separate from a core belief that people were not trustworthy and inevitably did hurtful things to one another. Even a place of education, a school, was contaminated by such a belief. I wondered if the vine might not be his last hope that psychotherapy could save him, although it was not enough in the dream to prevent his fall. Perhaps he also worried that he would find me to be unavailable (symbolized by the small opening), and thus dead and frightening to him, so he would have to flee in a dissociative retreat.

Over the subsequent months, Noah told me about a chaotic early life that only worsened after his father left. He recalled his early years as "turbulent" when "my parents fought a lot. I think my mother even hit my father. I remember once he had bruises on his face." He said that when he was 6, he went to school one day and later returned home to find his mother upset and yelling, although no one else was home. There was a letter on the table, and from what Noah remembered of that day, his mother told him that his father had left with his sister and they were not coming back. It seemed Noah's father had secretly planned to leave them, taking his sister with him to the European country his father was from. He had filed divorce papers before leaving and hired an attorney to assist in this process. Later, his father somehow obtained complete custody of Noah's sister, perhaps through the courts in his home country.

His father did not contact them at all until the divorce was final. Noah thought he might have sent his mother a sum of money so she would agree to the terms of the divorce, which probably included his keeping Noah's sister with him. Noah remembered his father as "tall, blond, and strong with big blue eyes." He said that his father had been good to him until the abandonment, and he felt him to be "kind and even generous." He did not think that his father started the arguments with his mother, but rather that she had "a hair trigger" and incited his father. Noah got a card from his father for his eighth birthday. His father included some money and a short note in which he said, "I'm sorry and I love you." He received cards and letters periodically until he went off to college. Only after college did Noah see his father and sister again, during a trip to Europe when he also visited the country where his father lived. He felt sad at the time, not at all angry because "what would have been the use of getting angry? He saw a chance and took it." Noah rarely expressed anger to anyone and instead presented with a nervous cheerfulness that felt artificial. He justified this cheerfulness by insisting that it was important "to stay positive" and to not let on that he was depressed.

When his father fled, Noah was left to live with his mother, whose mental condition only worsened. He said that she frequently talked aloud to no one, got agitated easily, and hit him and called him names for reasons he could not always discern. She had been trained as a nurse but had been fired from many jobs and ended up doing home health care for the elderly. Because she was often away evenings and nights, Noah spent time with an uncle whose family lived in a neighboring town. He recalled that these stays became upsetting when he was about 10 years old because his 16-year-old cousin began to abuse him sexually. The two of them shared a room with a double bed. One night "he just crawled on me, covered my mouth, and put it in me." Noah said that this sexual abuse continued for nearly a year. Later, he maintained, "I kind of got used to it, and I know this sounds bad but I liked it sometimes." The only reason the abuse apparently stopped was because his uncle's family moved to a town that was farther away and Noah no longer visited them. Noah seemed to feel that being raped by his older cousin was not all bad because he felt some attention from the cousin—part of a perverse world that turns things on their head. As Noah put it, "I know it wasn't love, but at least he felt something for me."

During this time that we worked together, Noah began to have fantasies about becoming a prostitute. The medications effective enough to treat HIV infection had not yet been discovered, however, so being HIV positive usually meant contracting a fatal illness. This theme of prostitution seemed linked to our discussing his father's abandonment and that his father had "bought off" his mother in order to get the divorce and keep Noah's sister. I inquired why, as someone with a professional career ahead of him, he might now be interested in prostitution.

He answered, "I like it when men want me because of my body. If they pay for it, somehow that seems even better. It's just a turn on that someone wants you, and then pays when you give them what they want."

I mentioned that he had been sexually abused and had perhaps misunderstood his cousin's attention to mean something positive when it was most likely very hurtful to him. Noah seemed to take this to heart because he gradually lost interest in trying to make this fantasy more of a reality. In retrospect, I suspect that he might have been trying to locate a bit of a good father in me, someone who would not leave him to a perverse fantasy/reality that would harm him. Noah was extremely interested in my work with children, and he often imagined that many of them were from traumatic backgrounds (which they were). I could feel his genuine desire to connect with me as a man in a way that would not turn into something horrible or distorted. At that time, I felt it important to let him explore that he might have wanted more attention from me, whether it was sometimes fatherly, sometimes brotherly, but caring and direct.

Noah reported then that he was feeling "more alert"—"like I'm waking up." The emotional downside of this turn was that he also felt more depressed and despondent. He said, "My life is so fucked up. How am I ever supposed to move forward? I mean, is it even possible for someone like me to recover from all this shit?" There was a hint of anger in his questioning. I understood this as a good development because he had a lot to be outraged about. Traumatized children and later adults often feel they do not have a right to their own indignation about what happened to them.[2] They often are missing an internal sense of normalcy; they don't know what one should expect from parents. This lack can make claiming a fuller emotional response to their situations more difficult. Noah certainly showed that he expected very little in a positive way from others, and he often thought of abuse as what was normal, even in his fantasy of engaging in prostitution, in which the best he could hope for was to be paid for his body.

In considering his newfound anger, I recalled the indignation of Noah's first dream, "This is no joke." I believed that to be a healthy part of his personality that wanted to stop a perverse expectation of how people behaved and instead locate acceptable humane behaviors in those around him. Donald Meltzer writes about the difficulty arising from perverse internal worlds that engender a fear and mistrust of goodness in others because the person dealing with this kind of perversion expects to feel persecuted and taken advantage of.[3] Such a patient's personality may, therefore, even defend against the prospect of change because it threatens how the patient has organized his or her internal world around bad objects that are full of abuse and mistreatment. Meltzer finds that a "unity" is created internally around the destructive part of the psyche and that it resists "being drawn into the sphere of good objects."[4] One can see this in Noah's dream in which the dead bodies surround him. Even his friend is cloaked in deadness, and when Noah protests "this is no joke" and later flees this world of deadness, he races to his own doom. Whatever health might be contained in his protest, in the former instructor's warning, or in his friend (or in the green shirt Noah is wearing) is not sufficient to stop this process. He seemingly cannot escape the perverse world of his early life. Others have written about how perversion functions to ward off unbearable psychic pain in protecting the patient from an imminent breakdown.[5] I think one could also say that Noah's father stole from Noah—stole his son's chance at a more normal upbringing and at developing the healthy parts of his young personality. When Noah's father left with his sister, he also kidnapped a valuable part of Noah.

Trauma from a Medea-Like Mother

After we had been working together for six months, Noah began to recount to me what had happened to him at age 15 when his mother's psychosis evidently worsened. One day he came home to find her rambling out loud in the kitchen. She yelled at him, telling him he was "worthless" and "no good." She said she wished he were dead because then she'd finally be free of "raising a shitty son who will never amount to anything." At these times, he told me he had often had tried to calm her down, but that as he moved more into adolescence, he found that leaving the house or retreating to his room was a better option. He turned to leave the kitchen when she suddenly rushed at him, grabbing him by the neck. She was "a stocky woman, strong as a bull, with thick arms and incredible power." He had often experienced this strength firsthand when she had hit him or shoved him against walls.

He recalled, "I wasn't muscular then. I was a skinny teenager, and she was a lot bigger than me." She had put both her hands around his neck and pushed him against a kitchen counter with his back to it. She would not let go, and he began to feel lightheaded. He said, "I couldn't breathe and knew where this was going. She was going to strangle me to death. One of my hands felt a saucepan on the counter. I don't know how, but I got hold of it and hit her with it." She released her grasp, and he remembered gasping for air as he hunched over and nearly fell. She reached for a kitchen knife and lunged at him. He continued this nightmarish story. "I tripped and fell. Because I fell, she missed me, and almost fell on top of me, but instead she scraped herself bad on the counter. I saw her bleeding where the skin had torn." Noah got up and ran out of the house.

This story appears more coherent as I write it years later than when he originally recounted it. As he told it, he broke down, sobbing at various points. His full account of this traumatic event emerged over many sessions. I often felt a sick, heart-wrenching pain while listening to him. He kept checking my reactions, as if to see how I was doing, and I commented that I suspected he was worried about whether I would be able to hear him tell it all. He remarked that he had been required to tell the police what happened but kept crying so much that "I think they thought I was an awful witness."

He ran to a nearby house, the home of a family that had three teenaged sons who were his friends. He had previously spent much time there and felt accepted and cared for by their parents. Noah did not return to his mother's. The police arrested her, and, although she spent a short time in jail, she was released pending a trial for assaulting her son. Noah was able to stay with his friends' family, and they initiated a legal process to become his foster family. Noah reported that he "felt like a criminal," which was a conflation of himself with his mother for her actions. He was confused because he felt he was supposed to cover for her and that his "betrayal" made him somehow guilty. This misplaced loyalty seemed to have been one of the tragic results of his earlier abandonment by his father. Noah had continued to feel obliged to protect and stand by his mother no matter how badly she abused him, even to the point of trying to take his life. He had great difficulty in psychologically separating himself from his Medea-like mother.

Why was she released? Why wasn't she tried for attempted murder? Noah only partly touched on reasons that might answer these questions. Perhaps he was, as he believed, not "a good witness" because of his expressed ambivalence at being called to testify against his own mother. This legal necessity puts any child in a terrible bind of accusing a parent, whom he or she may still love despite all the parent's failings and crimes. Noah called this predicament "a lose-lose situation." Meanwhile, his mother continued to work after her release. Noah remembered that he was interviewed by many detectives and attorneys during this time, but he acknowledged, "My memory of it isn't so clear. I was living in a haze." In all likelihood, he was frequently living in a dissociated state of mind. Whatever clarity he did have, he poured into his academics at school, where he achieved excellent grades. The split in his personality must have been remarkable because he did not collapse and was capable of maintaining his academic record.

During this period, one of the elderly women his mother cared for was discovered dead in a bathtub. The ensuing investigation led to her being charged with the murder not only of this woman but also of four others. Some of the evidence was found buried in the backyard of the home where she lived and included used syringes, empty bottles of potentially lethal medications, and vials of poisons. It would be hard not to imagine her as the witchy version of Medea. The family Noah lived with supported him through this difficult time, but after about a year, their father had to relocate to another state for employment. At first, they took Noah with them, but then they were notified that this was not yet legal since their application to be Noah's foster family had not been completed. This was Noah's recollection of the situation, but it again raises the question—why not? Perhaps there were other factors—financial reasons or some conflict within their family—that made it more complicated for them to take on the responsibility for Noah at that time. Part of what brought on Noah's more recent depression that led to his seeing me was a reunion with "his almost foster family." He said this meeting was "very emotional" for everyone. They told him how much they loved him and that they had wanted him to be with them. But Noah too seemed to have harbored a doubt about why this had not been possible.

At this point in his psychotherapy with me, Noah abruptly decided to stop and to also take a leave of absence from school. I attempted to talk with him about the timing of his decision, specifically that his telling me about his mother might have brought up confusing feelings for him about loyalty, betrayal, and abandonment. I thought he might be also feeling confused about me. I wondered, for example, if he were worried whether I would stand by him (or also become unavailable like his foster family and father) through his sorting out these events in his life that defied what anyone would think was reasonable or expectable for a boy. I also offered that remembering so many traumatic details might have felt like too much to handle. He was somewhat open to these ideas, but he insisted on stopping, telling me, "I'll be back. I just need a break for a while." I conveyed to him that I would be available, and I also thought it likely he might return. Sometimes, patients with histories of trauma have to tell their story and subsequently leave, as if to test the therapeutic relationship with a question about whether each of them can survive knowing what has been told. Trauma is a threat to survival. Would I still be there when he came back, or would I become another corpse? More terribly he might have wondered, would he survive after telling me his story?

After a Gap

Two years later, Noah phoned me to ask for an appointment. When I met him this time, he looked physically older, as though he had aged more than two years, and was also discernibly melancholic in his expression. He told me that he was again feeling depressed and listed several reasons for his depression: 1) although his class had graduated, he had to complete an extra term before he would graduate; 2) his boyfriend of one year had just told him that he no longer loved Noah; and 3) that one day following the graduation ceremony (in which he was able to participate despite not yet receiving his diploma), Noah learned that he was HIV seropositive. He was extremely anxious as he told me these details. I was reminded of his previously flooding me with material that felt unprocessed, raw, and like Bion's beta elements. Noah obviously continued to need much therapeutic containment. The medical news particularly concerned me as I remembered both Noah's fantasy about prostitution and the self-destruction within his initial dream.

Noah too was panicked about his HIV status (the retroviral medications to treat HIV were still a couple years away from distribution). He told me how he routinely had unsafe sex. "It's no wonder I got it." I asked why he was having unsafe sex. He said, "I don't know. You'd think someone with all my education would know better. I just seem drawn to tragedy." I inquired about that self-observation, and Noah told me, "It seems the more dishonorable the guy, the more I'm attracted to him. Like I can't keep myself from the sleazy types. I used to think it was just because I didn't think better of myself, but now, with this HIV, I'm wondering if I'm wired to self-destruct." He was despondent about the HIV, blaming himself for bringing it on—a cycle of fault finding and self-blame that felt familiar to him.

In talking about why he might be "wired to self-destruct," I mentioned that Noah's father had left him with a destructive mother and no one to really look after him. He said that his mother was still in prison and probably would be "for the rest of her life." Referring to his father, he added, "Yes, I kept thinking about something you once said to me over two years ago, that he had no right to leave like that. I always told myself he made a good choice to save himself and my sister, but I wouldn't let myself think about why he left me behind. He made a choice about me too, and look what's happened. I don't even know if I'll survive this HIV diagnosis. If I get sick, I'm probably done for." At the time, an HIV diagnosis was often viewed as fatal.

I found myself feeling guilty about Noah's HIV diagnosis. Had I let him leave therapy too easily? Should I have warned him more explicitly about my concerns that something in his psyche was too exposed to a world of dead corpses? Would it have made a difference to have insisted that he stay in therapy to work through the traumatic retelling of his mother's crimes? I think this countertransference guilt, while it did reflect some of my personal doubts, was also a response to a projective identification of Noah's helpless panic and terror into me about my now facing a damaged, sick object seemingly beyond hope or repair—in other words, like him as a boy trying to fix and take care of his mentally ill mother for all those years. I felt an implicit reproach in Noah's ruminations about how he got HIV, so I decided to ask him if he felt I had not stood by him strongly enough and warned him more urgently about the risks. He took this up, saying, "It crossed my mind. You knew I was medically informed. I might have wished you were stern with me, like brow beating me into good behavior." He believed that it wouldn't have worked because he probably "wouldn't have listened to you." When I heard this, I imagined that Noah's references to "stern" and "brow beating" were what he felt were desirable characteristics of a good father who would know just what kind of firmness his son needed.

I mentioned to Noah that perhaps he might feel angry with me for not "brow beating" him with obvious warnings. He replied that he had difficulty seeing anger as constructive because his mother's rage had been so upsetting and abusive. We talked about how anger is not only that extreme, and he appeared relieved by an idea that anger has degrees of intensity. I suggested that maybe he hid his anger too much from others, because he had learned to do so at a young age. Perhaps trying to normalize somewhat, I later said that he had had a life full of horrible misfortunes, about which anyone should rightly feel angry. Noah spoke about "betrayal—it's the theme of my entire fucking life, one betrayal after another, and I just wonder how anyone can live with so much of it." I thought this anger was healthy, and I told him so. I recalled his first dream and the remark he made about not joking. He spoke about his meekness and hesitation in speaking up when he didn't like something. During this course of our work together, Noah was more able to articulate how he felt toward me, although often this produced considerable anxiety for him.

Our discussion about betrayal turned to Noah's father. For the first time, Noah acknowledged that his father had betrayed him. He began to understand a connection between his father's abandonment and his attraction to "sleazy, dishonorable men." Noah saw these men as sooner or later mistreating him, much as he now felt his father had done by not taking him when he left. Noah wondered if his father saw him as less appealing and less desirable than his sister. He spoke about his father's taking his sister away and wondered why the legal authorities hadn't demanded he bring her back. He concluded that his father "got away with kidnapping her." At that time, I was not thinking about Jason, Medea, or the Golden Fleece, but his remark about kidnapping struck me as poignant and compelling because he was also a victim of his father's actions. I commented to Noah that he could now feel outraged by what his father had done, and he sighed, "Maybe. Could I be outraged about him taking her?" Then he paused, and after a long silence said, "And leaving me behind."

A Thieving Father

In looking back at our work together, I can now see that Noah was stolen from. His father behaved like a reckless Jason who seized the treasured sibling, stealing her. In the process, he also stole from his son the chance to have a father—who would have represented a greater sense of stability, normality, and healthy adjustment. In his absence, Noah did not get an opportunity to internalize such a father. Instead, he was left with a mother who acted like the vengeful Medea of Euripides's play. Quite possibly, she hated Noah because he reminded her of his father who left her so cruelly. Certainly, Noah was left with her to live a life of archetypal tragedy much like a Greek myth of old. That life also included his cousin's sexual abuse, which further stole from Noah—his body, his psychological integrity and boundaries, and the freedom to find out about his sexuality at his own pace.

I think a major part of Noah's difficulty, aside from the real and lasting effects of lived trauma, was that he internalized a stealing father. I suspect this figure lived on his internal stage in collusion with a perverting maternal object to turn Noah's life upside down. Bad became good, and good became feared or mistrusted. His father left to assert his power over a difficult situation. He stole a child in order to avoid possible shame over dealing with his very disturbed wife. He gave up his son to avoid the pain and complications of confronting his wife in a way that would have taken considerable time and effort. When Noah asked his father in a phone call why he had left so many years ago, his father answered that he was ashamed of Noah's mother. His father's theft of Noah's sister was done in part to gain an advantage over his wife, because it essentially put her in a weakened position in which she could be bought off by an offer of Noah and money. Noah seemed to recognize some of this thieving father in his attraction to "sleazy, dishonorable men." In addition, we might think that this thieving father, in Noah's unconscious, had continued to steal from him by derailing his ability to make healthier choices. This inner figure seemingly snatched good opportunities from Noah and left him vulnerable and betrayed.

His father's leaving when Noah was 6 years old would have burdened Noah's development at an important time. We might think of 4 to 6 as the Oedipal years, when generational limits are better integrated and when a boy has an opportunity to internalize good qualities and positive aspects of his father (or someone else close who symbolizes paternal functioning). To lose a parent is never easy, but to lose a parent at this moment complicates a process of internalization. Noah's only option was to attempt to attribute meanings to a father who stole his sister and in doing so, hurt him and his mother. Although Noah himself did not steal from others, he had within him a stealing object that deprived him of valuable internal resources like self-assertion, empowerment, desire for a better future, and a capacity to hold the line against dangerous interpersonal choices. Noah had lived as though he had to yield himself to hurtful objects in his life. He too often submitted when a stronger, more available internalized paternal figure might have helped him to speak up and say no.

In Noah's initial dream, he asks his instructor's corpse why she donated her body. This word *donate* offers an interesting contrast to stealing. To donate is to give freely for a good cause. One thinks of generosity and altruism in this context. We might consider in Noah's dream that it was as if he were trying to ascertain why someone would "donate" rather than steal, keep selfishly, or charge a fee (think of his prostitution fantasy). Noah understood all too well from personal experience what it felt like to feel ripped off. Perhaps embedded in this initial dream was something symbolic about how people might otherwise exchange things of value with one another. Noah knew about stealing from his father's selfish kidnapping of his sister, his mother's insanity, and his cousin's violation of him. In his mind, exchange had become nearly synonymous with taking, cheating, demeaning, and subverting. His puzzlement over the instructor's "donation" hinted at a desire to understand the normalcy of why someone might give freely without strings attached. In retrospect, I think that this question tucked into the dream expressed a wish in Noah to locate a nonperverse world in which stealing among people was not so brutal. Like Medea's brother Apsyrtos in the myth, Noah experienced that brutality firsthand when he became a casualty of thieving relatives.

Notes

1 R. Maduro, "The initial dream and analysability in beginning analysis," *Journal of Analytical Psychology*, 1987, vol. 32, pp. 199–226. See also C. G. Jung, "The practical use of dream-analysis," *The Practice of Psychotherapy, The Collected Works of C. G. Jung*, Vol. 16, Princeton, Princeton University Press, 1934, ¶¶294–352, pp. 139–61.

2 A. Alvarez, *Live Company: Psychoanalytic Psychotherapy with Autistic, Borderline, Deprived and Abused Children*, London, Routledge, 1992. See also her article, "Beyond the unpleasure principle: Some preconditions for thinking through play," *Journal of Child Psychotherapy*, 1988, vol. 14, pp. 1–13. In that work, she develops the idea that deprived children understand frustration and loss too well because it reflects their real-life situations. As a result, they frequently struggle with accepting positive aspects of emotional life such as pleasure, love, and excitement.

3 D. Meltzer, *Sexual States of Mind*, Perthshire, Scotland, Clunie Press, 1973. Meltzer writes:

> This is extremely important in understanding psychic structure, especially so when we approach the clinical manifestations of disordered sexual states and find evidence even in the most healthy of minds of loculated pathology. These loculations are connected with splitting processes and with the vulnerability of good parts of the infantile organisation to be fragmented by the divide-and-conquer techniques of the destructive part of the personality. However, experience suggests that these splitting processes are not operative in relation to the destructive part, which tends to retain a unity of structure and to be strongly defended against being drawn into the sphere of good objects.
>
> (p. 96)

Meltzer uses the word "loculated," which is a medical term for *compartmentalization.* He is suggesting that although good aspects of the psyche are vulnerable to splitting and division leading to compartmentalizing, the destructive aspect does not fragment and as a result is paradoxically more cohesive.

4 Ibid., p. 96.

5 S. Bonner, "A servant's bargain: Perversion as survival," *International Journal of Psychoanalysis*, 2006, vol. 87, pp. 1549–67. Bonner examines how perversion functions internally as an adaptation to survive when parents have not protected a child:

> In staying away from the exciting aspects of perverse acting out, I hoped to depict this cynical yet desperate quest for preserving a static worldview as a poor man's attempt to grab a moment under the sun in a universe that is believed to deny him the right to exist.
>
> (p. 1564)

In such a world, other persons are not quite real and, instead, exist to soothe and to live out a script that distracts from any psychological pain.

7

SHOPLIFTING

A 16-year-old girl sat across from me and, wiping the tears from her eyes, said, "I don't know why I took it. I always knew they kept money in the house, like in drawers and lying on the counters. And then, while we were playing hide and seek, I just thought I'd find Mark hiding in his mom's closet. But there it was. This huge jar stuffed with cash. A wicked huge jar—you wouldn't believe it—sitting on the floor by a bunch of her shoes. Before I knew it, I was emptying it. I ran and got a brown paper bag and filled it with all the cash. I had no idea it would be over $X (a low four-figure amount)." Phoebe was describing her third and most recent theft, which had just occurred weeks before while she was babysitting for a wealthy family. The prior two incidents were for shoplifting when she was 12 and 14 years old. In the first case, she stole a bracelet from a department store, and in the second, a pair of earrings from an inexpensive jewelry store.

Parents

When I met Phoebe's parents, they were distraught over her behavior and especially worried about her future because of the potential legal problems if the family she had stolen from reported her to the police. Her parents arranged to pay back the money on their own and apologized profusely to them. I inquired whether Phoebe had yet apologized, and they told me no. I asked why not, and they said she was resisting out of shame over what she had done. Apparently, Phoebe felt it would be emotionally crushing for her to speak directly with the family about the theft. I wondered about a written apology but could also see that I was subtly being drawn into issues of blame, guilt, and reparation before even meeting Phoebe. Perhaps I was feeling an initial countertransference in the form of a projective identification from her parents—a sort of helpless feeling in face of Phoebe's stealing. This situation could have reflected my taking in some of their own conflicted feelings about their frustrations in parenting Phoebe.

Phoebe's mother was a thin, wiry woman in her early forties, who came across as anxious, fragile, and judgmental. In contrast, Phoebe's father was a sturdy, robust man, somewhat older than her mother, and he was friendly but also evasive when asked what he thought about something. Phoebe's mother reported that she had been anorectic for nearly 30 years, and that she was currently extremely depressed about her own life, an impression that came across clearly to me. She had, six months before, attended an in-patient program specializing in the treatment of anorexia, which lasted for six weeks. In our meeting, Phoebe's father let his wife take much of the lead, and when I tried to get him to participate more, I noticed his hesitation expressed in short answers and abbreviated thoughts. Phoebe had an older half-sister from her father's prior marriage; however, she seldom had contact with this young woman.

Phoebe's mother told me that Phoebe was out of control. She added that their life at home was "a living hell" and that Phoebe had been "a handful" ever since she was a toddler. I asked what she meant by that, and she replied that Phoebe always had a defiant streak and now was "self-absorbed and irresponsible." Mother noted that Phoebe "swears at us and can get verbally abusive." At this point, I wondered about the effect of an anorectic mother on an infant and toddler, and whether her mother might have been emotionally unavailable because of an affective restriction parallel to the dietary one. Her mother continued, "Phoebe yearns for attention. She likes to be the *center* of any drama she can stir up." This comment again seemed to indicate a real problem in the maternal relationship in which mother might not have welcomed or wanted more interaction from her young daughter—feeling such needs to be indicative of a "drama."

Phoebe's parents told me about the two prior shoplifting incidents and that both times Phoebe had had to appear in juvenile court. The judge was lenient after the first theft, letting her off with just a stern warning. But after the second theft, he lectured Phoebe and threatened her with harsher consequences. He eventually sentenced her to participate in a group for first-time juvenile offenders at the jail and to complete 100 hours of community service. As was customary in this type of situation, both incidents would not appear in a permanent criminal record if Phoebe was able to maintain a clean record until the age of 18. The stakes were, therefore, higher after her third theft because if the family reported it to the police, then Phoebe would not get off easily. Her parents were almost panicked about this possibility and wanted to make amends with the family she had stolen from in order to avoid another court appearance.

I inquired if they might tell me more about Phoebe's wanting to be at the center of things. Her father smirked, "She's a little diva," but then did not clarify. Her mother, however, did. "Phoebe's had too much freedom. We gave it to her because we thought that was how you were supposed to be a modern parent. My parents watched me like hawks eyeing a chick. I didn't want to be like that with Phoebe. But she's abused the freedom we gave her." I thought that Phoebe's mother was telling me an interesting fact about her own experience as a child who was restricted by a kind of intrusive attention that felt overbearing and persecutory. Phoebe's mother told me that they suspected Phoebe had stolen money because suddenly she was spending freely on clothing and cheap jewelry. They received a phone call from the mother of one of Phoebe's friends, who told them that Phoebe had given her daughter over $250 in cash. It was after this news that Phoebe's parents confronted her about the money and where it came from. Phoebe broke down crying—like "a soap opera star," as her father put it—and confessed to taking the money while babysitting. She had also given several hundred dollars to her boyfriend who spent it on video games and electronics. When I asked how they reacted to hearing this story, Phoebe's mother responded angrily, "She's vain. A very vain girl, and that's going to be her downfall." Although many of these details suggested an impulsive adolescent with histrionic traits, I found myself full of unanswered questions. I wondered what might be behind this history of theft that had recently escalated. What kind of attention did this 16-year-old girl long for? Did she feel some nonverbalized need for firmer limits but fear they could become "crushing"? How had she managed to create "a living hell" at home?

Initial Contacts

Phoebe was an attractive girl, although she looked like a young woman far beyond 16 years old, and she seemed to know this about herself and use it to her advantage, especially around men and boys. She told me she earned money through babysitting and that she had been babysitting for a wealthy family for three years, the same family she had stolen from. I asked if she could describe what had gone through her mind later after the theft. She replied seriously, not at all cavalierly or defensively, "I thought to myself that I could use the money to buy clothes and jewelry." She added anxiously that she wouldn't ever do it again and that she knew she had to learn from it. Something in this interaction made me want to believe her.

I asked if she thought that the stealing could have anything to do with feelings she might have about her parents or her family. She was surprised and said, somewhat upset, that she didn't think so, but thought it was "a really funny question" because perhaps there was "something I don't know about myself." At this time, she was not behaving seductively toward me. I thought she was worried, concerned, and even frightened. I took her answer to mean that she was open to an idea about unconscious motivations, which struck me then as promising. I reframed my inquiry, asking if she might just say what first came to mind when she thought about her parents. She blushed a little. "Okay. I guess I can tell you that. My father, well, he doesn't want me to grow up. He's embarrassed by my development, um, you know, um, my physical development. I'm not your typical 16-year-old girl. And my mother, that's almost easier to say, she's a basket case. My mother is so so depressed, I don't know, maybe you deal with people like that, but I've never met anyone as depressed as her. And she has anorexia." I asked how being in a family with these problems was for Phoebe. She replied, "My mother is the *center* of everything." I wondered about that word *center* because both her mother and now Phoebe had used it to characterize the other. Both of them said it angrily too. I began to think that, in this family, emotional resources (for example, love, attention, nurturance) that usually occupy a central position in most families were regarded as rare, to be fought over, and potentially evoking envy toward anyone who appeared to get them at someone else's expense.

Phoebe went on to say that she didn't have "a normal family." I asked, perhaps too quickly, if she ever felt cheated by that. She denied it and instead said that she felt more embarrassed than anything, "Like I have to hide it." I asked what she would be hiding. "My mother counts her cereal pieces in the morning. I come into the kitchen almost every school day, and I find her counting the pieces of her Cheerios. There are measuring cups all over the counter, and she uses them to measure milk, yogurt, and even water. Can you believe it? I don't want my friends to know that." Phoebe told me that she enjoyed food and did not have an eating issue, although she added, "It's a miracle I don't." She confirmed that she felt depressed, both by talking about her parents and about her recent theft. She conveyed a vague sense of loss as she spoke—vague because, beyond an unformed idea about "normal," she was yet uncertain about what it was that was gone or missing from her life.

Winnicott writes about what essentially defines any "normal" child. For him, this concept goes beyond what most people might understand as normal:

> What is the normal child like? Does he just eat and grow and smile sweetly? No, that is not what he is like. A normal child, if he has confidence in father and mother, pulls out all the stops. In the course of time he tries out his power to disrupt, to destroy, to frighten, to wear down, to waste, to wangle, and to appropriate.[1]

We might infer that Phoebe did not have access to something approaching this definition of a normal childhood. Her mother's complaint about her being "a handful" and "out of control," however, might have indicated Phoebe's desire to pull out the stops and see how confident parents would react. More interestingly, Winnicott adds, "Everything that takes people to the courts (or to the asylums, for that matter) has its normal equivalent in infancy and early childhood, in the relation of the child to his own home."[2] Phoebe had been taken to court twice already, and her shoplifting could be understood along the lines of Winnicott's reasoning that she had not found an "equivalent" experience within her own home; in other words, she wanted to appropriate something "normal" there but had not been able to find it. This would imply a significant developmental loss that she had to endure, although she had not had an opportunity yet to make sense of it.

Phoebe did appear to pick up unconsciously on my question about her feeling cheated because, in subsequent sessions, she told me how she felt "cheated" by her boyfriend. She complained that she could not trust him. He became representative of a projective identification about feelings that arise when someone takes what he or she is not entitled to. Like many adolescents and children,

Phoebe relied on projective identification to communicate her experiences of the world. Thinking of Bion's idea about the normative use of projective identification as a means of communication (especially for infants and young children), I began to consider that Phoebe missed an important developmental experience—that of containment.[3] According to Bion, when an infant does not have someone receptive to its projective identifications, these then have to be evacuated by other means, and developing a capacity to contain them internally gets disrupted. I wondered about disturbances in her relationship with her mother that might have resulted in either a refusal or restriction of Phoebe's projections as unwanted and undigestible. In the countertransference, I felt overwhelmed at times by the amount of material she sent my way, as though she were very hungry to be the center of my attention.

Phoebe seemed to look outside her family for containment from others, for example, in her choice of friends. She told me they "are all older, more mature." She started puberty at age 10 and seemed to have missed an accepting family environment that would have held her through an early onset of this developmental milestone. On the contrary, her father seemed unsettled by it. Phoebe's older friends seemed, in part, to deflect her own feelings of loss and dependency because she related to them as if she were simply older, someone who had already left her childhood behind. She was sexually active with her boyfriend who was two years older. Her interest in older men might have suppressed the longing for what she felt she could not get from her father—acceptance of the little girl with childlike needs within an adolescent who is growing up. This acceptance challenges a parent to hold onto at least two beliefs about a daughter at once: that part of her is still quite young and that part of her is looking forward to becoming a woman. Many parents struggle at this juncture and feel compelled to choose one perception over the other.

Settling In

Phoebe decided on her own to write an apology letter to the family she had stolen the money from. When I asked if she wanted to meet with them to talk about it, she immediately said no. She blushed as though ashamed at imagining it, but when I asked about her feelings, she said that she was afraid and couldn't handle it if they were angry with her. She wondered what she would do "if they're mad?" She became increasingly anxious over the letter but eventually did decide to hand deliver it, which meant seeing the couple briefly.

She reported bouts of anxiety that she could not pinpoint a cause for. At this point, I suggested that she was anxious to some degree because she was beginning to see that she did things like stealing that she could not explain to herself. She asked, "Isn't it just bad judgment?" Phoebe began to speak more about her mother's judgments. This topic brought out Phoebe's anger at her mother's attempts to control her, which she felt were intrusive. I also experienced a countertransference identification with Phoebe because I felt her mother intruding into my work with Phoebe. Her mother sent me numerous long and formal letters about various concerns she had, and she seemed to ignore my suggestion that she call me so we could speak about them. These letters were complaints that I was not doing my job: "You are not addressing Phoebe's lack of integrity." I felt that if I reacted to these many provocative letters, then I would have undermined my work with Phoebe because I would be appearing to invite her mother's attention, rather than just tolerating a dilemma of her negative judgments about me and Phoebe. At the time I felt an identification with Phoebe around this issue; her mother probably noticed a similar change in Phoebe's visibly identifying more with me to get better. Her mother might have envied this because now Phoebe was the "center" of my attention.

I began to think more specifically about what it would be like for a child to grow up with an anorectic mother. Gianna Williams writes about a "no-entry system of defenses" that often characterizes individuals with eating disorders.[4] In this condition, a person restricts entry into his or her mind, making it difficult to exchange feelings and ideas because he or she is closed and impenetrable to what someone else brings to a relationship. Imagine, for a minute, a mother (or father for that matter, really any primary caregiver) caught in the grips of this defense system. Children naturally look to their parents for understanding, empathy, and helpfulness. Reciprocity of this expectation undergirds how people come to be represented in a child's mind. If this relational flow is consistently disrupted, then an infant or child is potentially left alone without a receptive parenting figure to help in processing emotions and sensations. A further complication ensues when a parent projects his or her own psychic material onto an infant or child, intruding into the child's developing mind. Williams describes the internal world of such children as one with "craters where the foreign bodies have landed, but around these craters there may be a desolate volcanic terrain."[5] Someone like this needs help, as she puts it, "tidying up," because they feel littered and bombarded inside. I suspect that Phoebe had some of this process because, to me, she felt hungry for therapy, and although I felt she sent many projective identifications my way, these did not seem to be to disable me but rather to help her when I held them.[6] This kind of interaction contrasted with the attacking "judgments" she had felt coming from her mother.

An anorectic parent can convey a confusing message about pleasure, enjoyment, and satisfaction because she regards these as potentially threatening experiences that have to be restricted and guarded against. In particular, satisfying hunger can be fraught with feelings of disgust and abhorrence. What would a child make of this? If a basic pleasure is denied, how is it to ever be gotten? When hunger grows, children will steal food to eat. I think an emotional correlate would be that when life's pleasures are too restricted, then there might first be some protest and then later stealing as a way to reach for a substitute or replacement satisfaction. I believe that Phoebe suffered from having a mother with a "no-entry" system of defenses and that, as a result, Phoebe remained in a state of cumulative emotional hunger, craving attention her mother both despised and envied.

Later Work

Phoebe's anger grew into rage and protest. She announced to me one day when I suggested she seek a compromise with a friend with whom she was having a disagreement, "I don't do deals!" This outcry became the refrain of a hungry child who wanted her nourishment without delay or infringement. She challenged her parents when they set a limit on use of her mobile phone. She challenged me when I suggested we think together about how she might find a way to compromise. She challenged her teachers who gave what she believed to be unfair grades. When I mentioned that we all face a task in learning to negotiate, Phoebe replied angrily, "Why, just why, tell me, would I ever settle for half a piece of gum?" To her, splitting a resource meant losing it all together, and she had little tolerance for that.

At the same time, Phoebe became more anxious about her own appetites and desires. She told me about an incident in a candy store when staff were handing out free samples. She went to take one, but her mother remarked that she might as well simply tape the candy to her waist, implying that Phoebe was not being careful about her weight. Phoebe was at the high end of the normal weight range for her height, but by no means overweight. She worried that if she was not careful, as her mother warned, then "I'll become a rhino." During this period of her therapy, Phoebe stole a friend's mobile phone (hers had run out of its monthly allotment of minutes). I noticed the phone as she nervously passed it from one hand to the other. I mentioned that it looked different, and she said, "It's Tiffany's." After a brief silence, she angrily shouted, "I'm just borrowing it." I said it was interesting that we had been talking about her mother's not letting her enjoy a simple pleasure like free candy, and she had again stolen something. Phoebe yelled, "It's borrowing!" Then she added more quietly, "Well, except Tiffany doesn't know where it is." I asked what Phoebe's plan was for returning the phone, a question that probably sounded to her both judgmental and persecutory—like her mother in the candy store. Phoebe exploded, "I won't keep it!" She returned the mobile phone to her friend the next day, apologized, and spontaneously offered to pay for any extra charges she had incurred. Perhaps her explosion at me was not entirely without insight.

Adolescent stealing can be seen as an immature response to dealing with problems because an ability to cope with delays, limited resources, and a need for sustained efforts has not matured sufficiently. Sometimes this inability may harken back to an earlier deprivation, although deprivation itself may not always be an underlying factor with adolescent stealing, some of which can also be an impulsive evasion of growth toward adult responsibility. Winnicott, as previously discussed in Chapter 3, proposes that the antisocial tendency includes hope: this is a radical statement about the positive value within a symptom. I might add that Promethean stealing is akin to an antisocial tendency. Part of Zeus's revenge on Prometheus was to have the gods create Pandora, who later unleashes all kinds of evil and misfortune on humankind, although the last thing left in her box, which did not get away, was—hope.[7]

Winnicott believes that stealing is at the center of the antisocial tendency.[8] "The child is looking for something, somewhere, and failing to find it seeks it elsewhere, when hopeful."[9] As mentioned in Chapter 3, he argues that what the child is seeking is "the mother over whom he or she has rights," adding "these rights derive from the fact that (from the child's point of view) the mother was created by the child."[10] We might surmise that instead of an anorectic and restrictive mother, Phoebe was searching for someone with signs of vitality, enjoyment, pleasure, and gratification that she could share. Her mother's dating of Phoebe's "being a handful" to her toddlerhood might have also been a reference to her mother's difficulty in letting Phoebe separate from her. Phoebe's unique needs as an individual were perhaps overwhelming to her mother then. Her mother's persecutory judgments might have expressed an intolerance for separation and a desire for a more infantile fusion with Phoebe whom she might have imagined she could continue to control. In Chapter 3, we saw that Winnicott examines the "nuisance value" of the many demands children can make on us. These are often noisy communications carrying a message about feelings of loss, unmet needs, and missing something important. Yet these "nuisances" also can be developmental opportunities when children, particularly toddlers, make messes to test out their limits and to explore what it is like to act independently.[11]

After returning her friend's phone, Phoebe's attention turned to fears of loss. She spoke about possibly breaking off her relationship with her boyfriend, which she predicted would bring her into "a tunnel of darkness." She was torn between discussing these deeper fears and keeping to a safer surface, which she knew well. She told me that with her friends, "We're all fake with each other. None of us could stand to talk about hard feelings." I commented on this conflict around showing herself to others, especially as she was trying to see and understand difficult parts of herself. She then reported this dream to me:

> *I feel an evilness in my boyfriend, but it's not exactly him in the dream. We get into a fight. He tries to kill me. I push him out a window, but my Dad brings him back. Dad is part of his scheme against me. My boyfriend attacks me, and he cuts off all my toes on one of my feet. I cut off one of his hands. There's a change, and we're at camp, and I'm teaching kids how to swim. I think I need him, and suddenly he's there. I don't think I can trust him. My friend Jane shows up to protect me from him. It was scary. I woke up feeling very nervous.*

A shadowy aspect of her personality is carried in the dream by the figure of the boyfriend who is not exactly her real boyfriend; he represents a self-destructive force that Phoebe would like to toss out a window (projection), yet he returns. Her mistrust of her father is evident and perhaps symbolic of her questioning what any man might want from her since she struggled to read her father's intentions in waking life. She imagined at this point that he was having an affair because he was away from home so frequently.

Phoebe's dream conveys a deep sense of persecution and fear related to her own aggressive and sexual impulses. In one way, the cutting off of her toes and the boyfriend's hand could symbolize a harsh punishment for her wayward stealing, a kind of talion justice for Phoebe's hands taking what she should not have (the hidden money). Such primitive retribution would, however, impair her moving forward in life (the missing toes) and finishing her education (the missing hand). In a different way, the dream might have also conveyed her feeling guilty about her sexual relationship with her boyfriend. A symbolic castration in the dream entails a loss of bodily integrity, condemning Phoebe's sexual desires and behaviors.

The topic of loss frightened Phoebe. After listening to a report on the television about threats to life span, she spoke about her mother's mental illness in terms of an anxiety that she might die soon. She also worried that if, indeed, her father was having an affair, he might leave the family, and then Phoebe would "be stuck with my wacko mother." This centrality of loss is something that Winnicott notes. "At the basis of the antisocial tendency is a good early experience that has been lost."[12] Initially, Phoebe dealt with her ideas about loss through much splitting, some of which is evident in the dream (her evil boyfriend and the protective friend Jane). She often spoke about friends, relatives, and her parents in polarized terms such as good and evil, safe and dangerous, protective or villainous, alive or dead.

Transference and Countertransference

An urge to steal eventually appeared in the analytic relationship. Phoebe became openly flirtatious and watched how I reacted. One day, for instance, she asked to show me a photo of her boyfriend, and while showing it to me, she knelt over the arm of my chair. I made some ambiguous remark about the picture and gave it back to her. Before moving away, she asked, "What's that cologne you're wearing? It smells terrific!" I blushed slightly, feeling some embarrassment, and replied that she was noticing something about my body while standing quite close to me. She went back to the couch and grinned slyly. I commented that her smile seemed to mean something, and she replied, "I hope I didn't embarrass you." Even though this interaction has an innocent aspect about it, I felt at the time that something had been taken—stolen—from me. I think Phoebe crossed a line to test me, and in this enactment, I felt clumsy and reduced to being a blushing teenager myself. Now, I can see that she had to bring an element of stealing into our relationship. I suspect some of this impulse resulted from her disappointment over what she perceived as her father's distance from her. How could she get what she might want from a boy or a man? Stealing an emotional response offered one possibility.

This trend in the transference and countertransference continued for several months during which Phoebe complimented me about various aspects of my practice (that I worked with children), my appearance (that my clothes appeared stylish), and my general manner with her (that I spoke intelligently with her and believed she would understand). I wondered what her seductive behaviors were trying to communicate to me. In part, I saw them aimed at idealizing me so she could then imagine herself basking in a glow from my attention and affection. This longing would seem to express her wish for an ideal parent/partner to nourish her. But I also discerned another aspect to this transference, namely that she was trying to gain—even take—something from me because she felt thwarted by her father's remoteness and her mother's restrictiveness. She was actively trying to find a way inside my psyche, which, at times, felt subversive and thieving. She saw a film in which a therapist was killed, and she suddenly became worried that she might lose me. Thinking about these developments in our relationship, I commented that perhaps she was trying to figure out how to relate to me without feeling she had to take advantage of me. She agreed with this and enumerated for me how consistently her parents disappointed her, although many of these complaints revolved around material wishes and her envy of others. Phoebe seemed to be saying that she was not at all sure how to get her emotional needs satisfied without some trickery or theft.

I carefully suggested that her current preoccupation with material desires might have something to do with what she felt was lost in her childhood. She replied, "Maybe that's right. I hate losing things. Last year, I just decided that I lost Christmas when my mother was in rehab. I didn't get any presents, and I just told myself, no Christmas this year." Her protest about "lost" presents is representative of the emotional deprivation and ensuing feeling something has been lost that Winnicott sees in the antisocial tendency. Phoebe also seemed beset by envious feelings, for example, of a rich girlfriend who "has it all. Her parents bought her a BMW for her 16th [birthday]." Envy thus entered into the motivations behind Phoebe's stealing, as well as her adolescent mindset and the earlier emotional deprivation. She talked a lot about this girlfriend, sometimes longingly and sometimes with resentment that startled her. Gradually, she became more inquisitive about "this crummy attitude toward someone who treats me nice."

She began to question why she remained involved with her boyfriend. He recently had been part of a purse-snatching incident in the parking lot of a store where he worked part-time. She was upset that he and his older brother did this to use the stolen money to buy equipment for cultivating marijuana. Phoebe wondered if "you can trust a guy at all." She related other incidents in which boys and young men got into rowdy fights at athletic events and parties. This led to her growing awareness of how she used her sexuality as something of a weapon. Parallel to this discussion about what was happening outside her therapy, she also continued to ask about me in more pointed ways. She asked about the rings I wore and wanted to know if I was married. She asked where I bought my shirts because they looked "classy." She said she was thinking about buying one for her father for his upcoming birthday. She spoke about my teeth and wondered if I had braces as a child because "they look so straight." She commented on my eye color and said, "I think blue eyes are best on a man. Brown eyes are shifty looking on a guy, and green eyes just weird." I could feel a mix of Phoebe's wanting attention from me, flirting with me, intruding into aspects of who I might be, and her anxiety about how I would react.

I reflected on her curiosity as something both positive and risky for her because she worried how I would handle her feelings toward me—perhaps concerned I might even take advantage of them. She rejected some of what I said as "too deep," but she also listened to me, and asked about lying on the couch. I inquired why she would want to, and she responded, "Well, I figure your old people [adult patients] probably lie on the couch. But I bet they do it because they're tired and have to rest. I bet they are not nearly as interesting as teenagers." Some of us might wonder about the sexual meanings of her choice to use the couch, and certainly these were present. I also felt that her request to try out the couch was something of an experiment that Phoebe presented about being more vulnerable in her own experiences with me. These turned to issues of loss that occurred within her relationships. She noted that she felt less desire "to toy with boys" because "it's just the same old, same old." Phoebe became more outwardly depressed, and when I commented on this, she cried, "My mother thinks hunger is normal. Can you believe that? In our family, if you eat, then you're a freak."

Phoebe began to think about her future and specifically if she would end up like her mother. She fretted that she could end up "like Holden Caulfield" whom she considered "a crazy person who is just plain mean" (she had just read *Catcher in the Rye*). Her mother tried to convince Phoebe to do a popular diet with her, as if she could not tolerate her daughter's continued separation heading in a positive direction. This maternal envy is similar to how a Medea-like mother sabotages or even destroys a younger generation's chance at growth. Both her parents behaved as if they unconsciously wanted to impede Phoebe's progress. Her father considered changing the family's insurance, a decision that would have ended Phoebe's therapy with me. Looking back at this moment, I speculate about her parents' desire to steal—to take their daughter's improvement and the positive changes they saw in her. This stealing dynamic may have formed an unconscious balance within her family.

Mary Brady discusses Bion's idea about group functioning as applied to families, and she notes how group processes operate within a family to maintain an impactful unconscious balance between family members. "Families can exert subtle unconscious pressure on individuals in order to preserve the functioning of the group (i.e., family) even to the extreme of a willingness to sacrifice the individual."[13] We might think of Phoebe's acting out through her repeated thefts as signaling attempts to break out of this kind of cycle, so her own development could break out of feeling trapped by the confusing messages within her family. Both her family and Noah's (from the previous chapter) are characterized by Bion's fight-flight basic assumption group, in which members feel terrorized by the threat of attack from others and in a hyperaroused state feel their only choice is either to fight back or to flee.[14] In such a circumstance, stealing might actually feel, to an adolescent, like one way to do both.

During this period when Phoebe used the couch during our sessions, the transference relationship intensified. A renewed seductiveness toward me was triggered by real threats to her treatment. It was as if she were desperately trying to convince me to keep her even if her family could no longer support her therapy. She told me, "You're savage [cool]. I think you're like one of the actors in that movie where the family falls apart because of what happens when they're swimming." She was referring to the film *Swimming Upstream*. This Australian story portrays a family's suffering under an oppressive father who overtly favors one brother over another in their rivalry to gain a single spot on the Olympic swimming team, in other words, the father's insistence about who should be at the center. I suggested that her complimenting me was because she was perhaps worried that she might lose me after we had been going against the current of her family not looking at hard feelings. She frowned at this interpretation. "No, I just like you and do think you look like that actor." I remembered that Phoebe had told me she hated "losing things," and I gently reframed my idea to say that I hoped we would find a way to be able to keep working together no matter how hard things got. In retrospect, I believe that a core conflict in the transference was around Phoebe wondering whether I would be on her team even when the odds seemed stacked against us, or whether she had to obtain this support in covert ways such as seduction and theft, behaviors that were familiar to her.

In particular, Phoebe pressured me through making a variety of demands to see if I would remain on her team—or if I might instead retaliate with my own demands of her. I could definitely see and feel her being "a handful." She insisted repeatedly, "Just answer my questions! You are so difficult!" Her questions became more directed at my personal life and tossed at me like a barb. I usually replied that it felt important for us to work through her anger with me and to talk about what it might mean. I often mentioned an idea of limits in a relationship, which seemed to feel for her like she was "losing something." Phoebe rejected this at first but eventually said, "Okay, maybe you have a point because I feel like when I'm told no, then I lose." Although these exchanges might have been based in the transference on an Oedipal frustration of her trying to steal a father-figure, I think they also harkened back to an earlier developmental period when she might have wanted to take what she felt had never been given to her, namely access to a nourished and nourishing mother.

Phoebe's academic grades improved significantly in high school. She broke up with her boyfriend, although she worried whether she was abandoning him, saying that she was afraid no one else would want him. She also feared that she could not tolerate losing him. Phoebe came in one day dressed very smartly and announced that she had gotten a job as a clerk in a professional office. This choice seemed interesting because it helped her avoid the temptation of another option she had considered—working in a department store full of clothing and jewelry. Her therapy ended about the time she began to apply for college. She was upset at stopping her therapy but observed, "I really learned a lot about myself." She added, "You weren't so bad after all." She thought about studying psychology because she was surprised she had come to see "there's so much I didn't know about myself, and a lot of it is yucky, but somehow it seems to have turned out okay. That's pretty cool."

Coda

Winnicott's concept of the antisocial tendency places a kind of primal stealing within the context of infantile or early childhood deprivation when the child cannot rightfully locate a mother in the environment. Growing up with an anorectic mother could likely cause confusion about what is at the core of a trusting maternal relationship. An infant in this situation would face challenges about what can securely be taken inside because "resources"—emotional and nutritional—can be heavily conflicted from the point of view of a mother with an eating disorder. Phoebe's case demonstrates that a parent who asserts that hunger is "normal" leads to a representation of an internal depriving parent against whom the child's options for satisfying needs are rather limited. This internal figure would steadily threaten a child's natural instincts to reach both for real nourishment as well as for nourishing relational objects. In such a predicament, when something cannot be readily gotten, then stealing is one way to obtain it. Phoebe's emotional hunger was, therefore, part of what her shoplifting communicated to anyone who might have been paying attention. In addition, an internal depriving parent can fuel envy for whatever might appear to satisfy any kind of hunger. Being located "at the center" comes to be enviously eyed as a simple cure-all for a situation of chronic hunger. What ideally should be at this center is a relationship with another person who offers emotionally nourishing interactions and who expects something reasonable in return. Phoebe struggled with her envy and entitlement, perhaps reflecting the desperation of the child's side of facing an internal depriving parent.

Phoebe's stealing also shows distinct adolescent characteristics such as impulsivity, convenient cognitive loopholes, emotional immaturity, and a need for quick gratification. Most adolescents grow out of these behaviors, which to some degree define the developmental challenges of adolescence, with time and support from their environments. We might think of this progress occurring in large part through a growing capacity to contain internally the impulses, urges, and turbulent emotions that an adolescent experiences. Phoebe was able to do a good portion of this work, but it involved recognizing the difficult and painful role that losses had played in her own young life. She had major resistance to looking at this theme of loss in her life. Her eventually becoming openly depressed was a step in the right direction because she could open up her mind to the sadness she was avoiding and defending against. This, too, is part of growing up. Her depression also brought along a discussion of her emotional needs within our relationship where some normalizing (reality testing) about what any person might need was necessary. It took some time for Phoebe to understand that her needs could be thought about as a natural dependence looking for a reliable enough person to respond to them. Phoebe experienced confusion about what might be "normal" emotional hunger. Although she wanted to depend on me, she was vulnerable to tipping into envious attacks at me—"demands" in her words—especially when she felt rejection toward the hungry and needful part of her personality. This demanding and entitled aspect of her psyche likely gained the upper hand when she stole.

Finally, Phoebe's stealing had a Promethean dimension as well because it created an opportunity for her to get psychotherapy where she could finally get help in understanding why she stole. The repeated nature of her thefts points toward something in her hoping for discovery because the hungry part of her wanted to be seen and nourished. A protest about what's normal or not waited in her unconscious to be heard and decoded. What I am calling Promethean theft may encompass Winnicott's concept of the antisocial tendency. Although he does not make reference to any myth, the tale of Prometheus seems to fit his reasoning in terms of a crime also creating circumstances for insight. Phoebe later felt consciously hopeful about her future but not in a grandiose, manic way. She had become realistic about her talents and her weaknesses. As she put it, "I have to be careful around men. And around shiny, pretty things that I can't really afford." That statement reflects an acceptance of social and personal limits that are easier to admit when balanced with hopes that don't seem so far out of reach.

Notes

1 D. W. Winnicott, *Deprivation and Delinquency*, eds C. Winnicott, R. Shepherd, and M. Davis, London and New York, Tavistock Publications, 1984, p. 115.
2 Ibid.
3 W. R. Bion, *Learning from Experience*, Oxford, UK, Jason Aronson, 1962.
4 G. Williams, "Reflections on some particular dynamics of eating disorders," in R. Anderson and A. Dartington (eds), *Facing It Out: Clinical Perspectives on Adolescent Disturbance*, 1998, pp. 79–97, London, Routledge; as well as her book, *Internal Landscapes and Foreign Bodies*, New York, Routledge, 1997.
5 Williams, "Reflections on some particular dynamics of eating disorders," p. 96.
6 Bion's attacks on linking would constitute a more disabling form of projective identification that aims to prevent the object from being able to think and is primarily done with aggressive force.
7 Edith Hamilton writes about Pandora's box, "One good thing, however was there—Hope. It was the only good the casket had held among the many evils, and it remains to this day mankind's sole comfort in misfortune." See E. Hamilton, *Mythology: Timeless Tales of Gods and Heroes*, Boston, Little, Brown & Co., 1940, p. 72. Timothy Gantz cites Hesiod in making a different argument about what was left in the vessel. He states that the Greek word in question could also mean "expectation," and he seems to believe that humankind's hope stems from "the withholding . . . of expectation." See T. Gantz, *Early Greek Myth, Volume 1*, Baltimore, Johns Hopkins University Press, 1993, p. 157.
8 Winnicott, *Deprivation and Delinquency*, p. 125.
9 Ibid.

10 Ibid.

11 Winnicott writes, "This leads to the proposition that the nuisance value of the antisocial tendency is an essential feature, and is also, at its best, a favourable feature. . . ." Winnicott, *Deprivation and Delinquency*, p. 126.

12 Ibid., p. 129. He continues:

> Surely it is an essential feature that the infant has reached to a capacity to perceive that the cause of the disaster lies in an environmental failure. Correct knowledge that the cause of the depression or disintegration is an external one, and not an internal one, is responsible for the personality distortion and for the urge to seek for a cure by new environmental provision.

13 M. T. Brady, "The individual in the group: An application of Bion's group theory to parent work in child analysis and child psychotherapy," *Contemporary Psychoanalysis*, 2011, vol. 47 no. 3, 420–37. Quote from page 434.

14 W. R. Bion, 1961, *Experiences in Groups*, London, Tavistock Publications, 1961.

8

SNATCHING A PRIZE

"Tell me glass, tell me true!
Of all the ladies in the land,
Who is fairest? Tell me who."
"Thou, Queen, art fairest in the land."[1]

But the mirror's answer soon changes, and the queen does not like what she hears when the mirror tells her, "But Snow White is lovelier far than thee."[2] The queen in this Brothers Grimm fairytale is Snow White's stepmother, who becomes consumed with envy for her stepdaughter's beauty and in a fit turns "yellow and green" with this feeling.[3] She orders a huntsman to take the poor girl into the woods, murder her, and bring back the girl's lungs and liver as proof. He pities the girl, lets her go free, and instead kills a wild boar. It is that animal's liver and lungs that the queen orders her cook to prepare and that she then eats. The boar is often considered a relative of the pig, but symbolically the boar is a different kind of animal because of its wild nature that is often associated with a spirituality belonging to forests and woods.[4] The queen wants to eat Snow White's vitality and strength (liver and lungs), the eating being a symbolic representation of enviously incorporating another person and, at the same time, destroying the source of her envy. In the paradoxical world of fairytale, the queen's mistakenly eating organs that instead come from a boar serves to emphasize her missing qualities of what the boar might mean, namely nobility, a spiritual attitude, graciousness, and understanding of a natural order that includes aging and transience. In this tale, the queen's envy leads her down a path of repeated destructive acts and eventual self-destruction.

Envy is one of the most complicated and difficult emotions to admit and to integrate consciously into how we might think of ourselves. Its connection with stealing may appear obvious. Even in the fairytale of Snow White, the queen believes she can steal and possess her rival's essence. We might also consider that she is eliminating a more obvious threat to her position in the royal household, in other words, stealing Snow White's potential future as a rival who could, in her own right, become the eventual queen. Behind envy is an emotional purpose of not only possession but, frequently, also destruction. Hanna Segal writes, "Envy aims at being as good as the object, but when this is felt as impossible, it aims at spoiling the goodness of the object, to remove the source of envious feelings."[5] This sort of interaction can quickly become toxic within interpersonal relations. In the Kleinian view, gratitude modulates our envious instincts, making them tolerable and less problematic. In "Snow White," we might consider the symbolism of the boar as carrying some of this particular meaning. Gratitude often stems from an appreciation of how we can enrich one another in the course of a relationship through a mutuality based on love, admiration, and acceptance. It softens the hardness of pure envy and offsets envy's destructive tendencies, which sometimes include stealing.

Envious theft can be targeted at tangible items such as money and valuable possessions, as well as at intangible things such as power, status, and personal attributes (intelligence, beauty, wit, and so on). The classic 1950 film *All About Eve* offers a riveting exploration of the latter situation when a young woman ingratiates herself to an established actress (played by Bette Davis) in order to slowly steal aspects of her identity so that she, too, can seize a place on center stage.[6] The film portrays the parasitical creep, like a slow infection, of an envy that cannot be held in check. Certainly, envy plays a role in Medea's ultimate vengeance on Jason because she cannot accept his rejection of her for another woman and the shame she feels about this. Jason, himself perhaps also envied by Pelias and Aietes who fear what he might take from them, seems emotionally blind to how envy can play itself out in relationships. Within families, envy can linger as a leftover in a primary caretaking relationship when a child, for example, envies his or her mother but does not feel sufficient positive feelings like gratitude or admiration to balance the negative effects of envy. In such instances, a young child may feel such distress that a desire to spoil anything perceived as good takes over:

> Since strong envy in relationship to the primary object gives rise to such acute pain and hopelessness, powerful defences are mobilized against it. Spoiling, which I described as an aim of envy, is partly a defence against it, since a spoiled object arouses no envy.[7]

This kind of negativity is, to say the least, problematic for such a child's future capacities to relate to others.

Parents can, of course, feel envy toward their children, a circumstance that sows seeds of major confusion for a child, particularly given a parent's usual position in the family of power and authority. The Snow White story in many ways shows the influences of an envious parent who cannot bear to see her daughter surpass her in terms of beauty and desirability. Snow White is left as a girl to experience her stepmother's thieving and hateful impulses, born of envy, directed against her. This situation also happens in real families not at all of the fairytale genre. We saw some of these dynamics already in Chapter 7 as they occurred between Phoebe and her mother, who had an eating disorder; in that case, significant conflicts centered around what were perceived as attentional, nutritional, and material resources within the family. The following case example explores in further detail what happens when a mother envies her daughter's femininity, which she feels somehow threatens her own psyche. Something was stolen in this daughter's development, an important piece of her own identity belonging to her femininity that she had to laboriously reclaim.

Meeting Marie

The first time I met Marie she had trouble finding my office and drove past it several times because of thick fog that evening. This became a metaphor for our early work together when she would tell me she was "lost in a fog" and I was unsure how to find her when she was sitting there with me. Marie was then in her late thirties and decided to begin what would become a nine-year analytic experience with me. She was an educated professional, married to a man who worked in a lower-skilled job, and together they had twin sons. Her father was dying after a series of strokes. Her mother had died suddenly in her late forties of a heart attack. Marie grew up as the only girl with five brothers, and she was in the middle, with two older and three younger siblings. Her father owned a small business and was quite successful. Both her parents were well educated with university degrees. Marie had a cousin married to a man who bore many superficial similarities to me, such as ethnicity, professional background, and the sound of our voices. As she was very fond of this cousin and her husband, these similarities eased some of Marie's apprehensions about me during our initial phase of working together.

Marie described her father as distant and remote. She felt he actively pushed her away. As evidence for this, she told me about an incident when she was 13 and received a perfect score on a challenging math test. Showing him her score, she asked if she might help him at his office. He said no in a derogatory manner that left Marie feeling foolish for having mentioned the idea. She reported many difficulties with her husband, who had a very different background from her own and struggled with staying employed. She related many versions of how he dominated their home, leaving his athletic equipment lying about, insisting on which television channel was turned on, hanging up posters she did not care for, and so forth. She felt there was not even space for her in a house she had bought and owned. She also told me that she felt helpless discussing these conflicts with him because he would likely put her down and dismiss her for acting "uptight." She rarely spoke to him about her angry feelings, preferring to keep them hidden.

Her initial dream seemed to convey her ambivalence about the therapeutic process. Although this dream involved swimming at sea, a good metaphor for delving into her unconscious, it also had "comedians" as characters who possibly represented her own anxiety about taking her pain and suffering more seriously. In this dream, "*a young man takes me to a cake factory out there in the ocean, and I think it'll be great to bring back a piece.*" Marie associated the young man with both me and her cousin's husband, and she commented on some of the resemblances she saw in us. Although she thought the dream "funny," I wondered about a possible initial attitude of skepticism and mockery toward herself and toward psychotherapy. The phrase "it's a piece of cake" denotes something easy to accomplish. It occurred to me that some part of Marie might devalue or underestimate what a therapeutic endeavor requires. Her driving past my office several times in the fog also brought to my mind a nonverbal communication about her uncertainty toward the process.

Soon thereafter, however, a more serious attitude emerged in Marie. She revealed the depth of her suffering in the following dream:

> *A dirty homeless woman is admitted to a hospital for her depression. I help to get this woman into bed and can see she has an infection on her left thigh. I realize I can see right into her pelvic cavity. It's all empty, no organs, nothing. I feel dizzy. Another nurse asks me to make a note in the chart, and I open it and see all these small objects that I think are from your office.*

Marie was upset as she spoke about the empty pelvic cavity. She asked, "What if that's me?" and cried. She continued, "I wonder if I'm that wounded. In the dream, this woman was missing all the internal organs that would identify her as a woman. No vagina, no uterus, no ovaries. It was all empty." We discussed her anxieties about the dream, and I made no interpretations. I was struck by the horror Marie felt at this image and wondered what it was telling us about a feeling of missing female parts inside. Marie spoke some about losing her mother years before and how sad she was that they had not had a chance to resolve many openly intense conflicts between them that Marie dated back to her childhood.

Marie's next dream continued this discussion about the mother–daughter relationship. She reported that she was in the backyard of the house where she grew up and

> *on the roof of the garage, three boys were throwing down big pomegranate seeds for me to catch. They were purple and sweet. The boys pointed into our neighbor's yard, but I couldn't see what they were pointing at.*

Marie had researched the significance of pomegranate seeds and found a connection to the myth of Demeter and Persephone, a mother–daughter story about separation and grief. In the myth, Hades kidnapped Persephone, taking her to the underworld. Demeter, a harvest goddess, would not let anything grow because of her grief over losing her daughter. When Persephone later was allowed to leave, Hades tricked her into eating a pomegranate seed, which meant she could not permanently leave. Marie told me that Persephone's mother

Demeter recognized the trick and conceded that Persephone must return. In the deal eventually worked out, she would be permitted to leave each year, but she would have to return for a third of every year, and during that time, there would be darkness and decay on earth. I wondered to Marie about her relationship with her mother, and she reflected on her mother's "being taken" from her at too young an age—her mother would never return. I also wondered what the boys were pointing at, and Marie was unsure until she remembered the neighbor's surname, which was a homonym for a word indicating grief. She cried, adding "That makes it pretty obvious." Unaddressed conflicts with her mother would become a major focus of our work.

Interestingly, the Persephone-Demeter myth is also a tale with a theme of theft, both in Hades's taking Persephone (stealing the daughter) and in Demeter's revenge of taking the earth's crops (stealing the earth's bounty) until she once more sees her daughter. Marie's curiosity about this myth may, therefore, have indicated more to be discovered about stealing in her relationship with her mother, more than that caused by a premature death.

Marie reported that she almost constantly monitored herself to check for faults that others might also see. She would berate herself when she found evidence of a shortcoming, especially one that related to how she thought she might have appeared inadequate to someone. In our relationship, I saw that she also graded herself for potential missteps. When I asked if she was aware of this, she replied that she worried about coming on too strong with me about her sexuality, a topic she was at first hesitant to discuss much, even though she told me "it's always on my mind." I wondered then how she was managing to avoid it because we barely touched on it. She said she felt "iffy" about trusting me, although she found my "middle distance" somehow comforting. She began to tell me more about her sexual history, but we were interrupted in this process when Marie had a dissociative episode. Her eyes glazed over, and she fell silent. More concerned, I noticed her staring at the ceiling of my office. I asked if she could tell me where she was going, and slowly, she refocused on me. Marie replied, "I was 19." Like the mythical Persephone, Marie had also been sexually assaulted at a young age.

This traumatic event was followed by a nearly complete lack of proper response from anyone she might have counted on, including her family, the local hospital, and the authorities. The police advised her "not to tell her boyfriend." Medical staff gave her only cursory treatment. Later, her parents were mostly uncommunicative about what had happened to her, although they found her a male psychiatrist, who never said a word to Marie during the three sessions she saw him. When she left the last appointment with him, she said, "I guess I'm done here." She felt damaged psychologically by what had happened to her and felt it contributed to her sense of "wounded femininity." As she revealed these memories, she dreamed about a woman "*with a wound in her groin. But I examine it, and the wound is clear. I tell her 'it's looking better.*'" This dream reassured Marie because she thought, "At least this patient has all her organs." Perhaps, she wondered, the dream could be a sign of improvement because the patient was not as damaged as in her earlier dream. She hoped that by talking with me about the sexual assault, she was taking a step in the direction of trusting me.

Marie recalled that relying on men had been difficult since her adolescence. She recalled one weekend during her teenage years when she got injured during an athletic event. She was upset, but her father only said, "Into every life some rain must fall." She was angry at remembering this, and that later her father never once spoke about the assault with her. She had come to believe that all men were similarly insensitive and emotionally remote. She grew up in a very masculine household that her mother seemed to relish. Her oldest brother was the golden child who everyone envisioned as a rising star. He did well at college and began a promising career that he abruptly gave up to move to a rural area where he took up another occupation. Perhaps the parental expectations were too much even for him. As I brought this discussion back to our relationship, she voiced a more specific concern about me: that I might laugh at and humiliate her. She noticed she enjoyed my interest and empathy, but she also was unsettled by this experience. She reflected that she was in a "can't win situation" in which she wanted something from me (attention, availability), and if I gave it to her, she would become anxious because it did not fit readily into her ideas of how men typically behaved toward her. She expressed this anxiety relating to me as "being out on a limb" and worrying I might leave her there to fall. Around this time, her father died, which Marie experienced as something of a relief because he had seemed to be suffering more.

The Rule of the Inner Critic

Following this initial period in our work, Marie became more comfortable and less ambivalent about our working together. She dreamed of "*a young man who teaches me how to swim near shore. I enjoy that he shows me this. He even tells another guy to wait until he is finished with me.*" Marie found the dream to answer somewhat her worry about feeling "out on a limb" with me by showing a safer place (in shallow water) to swim with an attentive teacher, who she thought might be me. Interestingly, the locus of her internal criticisms also moved away from men and her father more directly toward women and her mother. Marie dreamed then about a woman friend, with whom she had once been quite close in a way that reflected a kind of longing for maternal acceptance and mirroring.

> *I'm standing outside headquarters for Sauron, and I greet Nancy who tells me that's no way to say hello. She thinks I was rude. She tells me another woman Avalon can no longer stand it. Then she lets me have it, saying "You are so unreachable, bottled up, and dense!" I tell her it hurts me too, and she gloats, "I'm glad."*

Marie had a complicated friendship with Nancy, and although they were peers, Marie idolized Nancy, somewhat like a mother. She relied on Nancy for advice about many of her life's important decisions. Nancy had quite a bit of power over Marie for several years until Marie realized that the relationship was very one-sided. She saw the character of Nancy in the dream as an authority for "the feminine art of keeping track of important social details," over which Marie doubted her own competence. She explained that Sauron was the dark wizard from *The Lord of the Rings*, and she wondered if his presence in the dream meant she was heading into psychological material about what felt to her like a setting for good and evil. Marie thought of Avalon as a female spiritual authority who was "Druid, definitely pre-patriarchal." She associated Nancy's judgments as indicating that Marie was "petrified" and unable to grow. The dream overall seemed to suggest to Marie that her femininity was a part of her psyche looking for more conscious integration and acceptance, but she had little idea how to go about this. She found it to be a scary topic filled with self-doubts, self-recriminations, and terror that she would never be able to develop further.

This terror appeared in a subsequent nightmare that hinted at depression and a troubling aspect to Marie's self-image. In this dream, Marie reported:

> *We have gone to the downs and an older man leads us around. There's a tree growing in the midst of a rushing river. I think, it started growing roots before it grew up into the current. The guide throws a stone at the base of the tree and awakens a water serpent. I hope it doesn't get me. But it comes up in front of me looking at me like something to eat. Hit him! Says the guide. I can't. I'm frozen in place, and it comes at me.*

Marie thought of the older man as being a bit like her father, but not completely. He was a healthy man and "definitely not a geriatric case." She thought the water serpent was "a sea monster" with ram's horns. The "downs" were a "scary place where ghosts appear." About the tree, she remarked, "I think that's me," and the roots indicated "the base of my vulnerable spot." Marie thought her comment to the guide, "I can't," meant that she was unable to cope with her vulnerability. I wondered if the guide was also a representation of me, and that I would expect her to do something she did not yet know how to do. At that time, I believed that the tree growing in the middle of a rushing current was a possible reference to her own development as a girl—that her conflicts around her gender originated when her "roots" would have been taking shape, an idea that made me think more about Marie and her mother.

Marie recalled that when she went into puberty at age 12 both her parents seemed to pull away even more from her. She felt that she was becoming "a misfit" and experienced a deep shame about menstruating. I asked who helped her to understand what changes her body was going through, and she answered, "No one, really. A friend told me a little, and when my friend's mother saw how confused I was, she explained about tampons and sanitary napkins. My mother never said a word about it." Marie intuited, I suspected, that I thought this was odd, and she asked, "Wasn't that normal for the time?" As we explored this topic,

Marie described her mother as "an abstract thinker" who was not comfortable with emotions. She added that her mother was "legalistic" and might have enjoyed a career as a lawyer. Her mother read voraciously and appeared to prefer ideas over feelings.

For Marie's mother, expressions of feeling led straight to recklessness. Marie recalled the few times she could remember her mother showing a strong feeling, for instance, around the death of Marie's maternal grandfather, although she then told Marie dismissively, "You won't understand until you're older." Her mother had high standards for social etiquette, appearance, and manners. Many of Marie's self-criticisms seemed linked to having taken on these standards from her mother. Marie fretted about her appearance, even though she was very attractive, and early on in our work, she dreaded the times when she had to shop for clothes because she could not trust her own judgment. This changed later when she began to dress stylishly and took enjoyment from purchasing clothes made of more colorful fabrics. But before this occurred, Marie suffered from an almost constant drumbeat of negative self-criticism about not being feminine enough.

As we spoke more about how she had unconsciously accepted her mother's expectations and standards, Marie wondered if a type of repetitive dream she had had since adolescence might be about that. In these dreams, a boat or ship inevitably went aground, and Marie usually felt at fault for these accidents. She wished to be a ship "that can sail smoothly" and faulted herself for being socially clumsy, particularly as a woman. A more recent dream, without a ship, but again with another homeless woman, seemed to speak to some of these anxieties. Marie was

> *in the ocean and jumping waves. It was fun but edgy. Sometimes the waves crash over me. When I'm back on the shore, a homeless woman is angry because the city isn't maintaining the bathrooms. She is wearing filthy layers of clothing.*

The dream image of waves crashing on her perhaps represented the experience of being judged over and over and barely having a moment to catch her breath. Although "fun" in the dream, that aspect might have been something of a manic defense to cope with a process of self-criticism that felt never ending. She said being in the water was "surreal," which might have reflected some dissociation when she felt assaulted by waves of parental judgments. Marie thought the homeless woman was an image of a wounded woman who was "fragile and broken." She believed her to be another version of the woman with the groin wound (in the dream from the beginning of therapy), and Marie felt hopeless because these sorts of dream images seemed to haunt her. I wondered if Marie was frustrated about the slow pace of our work, which had yet to find a way of cleaning what felt to her like a dirty area.

Marie spoke about her mother's life that was cut short when she died in her late forties of a heart attack. She felt this was tragic because her mother seemed to have just begun to open up a little bit. Her mother had taken up painting and showed some talent. But her creativity "was snuffed out," and Marie worried "if the same is in store for me." This idea of their fates being fused together seemed to hint at a problem in Marie's mind, one in which she and her mother were too closely linked with not enough space between them. She recalled that her mother had painted from a photograph a picture of Marie with a violin, and Marie felt very moved by this, both at the time and in telling me about it. Marie began to make collages of her own and took up an interest in photography. This seemed to connect her with her mother in a positive way and also allowed a sense of separateness to come into her mind about the two of them choosing different ways to express something creative.

In her first dream directly about me, Marie reported

> *Robert has a therapy group I'm in with five other women. I've shared a lot and now I listen to the other women. He is also teaching a class, but I decide not to go. I don't want to change my relationship with him that way. The class is called rectifications. In the group, Robert seems inattentive and grabs a book from his shelf.*

Marie reflected on how much her trust in me had grown, although I saw traces of her continued doubts in the dream, such as my being inattentive and teaching what sounded like a course in correct attitudes or proper behaviors. Here, I saw myself as like a judgmental parent who cannot be bothered by a child's needs for attention, at that time more akin to Marie's mother than her father. Importantly, when discussing this dream Marie noted, "The other women, they're just different parts of me, I think. So in this group there's an opportunity for us to get acquainted." To me, that seemed like a hopeful view of what the work was becoming, a way for Marie to gain different perspectives on femininity and how she had come to fear some of these parts of herself. After discussing this dream, Marie mentioned she felt "bad" about a professional conflict with a colleague where she worked. It turned out that there were some competitive feelings between them, and Marie told me she typically shied away from this kind of interaction. After this particular incident, however, she was aware of feeling inexplicably saddened. I inquired more about this sad feeling, and Marie said she felt that she had learned "somewhere before puberty" that "it's unladylike to compete." As a result, she consciously held herself back from competing with her oldest brother, who carried many of the family's ambitions and hopes. She also clamped down on competing with her closest girlfriend from childhood, for instance, in sports activities, by letting that friend have an advantage. She explained this inhibition, "I guess I told myself I was second rate." She also mentioned she felt embarrassed discussing this with me, which I had a hunch meant she was feeling competitive with me. I reflected this back to Marie, and she said wryly, "I guess that's obvious." In retrospect, I wonder how much of this feeling was truly competitive as opposed to envious, which would have spoken more to her desire to possess something of me as an idealized object.

Idealizing, Competing, and Envying

Themes of competition and envy soon became more prominent in our work. Marie told me a dream in which

> *I share an office with Dr. B, but he's redecorated and all my things are gone. I confront him, and he tells me he should have a more impressive office, but I ask, what am I, chopped liver? After this, young parents show me a picture of their kids dressed in pirate costumes.*

I thought at the time that the dream expressed some of what happens when a parent is idealized too much—they take over a child's psyche crowding out "her things." Marie, however, spoke about professionals who cheated and behaved "like pirates" because they stooped to taking credit not due them. She associated Dr. B with her maternal grandfather, recalling that her mother was his favorite. Her "lost things" in the dream reminded Marie that when she was 16, she lost a gem bracelet that had been handed down in her family to her. She had taken it to a jewelry store to be polished. For reasons she could never explain to herself, she left the bracelet at the store and never retrieved it. This precious item was cast aside unconsciously, an action perhaps representing a devalued attitude toward her own femininity. Marie may have done this because she had felt stolen from in other ways that she could not understand, "pirated" by a mother who took from her and left her feeling impoverished. Losing the bracelet in that way, essentially leaving the treasure for someone else to claim, might have expressed in symbolic form a transaction in which Marie felt robbed by a parent who seemed to act like a pirate. Marie did feel "like chopped liver" in many ways when she compared herself to her mother. A parent who takes up too much room in a child's psyche creates a particular difficulty when, later in life, the parent dies and the child, now grown into adulthood, may feel either a gaping absence or emptiness, much like the vision from Marie's dream of the homeless woman missing her internal organs.

Marie dreamed about having dangerous wounds, cancer, and being in need of medical attention. The women doctors who tried to care for her were often suspicious or incompetent. They acted aggressively toward Marie in these dreams, not caring for her at all. They seemed to symbolize how intruded upon Marie had felt by her mother, who was not available in helpful ways that Marie could remember. To the contrary, Marie now grew angry at what she came to view as her mother's attacks on her because she happened to be a girl and not another boy. She openly worried that I quietly judged her, but then she rushed to idealize me in various ways that I tried to help her see as elevations of me in relation to her. Sometimes this tack helped; sometimes it did not. Marie came to see that she idealized me as "having all the answers" or "knowing the five keys to life," and I interpreted that she seemed to be inviting me to take up a lot of room in her psyche, much as Dr. B did by displacing her in the dream, or as her mother had earlier in her life.

Commenting on this seemed to bring about a change because Marie subsequently began to pressure me by asking why I did not answer certain questions. For example, she wanted to know where I attended college, how I had become fluent in a foreign language, and whether I was gay or straight. On the face of it, many of these inquiries appeared to speak of a competition between us, for example about intelligence, education, and desirability. Yet, an anxious insistence behind her questions also conveyed that these were projective identifications onto me about what it is like to be an envied object. I began to wonder more about Marie's having felt similarly in relation to her mother. Had her mother intruded into Marie's psyche to deprive Marie of developing a more overt, expressive femininity that would have rivaled her own? What would it be like to grow up as an envied daughter with a potentially stealing mother in her mind and in her family? As if intuiting that I was considering these kinds of questions, Marie dreamed, "*I'm driving and pick up a young woman who needs a ride. She fumbles with my purse, and I say something because I want her to know she shouldn't steal from me.*" This dream made Marie very anxious because she feared that she was the young woman, in other words, a potential thief. Although that might have been true, I wondered instead about Marie's young mother wanting to pocket items from Marie's "purse" of developing femininity—a purse that could hold a girl's sexuality, emerging attractiveness, and gender potential. What if her mother had wanted to steal some of what was in that purse from Marie? When I mentioned to Marie that perhaps she was not the thief in this dream, she cried saying, "It makes me sad that I feel it's easier for me to see myself like the thief rather than . . ." After a pause, she finished, "my mother being it."

Marie related that she considered herself "a defective girl, especially as a teenager." She said she grew to believe that her mother was embarrassed by her awkwardness and that her mother judged her as a "poor example of what a girl is supposed to be." She also offered paltry few instances when her mother showed interest in her as a girl. She contrasted this with how excited her mother was around Marie's brothers, lavishing them with attention, praise, and even "being sort of flirty with them." Marie attended a girl's school during her adolescence, and she came to feel that this was a healing opportunity. She found friends and teachers who showed great interest in her mind and her athletic skills. But at home, she experienced an icy silence from her mother who rarely asked about school and Marie's achievements. Instead, Marie concluded, "My mother had such low expectations for me, the bar was so low, that I would have to trip over it." She laughed about this paradoxical notion of tripping in self-defeat because so little was expected, but she also admitted it was painful to think about.

What began to emerge for Marie was a more specific curiosity about how she had developed as a girl and woman. She came to recognize that she gravitated to idealistic portrayals of being a woman but found that these were ultimately disappointing because when she compared herself and was found to be wanting, "it all collapsed." For example, Marie dreamed that she was

> *in a fancy restaurant where I'm honored as being like a new Lauren Bacall. Later though, the pants I'm wearing keep falling down. A guy loans me an extra pair, but they're odd.*

The falling pants convey a meaning about the difficulty of maintaining such an idealization, whereas the next piece of the dream suggests a possible wish for refuge in assuming a more masculine identity, although that, too, does not quite hit the mark (is "odd"). She thought of the actress Lauren Bacall as "freely female" and not bound by old-fashioned gender constraints. In contrast with her ideal, Marie worried whether she was attractive to men and grew despondent at what felt to be a remote possibility that she could present herself as sexy and confident.

Marie's anxiety and disappointment about her attractiveness to men also appeared in the transference. She imagined me, at times, to be critical—specifically that I "pitied" her because she was not "woman enough." She pressured me through a type of interaction we often had when she would state that she was confused and insist that I clarify her confusion. In this process, I often felt that I could not think clearly, and I got a taste through this unconscious tangle of what Marie meant by being "in the fog." When it happened, I felt that this was a projective identification, but only later could I think about what was occurring in a way that eventually made sense to me. Marie had a fantasy of me as idealized, all knowing, even omniscient. She emptied herself at times and presented this disembodied self to me with forceful insistence that I address her emptiness. When I resisted, she grew even more confused and increased the pressure on me through nonverbal indicators of anger, such as glaring, frowning, and sighing impatiently, and by adopting an accusatory tone. I suspected these exchanges represented attacks on my ability to think analytically, as a kind of psychological spoiling that I referred to earlier in this chapter, when destructive envy motivates a person to damage the very thing she or he wishes to possess. In these moments, I became, for Marie, an envied and idealized object who she unconsciously imagined could perform a desired function, that is, to fill her up in ways she longed for and do her thinking for her, not believing she had resources to do so herself. This is certainly not an uncommon analytic experience, and I suspect in Marie's case, she did envy me, but I think she was also communicating what it had once felt like for her to be in a very similar place, envied by her mother, filled with her mother's unconscious projections, and unable to perform or, more importantly, to develop as a girl. In a child's development, the overall direction of most projections should flow from a child to her or his parents, not the other way around. A reversal in this projective flow can greatly impede psychological development with the effect of overcrowding such a child's own mind, which is then not free to express itself.[8]

Finding Her Voice

Around this time, Marie's sons were leaving for college, and she wished that she could feel closer emotionally to them. She felt pushed away by them and by her husband, whom she experienced as excessively argumentative for trivial reasons. She began to notice how much he crowded her out (as I felt she sometimes did with me or her mother had probably done to her). She said he was becoming "mean and nasty," although it was possible that she was now less tolerant of him and was instead asserting her needs to be heard because of what she was learning about herself through our work. She even dreamed about singing in a church and "*the choir leader asks me to sing louder.*" Marie associated the "church" to both her childhood and family, and this connection led her to say, "I learned to sing softly at a young age." Soon, after much contemplation, Marie decided to divorce her husband.

Her main response to this decision was relief. She felt freer and subsequently had this dream:

> *Now I'm writing a brief autobiography. I'm swimming at the shore with Dad. There are photos of us standing naked, my oldest brother too.*

She was pleasantly surprised by the dream, which brought out fond memories of her father when she was quite young. The autobiography affirmed for her that she could author her own story, and the nakedness implied that she was once free and could learn to be that way again. Her confidence in her decision about the divorce wavered on occasion, but generally she remained strong in her choice. She reported dreaming of

> *a dying rose bush at a house near ours. I plant a new one. My father won't be fooled because he's been watching the rose every day. But I realize the plant will flourish because I tend it well.*

The house reference was a current one, and Marie thought the dying rose meant her marriage was over, but all was not lost. She found this dream hopeful and liked her father's role as guardian, not so much policeman. She was sad at the thought that she might be disappointing him by getting the divorce, but felt confidence in this dream because the new plant does well owing to her efforts.

A new sense of freedom led Marie to explore her feelings of rivalry with other women. She reported a dream in which she elbowed a friend's pubic bone while playing soccer and later made a lame pass that was intercepted. This image made her think about the wounded feminine images that pervaded many of her dreams. She asked herself, "Am I lame as a woman? Do I not know how to compete as a woman?" She realized how much her mother would have disapproved of her divorce if she were alive. Although her father appeared in her dreams and fantasies as supportive around this choice, her mother showed up as hypercritical and disparaging about it. The dream might have meant, in her deepest worry, that she could never hope for better because she had never properly learned to play the game (of being a woman who could interest men). According to this fear, her mother would evaluate her as "lame" and fated to be intercepted by someone more desirable.

In considering what her mother would have had to say about her divorce, Marie became depressed, and homeless women returned to her dreams in need of stitches for various wounds, cuts, and injuries. Sometimes the women seemed to deserve what had happened because they were "trampy" or "promiscuous." The timing of these judgments seemed to me right then to characterize Marie's internal mother who stole from her, especially when a positive development appeared for Marie. Marie lamented that her mother would have asked if she were crazy to divorce because she obviously had limited prospects to remarry. And she would also have asked whether Marie knew what it was like to grow old as a single woman. These thoughts plagued Marie and brought on a period of suffering when it seemed that the force of her stealing internal mother had gained the upper hand. She even dreamed of her mother pushing her back to a table and telling her "no hands." The hand reference fit a view that Marie had of herself, "disarmed," because she had been taught by her mother to play with one hand tied behind her back (it being "unladylike" to compete assertively).

Gradually, though, Marie found a determination to challenge her mother's predominant standards, which overwhelmed her mind like the rushing currents and crashing waves that occurred frequently in her dreams. She bought a new car in a color that she knew her mother would not approve of, but that Marie found exciting. She felt proud that she negotiated a good deal on the car with a man—she did not allow herself to be pushed around. She also rebuffed her husband's latest attempts at reconciliation because "he wants it just on his terms; he didn't even listen to what I might want." She had the following dream around this time:

> *I'm trying on a high-heeled shoe. I'm looking at nice femmy things a woman friend (C.) has, and I tell her, I'm going to have some things like this too, but I'm still making space for them. She agrees I should have them. Other women come and I suggest we make a dinner and color it up with green beans, red peppers, and spikes of anise.*

Marie mentioned that her friend C. was also divorcing. She felt the dream was an invitation to explore more in sensual and sexual ways that struck her as feminine, like with color, food, and fashion. The high heels seemed to me a good representation of letting herself feel uplifted without getting carried away by an idealized inflation of what a woman with her mother's standards *should* have desired or *should* have worn. Marie said about this dream, "It's new! To have permission like this, that's new for me. It feels liberating." In contrast, she recalled her recurring dreams about ships running aground, which to her represented a kind of femininity damaged beyond repair.

Marie wondered too whether I might have found her desirable and also showed some envy of whoever I was privately in a relationship with. She had dreams about our overstepping a boundary, usually in intimate contact, and Marie's accidentally seeing who she dreamed to be my wife and children. These dreams seemed to express both a wish that I desired her and envy of whomever I shared my life with. Her contact with my family in these dreams often made her feel guilty as if she had "stolen something" from me. Guilt was often disguised by an agreement we made in the dreams to keep secret what had happened.

She began to think that her idea of "broken femininity" originated within her relationship with her mother, whom she now came to believe related more naturally to her brothers and was unprepared for raising a little girl. Marie mentioned a dream in which "*I add three inches to costumes for a movie*" and she associated boys' penises with the three inches of material she was sewing on. She remembered from an early age wishing, "If I could have that, things would be right." We discussed that she might have gotten this feeling because neither parent had admired her being a little girl with her own special parts. Out of these discussions, Marie began to consciously appreciate that many of her long-held ideas about what constituted femininity arose implicitly from how her parents interacted with her and her brothers. She emphasized that their home environment was very masculine-oriented, a kind of boy's land in which a little girl stood out. In this situation, her mother became idealized, queenly, and unattainable for Marie. Her mother did not much care for Marie's attempts to get attention by her own achievements and actively discouraged Marie from showing her feelings. She recalled her mother's oft-heard warning: "Dear, it's better if you don't bring up such things." In spite of how different she actually felt from her mother, Marie had long felt an uncomfortable sense of being joined with her, as reflected in a dream in which her mother "*makes a sailing error and the boat we're in capsizes.*" She interpreted this dream to mean she was too accommodating in steering her own life by her mother's rules and that she might "go under" if she did not stop this. Marie also thought that the dream's sinking boat "is my gender identity and I can see that she [mother] didn't want it to stay afloat." Marie seemed to understand that her mother's early intrusion into her psyche had now made aspects of her own life related to gender feel impossible, especially in terms of accepting who she was as a woman.

After this dream, Marie brought in an old family photograph of her mother on a sailboat. Her mother was smoking a cigarette and appeared attractive, thin, and somewhat coolly aloof—similar to how a female film star from the 1940s might have appeared. As we processed her feelings about her mother at this time, Marie brought up the word *heartless*, which was interesting not only because of its obvious meanings but also because of Marie's dreams about women with missing organs. She did not feel that her mother was this way with everyone in the family since Marie could tell "she was smitten with my oldest brother." It seemed that *heartless* was an aloof, distant, and envied/envying position that her mother mostly had vis-à-vis Marie. During a session when Marie was upset with me after a date fell through with a man she wanted to meet, Marie also used this word to describe how she experienced my reaction to her disappointment. Her anger at her mother became part of her transference to me, that I would be aloof and cool to her when she was upset because I might also believe Marie would eventually "go under" as a woman. It was as if Marie imagined I would envy her success in dating, so I could, therefore, only hope for her failure (and conversely, she envied me for what she perceived as my ease in this area of experience where she believed herself to be lacking by comparison). It is important to note that the idealized aspects of her mother (looking like a film star) seemed associated with Marie's feeling envy, whereas the persecutory aspects ("heartless") were connected with feeling she was instead the object of her mother's envy.

Somewhat later, Marie was able to recognize the projective aspects of her believing me to be persecutory in these various ways, although this involved overcoming the aftereffects of a synchronicity that unsettled her quite a bit. Before that occurred, she reported a dream about a kidnapper, a dream that evoked strong memories of the sexual assault as a young woman. She noted that she was relieved on waking and thought the dream represented her currently feeling unattractive to men she was hoping to date (because the kidnapper ultimately did not take her after palpating her ovaries). Significantly, she also said the kidnapper was part of her, something in her that "kidnapped the youthful, nurturing, and beautiful parts of who I could be." This elaboration of the dream felt like a shift in Marie's understanding about what I then thought of as her internal envious and stealing mother, not the idealized one. In further discussing this dream, Marie noted that the kidnapper rejected her because she failed an evaluation of her reproductive organs. She felt this rejection represented the feelings of inadequacy that she probably experienced as a small girl within her family. She wondered if all children feel ashamed of their sexuality. When I asked about her impressions of her twin sons, she recalled that this was not true for them. She remembered fondly many incidents when they paraded around naked and joked proudly about their penises. Following this, Marie had several dreams in which different injured parts of her were healed, and she interpreted them affirmatively to be "a good progress report about the woman who once had no organs in her pelvis."

What is a Woman Supposed to Be?

Marie recalled here another detail about how her father treated her being a girl, namely that her occasional nickname was "Lady Agnew," which was possibly meant as a covert putdown of Marie's feminine identity—that she could never be like the real Lady Agnew, who married a Scottish lord in the late nineteenth century. Marie brought in a copy of John Singer Sargent's painting of Lady Agnew for us to look at together.[9] This classic portrait by Sargent shows a confident woman seated and looking straight ahead beguilingly. She seems a distinct feminine ideal representative of upper-class beauty and elegance, in a soft white chiffon dress with a lilac sash and wearing a jeweled cameo pendant. Marie said she considered the painting "lovely," but sadly too she felt, "I'm not like that." She recalled her father's tone when calling her "Lady Agnew"—that he was not quite sarcastic, but just deflating enough that she could feel whatever excitement she might have felt drained out of her. She had a sense he might have wished she could be more like Lady Agnew, and she felt the burden of his impossible idealization. For example, she had a dream about the two of them on top of a high mountain. In that dream, she had to take over driving them down from the top, and Marie realized that this spoke to her letting go of that burden created by an overly idealized picture of what he might have wished to see in a daughter.

Discussing these themes, we experienced a synchronicity that both amplified and complicated this process. Jung defines synchronicity as a temporary coincidence of acausal events that nonetheless can appear meaningfully associated.[10] Put another way, something happens in the physical world that seems to mirror an associated linkage in the psychological realm. For Marie and me, this synchronous event involved our finding ourselves in the same jewelry store one weekend afternoon. I was looking at watches and had removed my eyeglasses. While looking at a model the salesman had set on the counter, I glanced up and noticed that Marie was at the opposite counter looking at watches herself. She smiled at me and waved, and I smiled back and nodded my head in acknowledgment, but did not say anything. I felt awkward and foremost thought of being mindful that we were in public. I returned to looking at the watch, and a little while later, she passed me as she left the store. We said goodbye at that point, my goodbye perhaps said more quietly than hers.

In the session immediately thereafter, Marie was furious with me. She said accusingly, "How dare you snub me!" She left me little room to reply and expressed a great deal of anger that I "disrespected" her by not chatting with her. She imagined that I had done this because I hadn't thought her socially capable of handling a superficial conversation. She claimed, "You probably think I'm socially inept." She threatened to quit her therapy and said that it took "will-power" for her to not act on that impulse. I felt the brunt of her anger over several sessions, and I was aware of feeling defensive, attacked, and being characterized as an ungracious snob. Deciding to dig into it, I encouraged her to continue telling me more about her anger, which was simultaneously spilling out at male colleagues and her ex-husband for what she regarded as insulting behaviors.

I began to see this event as an analytic enactment of what we had been discussing around her father's putdowns of Marie when he used Lady Agnew as an idealized reference. The jewelry store became in my thinking a place where someone like Lady Agnew might have sought to purchase something to adorn herself and would have probably felt quite natural in doing so. But, for Marie, this place represented vulnerability, where she felt I acted like her father and disregarded her ability to show social grace. In her mind, this meant that I found her inadequate as a woman. To her, the "jewelry store incident" confirmed her worst suspicions that I viewed her as suffering from a wounded femininity beyond recovery.

My accepting her anger and hostility came as a surprise to Marie. She fantasized that I might choose to retaliate and "kick [her] out" of the office, thereby ending her therapy. Afterward, I came to see that her expressing her feelings about this event helped bring into focus some destructive aspects of her envy, in particular her fantasy of me as someone idealized and out of her reach—as if I were socially situated above her like Lady Agnew. In such an unconscious scenario, I might even be Lady Agnew's husband, and together we would form a royal couple, who, to Marie, would exclude her. Hearing Marie's anger in various ways seemed both to bring me down from the mountaintop and to bring her envy of me into the open. This anger appeared relatively undisguised in dreams, for instance, when she visited my house and found "*your kid is a biter. He has a bad reputation. Your name is actually Mr. D, and you're a musician playing a Renaissance guitar.*" Marie thought I would be "a bad parent" to have such a child, and she associated this with her feeling that I had been "a bad therapist" around how she perceived me during the jewelry store incident. She also thought of herself as my "kid" in the dream and that I now had to deal with her "biting anger" at me. My musician identity in the dream evoked for her someone who is "wimpy" and "emasculated." This sounded to me like a manifestation of the destructive side of her envy, which transformed the previously idealized object through spoiling into something undesirable. Marie's willingness to imagine herself as my "kid" seemed, however, to also be a promising way for her to integrate into her own narrative how envy had played a major role in her early development.

Months later, Marie spoke about this encounter differently, and she gained a perspective on why it had felt "violent" to her. Her tone in talking of it became more humorous, as she affectionately teased me about my reserve, and also noted, "I really turned a corner and you hung in there with me." She began to understand how anguished she had felt for years by the projections of idealized femininity that she had absorbed from her mother and father. She said, "I had these preconceived notions that you were like them in relation to me—that I was puny, you were unassailable, and I could never grow into anything you would appreciate." Certainly part of this was the Lady Agnew complex referring to Marie's father and his implicit disregard of her. Another part involved her relationship with her mother and the major role envy played between them. At first, it seemed clear to Marie that as a girl she, of course, envied her mother, who had seemed both aloof and glamorous. But gradually Marie came to see another side to this relational dynamic—that her mother envied Marie because Marie was a "future rival with possibilities." She spoke of her mother's disinterest in her excellence at sports and academics, a disinterest that did "not make sense" because "everyone else saw it—my grandparents, my aunts, even my brothers. Why would my mother have avoided seeing what they could see about me?" Such self-awareness helped Marie to begin appreciating the depth of her mother's envy of her as a girl, teenager, and young woman, when Marie's considerable achievements were evident both inside and outside her family.

An envying parent can deposit something of a stealing object in his or her child's psyche, and the resulting identification can assume rather large proportions for the daughter or son to contend with later in life. Sometimes, as adults those so affected report feeling confused inside because they feel stolen from, impoverished, and that they are missing something vital to their identity. Part of this mystery includes figuring out what the internalized stealing object has taken. Later in her analysis, Marie dreamed:

> *I'm in a forest and see a skunk. It moves toward a downed tree where a mother pig is giving birth. As her piglets come out, the skunk eats them one by one. I see it chewing with its sharp teeth on a liver. Maybe the mother pig will die too.*

We could say that Marie's situation in her family did not smell right and evoked a bit of a fairytale world like in this dream. One aspect of the dream tells us about a conflict between two animal instincts such as hunger and a brutal competition for survival, which could also indicate envy. At one time, Marie may have felt that her hunger for her mother was dangerous, although we must ask how she came to learn that. Might this feeling have originated through the role of envy in their relationship? To have an unsatisfied and chronic hunger, even for affection and attention, can stimulate envy. The downed tree could represent a period in Marie's development (recall that in the water serpent dream she identified with a tree) when difficult feelings of hunger, envy, and danger got confused, and she might have wondered which belonged to her and which to her mother. Marie felt both fear and revulsion over this dream, and both those feelings would have been natural responses when faced with a mother's primitive envy directed at her. Interestingly, the skunk is eating a liver, which might remind us that the queen in the Snow White fairytale ordered the huntsman to bring her the stepdaughter's liver so she could eat it. At an archetypal level, this skunk may then symbolize the struggle between an envious and queenly mother/stepmother and her hungry and talented daughter. For Marie, sorting through this struggle meant also clarifying her identity separately from her mother's. In that way, the internal thief in Marie's psyche had blurred an important boundary between them.

As this separation became clearer to her, Marie also discovered helpful aspects of her internal mother that ameliorated the envious ones, which she now recognized as stealing from her. In a dream from the middle part of her analysis, Marie is

> *in a race with other women. We have a friendly feeling among us. I'm holding bottles of hair products that I hand to my mother. She's happy to hold them and help me in the race.*

Marie felt that "it was a wonderful moment" with her mother in this dream because she was supportive and attentive to Marie. She spoke about the positive camaraderie she experienced with the other women in the race, "It's new, upbeat, and unfamiliar, but I like it." Marie viewed this dream as an indication of self-acceptance and less ambivalence about her feminine identity, which to her seemed to be healing. The act of handing something off to her mother seemed also to define what Marie was doing in her analysis—namely giving back to her mother many of the artificial and perfectionistic standards that Marie had unconsciously absorbed from her.

Marie's analytic process continued for several more years, with expected challenges and inevitable detours, but fewer waves crashing her aground. Importantly, Marie felt greater access to what internal resources she had and was less worried about their being stolen from her. She found it frustrating that the envious internal mother—with thieving tendencies—would never disappear, but she took comfort and pride in realizing how open she had become to the depths of her emotional life. She also felt far less compelled to search for ways to live out what she might have conceived as idealized wishes for something more perfect. She continued to find compensatory qualities of her internal mother that helped to construct a revised narrative of why her mother had been the woman she was. In a much later dream, Marie reported:

> *I'm at a summer house on the bay, and it's mine. I've inherited it. It's a bit run down, but beautiful. I'm thinking of remodeling it. On the post by the porch stairs, there's a red jewel on top of it, ruby red.*

The jewel on the post, a sort of finial, brought a redness to the entry to this house, perhaps symbolizing Marie's passion for life and a precious sparkle inside her, one she could now locate. This small jewel on the way into a rundown house provided a fitting contrast of a different kind of self, distinct from the inflated vision of Lady Agnew. This was a self-image that could be beautiful and remodeled through repairs to what had been inherited from her parents. Marie now saw in herself two things at once: beauty and imperfection. Her recognition of the positive and the negative in her experiences gave her increased confidence in relating to others as well as in relating to her own psyche. Commenting on the dream, she noted, "I can do both," which reflected this capacity to hold opposing views on the same thing.

Finally, the word *inherited* offers an interesting comparison to stealing. There are many ways a person can acquire something of value (or lose it for that matter), such as earning it, receiving it as a gift or honor, taking it, and inheriting it, to name a few. Marie had, through her dedication to a healing therapeutic process, come to understand that her internal mother had a potential to steal from her something valuable and close to the roots of her feminine identity. We might recall here that Snow White's envying stepmother could not pass along an inheritance that was owed to a stepdaughter she felt instead to be an existential threat. Perhaps, like Medea, such a mother will try to rob a child's future of anything that suggests she will eventually be replaced. She may well believe that resources are not intended to be passed along to children but have to be greedily hoarded. Inheritance would be foreign to her. Marie's dream suggested a different outcome, namely that when a daughter finally puts such a mother to rest, she might at last claim her inheritance and find the value in it.

Notes

1 The Project Gutenberg eBook, Grimm's Fairy Stories, by Jacob Grimm and Wilhelm Grimm, illustrated by John B Gruelle and R. Emmett Owen, release date: February 10, 2004, eBook #11027, original from 1922. Online, available HTTP: <http://www.gutenberg.org/files/11027/11027-h/11027-h.htm> (accessed August 16, 2013).

2 Ibid.

3 en.wikipedia.org/wiki/Snow_White (accessed August 16, 2013).

4 J. Chevalier and A. Gheerbrant, *Penguin Dictionary of Symbols*, trans. J. Buchanan-Brown, London, Penguin, 1996. Boars often appear on the crests of nobility.

5 H. Segal, *Introduction to the Work of Melanie Klein*, New York, Basic Books, 1974, p. 40. She goes on to add:

> But envy does not stop at exhausting the external object. The very nourishment that has been taken in, so long as it is perceived as having been part of the breast, is in itself an object of envious attacks, which are turned upon the internal object as well.
>
> (p. 41)

Thus, envy, when unchecked, releases a self-destructive component.

6 *All About Eve*, written and directed by J. L. Mankiewicz, produced by D. F. Zanuck, Twentieth Century Fox, 1950.

7 Segal, *Introduction to the Work of Melanie Klein*, p. 45.

8 See Antonino Ferro, *The Bi-Personal Field*, London, Routledge, 1999, especially pages 168–81, for a discussion of this phenomenon, which he refers to as an "inversion of flow" in the field of projective identifications. When this occurs, Ferro conceives a reversal in the normal activity of a dyad or couple, for example, a child now having to receive a parent's unprocessed emotional elements, rather than the other way around.

9 Accessible online at <http://www.jssgallery.org/Paintings/Lady_Agnew.htm>. The painting belongs to the National Gallery of Scotland in Edinburgh and dates from 1892–93.

10 C. G. Jung, "Synchronicity: An acausal connecting principle," *The Structure and Dynamics of the Psyche*, *CW* 8, 1973. Jung regards the connection, occurring as the result of what appears to be just a coincidence, as instead meaningful and potentially suggestive of an underlying pattern that has yet to be revealed to conscious understanding. In this sense, a synchronicity can be a manifestation of an unconscious relationship between people that bears implicitly upon the circumstances of the actual coincidence.

9

TECHNO-THEFT

Modern communications technology has made the stealing of information more likely to occur and much easier to carry out. Email messages can be sent to unintended recipients. The same is true for text messages, which can be forwarded without regard to the sender's wishes. Webcams now make spying on others not only the purview of government surveillance agencies but also possible in ways we might have thought more typical of science fiction as recently as 15 or 20 years ago. Identity thieves create ever-more refined scams in order to lure trusting consumers into revealing enough information about themselves so the thieves can create alternate and phony identities with access to victims' credit cards, bank accounts, and even income tax refunds. Lizette Alvarez reports in the *New York Times* that the U.S. Treasury found "940,000 fake returns for 2010 in which identity thieves would have received $6.5 billion."[1] In addition, determined hackers often find ways to gain access to an unsuspecting person's private world, not just to someone's financial transactions, but also to his or her email accounts, social networking sites, and electronic commerce and shopping accounts.

Much of this technologically assisted theft is opportunistic, frequently based on greedily fleecing another with minimal effort, and thus appears sociopathic and primitively narcissistic. A different aspect of using technology to steal personal information, however, often includes motives such as hacking someone's electronic accounts as a way to get revenge, forwarding private messages to provoke someone, uncovering secrets as a way of wielding power to discredit someone, and snooping into another's private life to gain some sort of advantage over or to potentially blackmail him or her. Stolen letters have a long literary history; Edgar Allan Poe even named one of his more famous short stories *The Purloined Letter*.[2] Letters that are shown to people from whom the sender wants to hide the contents are another well-known plot device, for example, in Shakespeare's *The Merry Wives of Windsor*.[3] Personal information is like currency when it can be traded, bought, sold, and stolen. Contemporary adolescent experience is often quite conversant with all these aspects of how that can happen.

Hazardous Texting

Jack was 17 years old, a charismatic, extraverted young man, who was also rather impulsive and prone to drinking and using drugs in ways that repeatedly got him into legal troubles. He began treatment with me after he had been hospitalized for a stab wound to his shoulder. He recently had testified in court for charges brought against his former girlfriend who had attacked him.

Jack told me his story, one that is not uncommon in its ordinariness—until the point when his girlfriend decided to avenge herself. They had been dating for over a year. She was a year older than Jack and attended a different school. They had met through mutual friends at a party and began a stormy relationship that included many volatile breakups and sentimental reunions. Jack described his girlfriend as "mad jealous," meaning she was extremely jealous. He said that most of the breakups had come about because she perceived him to be flirting with another girl. Jack confessed to being a flirt. "I am a flirt, a big flirt, but man, that's cool, right? So what's her problem? I figure it's got to be good for her that so many other girls like me." Jack felt his girlfriend should have admired his desirability and considered herself fortunate to be with someone like him.

Part of Jack's flirting with girls often involved text messages. Typically, a girl would obtain his mobile number from someone who knew Jack and then initiate a thread of text messages to him that indicated both her availability and her attraction to Jack. Jack usually erased the conversations from his phone because "She [his girlfriend] checks it. I've caught her red handed." However, he had no control over what happened to the other party's copy of their texted conversations. One girl was put off when Jack stopped returning her messages after he had been sending her texts about how "hot" she was. Their exchange had included a message from him that he would consider ending his relationship with his current girlfriend just to be with her. This girl complained to him in person, but he basically ignored her because he thought she was overreacting. She apparently did not feel that way because she then forwarded the incriminating text messages of her conversations with Jack to many other teenagers who were friends of both Jack and his girlfriend. Jack's girlfriend soon discovered the contents of those texts.

She was infuriated at Jack, confronted him, and threatened to break up with him. He became upset when she shoved him, and although he told me "I wanted to push her back," he did not because "that's not cool to hit a girl." Instead, he walked away. As he headed toward a bus stop, he recalled hearing the sound of breaking glass behind him. His girlfriend had broken an empty glass bottle to use as a weapon. She ran after him and stabbed him in the back, a wound that barely missed his spinal cord. She ran away as Jack writhed on the ground, eventually losing consciousness. Later, he woke up in a hospital bed. At first, he didn't know what had happened to him; then he remembered: "She tried to take me out." He was furious.

In the subsequent court proceedings, Jack's now ex-girlfriend pleaded guilty, and as part of her sentence she was forbidden from texting Jack for one year.

He, too, was admonished by the court not to send any texts to her because that could be interpreted as his deliberately trying to incite her. The judge seemed to believe that a source of their problem had been the misuse of mobile texting, although Jack did not agree with that conclusion. He instead blamed his former girlfriend in harsh terms that conveyed both his anger and feelings of being persecuted by her. He vacillated in his judgment of the other girl who had spread his flirtatious texts among their circle of friends. Sometimes he argued that it was entirely her fault "because she took those private texts and blasted them for everyone to see. That's a fucked-up kind of revenge." At other times, he professed more understanding for what she had done. "I was a jerk to her, I guess. She should have just told me I was an ass." In this moment of self-observation, Jack seemed more open to an admission that he had also stolen something from both girls—his girlfriend's trust and the other girl's interest in his availability.

How did the girl who felt rejected steal from Jack? She decided to distribute Jack's side of the text exchange, which consisted of his private, immature, and boorish declarations about her. She stole Jack's assumption of trust, however rudimentary, and a degree of Jack's freedom from retribution, that is, his safety because her theft worked to turn his comments into a weapon that was used against him. Her theft, therefore, violated an implicit agreement as to what Jack might have held to be a relatively private communication, becoming a cudgel for both her revenge and provocation of Jack's girlfriend, whose reputation for having a temper preceded her. Those in their social circle would have assumed she would react quite badly to the flirtatious text messages. As danah boyd (sic) and Alice Marwick find, "There's a widespread myth that American teenagers don't care about privacy . . . All teens have a sense of privacy, although their definitions of privacy vary widely."[4] In this example of wayward mobile texting, Jack believed his privacy had been stolen. Then the contents of this theft were used against him in a way that proved quite dangerous.

A Social Network Turned Rotten

A project report for the Pew Research Center finds that "[m]ore so than their elders, the internet is a central and indispensable element in the lives of American teenagers and young adults" with 93 percent of teenagers going online and 73 percent of "wired American teens" using social networking sites.[5] Social networking sites have, however, also emerged as potentially shadowy places where cyberbullying, stalking, and predatory pursuits occur. In this virtual realm, there exists a complex maze of privacy settings and accompanying designations, for example, about who is regarded a "friend" and what a "friend" can see, post, and share with others. With their near ubiquitous use among teenagers, these sites now substitute for real-world social interactions, although the latter still pose their own challenges and obstacles, especially when something from a social networking site comes to haunt a particular teen. boyd (sic) and Marwick write, "The flattening of diverse social relationships into monolithic groups of 'Friends' makes it difficult for users to negotiate the normal variances of self-presentation that occur in day-to-day life. Social media participants regularly lament moments where worlds collide."[6] These researchers emphasize that the complexity of real-life social interactions cannot yet be fully captured in range and nuance by an online set of virtual exchanges. Because of this de facto constraint about what we really need to process interpersonal relationships, in an online environment, exaggeration, hyperbole, and dramatic portrayals often substitute for what is missing, resulting in much personal hurt and emotional pain.

When Ben first came to see me for therapy, he presented as a disheveled, silent 16-year-old boy who looked very depressed. His parents told me that he had become increasingly socially isolated for reasons they could not explain since he had been popular at school during the previous academic year. All they knew was that there had been some "drama" (Ben's word for it), and Ben had been shunned by many of his peers. He now spent long hours playing video games and also hung black curtains over the windows of his room. He kept them drawn so no natural light could get in. He slept ten or more hours daily and refused to take part in any enjoyable family activities. Ben's parents told me that he had had a girlfriend, but his relationship with her had been turbulent, and they were not currently seeing one another.

Ben soon informed me that his girlfriend had been "hella bad, evil" and that he felt she was the cause of much of his current suffering. He explained that six months ago he and his girlfriend had decided "to take a break because we were stressing each other. She was all emo [emotional] and I just couldn't deal with her. We both agreed, but apparently afterward she thought we were still dating." Ben changed his relationship status on the social networking site he used, indicating that he was no longer in a relationship. When his girlfriend saw this, she became angry, sending him a long text message about how betrayed she felt because she had not considered "taking a break" to mean that they would be formally separating. Ben replied that he thought otherwise and that she could not control him—although his language in conveying this was coarse and vulgar.

His girlfriend knew Ben's password and ID for the social networking site he used, and she proceeded to post many lewd, insulting messages on his "wall" (an area where messages and photos can be viewed) about various other girls, including many whom his male friends were dating. She signed these forged entries as if Ben had, in fact, written them. She then altered his privacy settings so all of these posts were public to anyone instead of limited to Ben's designated "friends." The posts quickly circulated in his school before Ben even knew what had happened. Two boys threatened him physically because they believed the posts had come from Ben. By the time Ben figured out what his ex-girlfriend had done, a fair amount of social damage to Ben and his reputation had occurred—even friends who attended other schools and Ben's relatives (though not his parents) had been able to read these posts intended as salvos.

Ben deleted the offensive posts, but he neglected to post for himself any explanation or apology. His ex-girlfriend again hacked into his account, repeating what she had done. Only after that episode, did Ben understand that he had to change his ID, password, and privacy settings because his account was compromised. The fallout continued to be significant, in part because of Ben's immaturity and unwillingness to apologize in some public way that his peers could appreciate. He demonized his ex-girlfriend: "It's all her fault. Why should I have to apologize? She should put it up on her own wall." Most of his friends distanced themselves from him, and he suffered considerable isolation and derision, both at school and online since many of the forged posts continued to circulate even though he had erased them from his own "wall." (One thing we are all learning in this Internet age is that, once put online, contents can assume a life of their own.) Ben was referred to as a "cheat," a "perv," and much worse, as people he barely knew reacted to the content that his ex-girlfriend had posted under his name.

Ben recovered from this incident, although it took time and work in therapy, and he eventually decided to transfer to another school. He was clear in expressing that he felt his ex-girlfriend had stolen from him: "She ripped me off, took my rep [reputation] and my buddies from me." Her vindictive intent appeared to have been to inflict social pain on Ben. She succeeded in making him pay a high price for what she felt was his betrayal. In these situations, adolescents can act impulsively and harshly—they rarely reflect about the long-term effects of their actions or the degree of hurt they can cause someone else, both of which are cognitive and relational capacities that continue to develop during later adolescence into early adulthood. His girlfriend's stealing—which included her taking Ben's password to forge the online posts and changing his privacy settings to make them public for anyone to see—has unconscious motives of a spurned romantic interest who gets revenge by symbolically castrating the boy she feels rejected by. These motivations are similar in ilk to what moved Medea's revenge on Jason when she took all that he valued and rendered him powerless. The fake postings damaged Ben's social standing and status among his peers, and when they shunned him, Ben felt ashamed and weak. Her theft shows a danger inherent to online technology, in that valuable information can be stolen in order to leave a victim not only poorer but also socially diminished and outcast. This kind of stealing illustrates how the virtual world does not adequately approximate the emotional complexity of real-world social relations, a point that the next example also makes all too poignantly.

The Rutgers University Webcam Spying Case

At the outset of exploring this example, I think it is important to emphasize two points. First, this case was an awful and heartbreaking tragedy, especially for Tyler Clementi and his family. Clementi committed suicide in the immediate aftermath of the Rutgers webcam spying case. Suicide is an incredibly complicated topic—psychologically, culturally, and socially—particularly during adolescence and early adulthood. It is the third leading cause of death among those aged 15 to 24.[7] Although each circumstance is undoubtedly unique, frequently suicide results when an internal struggle tips a fragile psychic equilibrium more toward a destructive part of the personality that is able to assert itself in face of what is felt to be unbearable emotional pain, loneliness, and isolation.[8] Suicide is usually multidetermined, and as such, attempts to attribute it to single causation are rarely sufficient.

Second, I am using published secondary source material that I gathered about this case in order to examine another way in which stealing occurs through the use of modern technology. I can offer no diagnostic conclusions about either Tyler Clementi or Dharun Ravi because I am in no position to do that since I have never had any clinical or personal contacts with either young man or their families. Where I might speculate about motivations, I hope to acknowledge fully that these are based on conjectures that I am trying to relate to the broader topic of theft, in this case, theft of one's privacy through a sophisticated application of computers, webcams, connectivity, and Internet social networks.

In August 2010, Dharun Ravi and Tyler Clementi, both just out of high school and in their late teens, were assigned to be roommates in a dormitory at Rutgers University in New Jersey.[9] Prior to the start of school, Clementi came out to his family as gay. He was the youngest of three sons, and he appeared to have felt "rejected" by his mother when he delivered this news.[10] He seemed, however, to have felt accepted by his father at that time. Ravi appeared to have ascertained through Internet searches of various postings that his new roommate was gay, although ironically he seemed to have also mistaken Clementi for another gay student about to enter Rutgers. Ravi was the son of Indian immigrants and the older of two brothers. The two young men were quite a contrast in many ways—socially, culturally, and in terms of their personal interests. Ian Parker, whose article in *The New Yorker* explores in excellent detail the events between these young men, writes, "If Clementi had a touch of middle-aged fastidiousness, Ravi was fully a teen-ager: rangy, physical, with a taste for public regard."[11] It might have appeared that these two were fated to collide in some way sooner or later, although many young college roommates, thrown together by chance, have to grapple with real and imagined differences that can look unbridgeable yet they manage to do so.

Approximately three weeks after they had met, Clementi sent a text message to Ravi requesting the use of their shared room so he could entertain another man with whom he had initiated romantic and intimate contact.[12] Ravi complied, but he had set up his computer to activate its webcam automatically whenever an incoming video chat request was triggered. In addition, when he left the dorm room that evening, he turned off the computer's monitor so the screen would not reveal that someone was watching through the camera. Ravi had something of a history of trying to spy on friends this way, and we might infer an identification as an adolescent prankster or trickster in these activities.[13] Such a trickster would plausibly be a privacy thief who steals like a Peeping Tom, but in this networked, Internet version, not only for his personal gratification, but also for a potentially much wider audience—as a jester or clown visually reveals a gag to a waiting crowd.

Ravi went to a neighbor's room, where they launched a program on her computer to begin a video chat with Ravi's computer across the hall. Having been secretly enabled, his webcam now gave them a view of what was happening in Ravi and Clementi's room. They spied Clementi in an intimate embrace with his guest. Their surprise, and perhaps anxiety over how they were trespassing, led them to quickly turn off the prying webcam that they had remotely activated. Ravi then posted this message on Twitter: "I saw him [roommate] making out with a dude. Yay."[14] Later, after Ravi had left, his accomplice invited four other young women to join her when she reactivated the camera. They again saw Clementi in an intimate situation and apparently turned off the camera after a short viewing time.

Clementi had discovered that his roommate had a Twitter account, and the following day, he read the Tweet exposing his liaison the evening before. He had likely noticed the electronic glow of a tiny dot on Ravi's computer, indicating the webcam was turned on, because he had an online chat with a friend that day in which they discussed Ravi's invasion of his privacy. During this time, Clementi seems to have reached out to this friend, to an online discussion group for gay men, to the housing office at the university, and eventually to his residential adviser. Two days after the initial spying incident, Clementi again asked his boyfriend to visit and requested the private use of the dorm room from Ravi. Ravi spotted another opportunity to spy on Clementi. He then posted another Tweet, notifying others that they could join him in secretly viewing Clementi with his boyfriend. Clementi, now wise to this salacious game being staged at his expense, shut down Ravi's computer. His boyfriend came to the room, and later, after he had left, Ravi returned to their dorm room.

The following day, Tyler Clementi jumped off the George Washington Bridge in New York City. University officials notified Ravi that he was in trouble because of a complaint from Clementi. Ravi then appears to have made revisionist efforts to cover his tracks, including writing apologetic text messages to Clementi and attempting to make it look as if he had never intended to send his Tweet inviting others to join him in spying on Clementi. He also tried to persuade the neighbor across the hall, from whose room they had first spied on Clementi, to give a doctored version of events to the university police. He seemed to have been scrambling to create a cover about having been involved in accidental occurrences, as well as trying to erase anything looking more dubious or sinister about himself. Less than one week later, Ravi was charged with invasion of privacy, the day before Clementi's body was found in the Hudson River.[15] Later charges would be added: bias intimidation (a hate crime statute, in this case based on Clementi's sexual orientation), witness tampering, and evidence tampering.

Ravi rejected two offers for a plea bargain, perhaps, in part, because he believed that he had not willfully intimidated Clementi over his sexuality.[16] There might also have been a family concern that if Ravi had accepted a plea deal, then he would have been at risk for deportation. Nonetheless, on March 16, 2012, Ravi was found guilty on all counts, and he was sentenced to 30 days in jail, three years of probation, 300 hours of community service, counseling about cyberbullying, and $11,000 in fees. The judge remarked, "I haven't heard you apologize once," and to the courtroom he added, "I do not believe he hated Tyler Clementi. I do believe he acted out of colossal insensitivity."[17] When his mother cried, "Mr. Ravi himself broke down crying, the first time since the beginning of the trial that he had publicly shown more than a glimpse of emotion."[18]

Ravi might have been frozen, fearful, maybe contemptuous, seemingly stubborn—there is no real way to know short of his speaking about it. A looming mystery of this case is that no one knows certain secrets that each young man kept, for example, Ravi's motives when he spied on Clementi, the choices he made during the trial, or even those that drove Clementi to take his own life. That, in itself, is a bit of irony considering that they were young men at home in using various forms of Internet and communication technology to make their lives superficially more public. Ravi's attorney maintained as part of his defense that Ravi was "not antigay." In his opening statement, he argued, "We do stupid things, we make mistakes, especially when we're young—it doesn't mean we're hateful, we're bigoted or we're criminal . . . In fact, Dharun never intimidated anyone."[19] Oddly, in their inability to make a real-life connection, both young men showed the glaring limitations of relying on virtual "friends" and virtual contacts to try to bridge obvious differences and the conflicts that might be lurking beneath those differences. Kate Zernike notes, "The testimony painted a picture of two college freshmen . . . who could not have been more different."[20] Given such an interpersonal dynamic, depth psychologists would recognize fertile ground for mutual projections to overtake meaningful relating; the intensity of these projections usually clouds our ability to understand one another. Parker concurs, "Clementi and Ravi seem to have responded in similarly exaggerated ways to perceived hints of modest roots in the other."[21]

If we believe that Ravi was not acting out homophobic intentions or feelings toward Clementi, then what might have predisposed him to steal his roommate's privacy and reveal these secrets to a virtual audience? What made Ravi "unsympathetic" in court, instead falling into an apparent role of villainous thief caught red-handed? During adolescence, because of the strength of developmental impulses, vulnerability frequently arises when something archetypal seizes a teenager's mind and makes him or her run amok. Like Jason stealing the Fleece (and, in many ways, Jason was a late adolescent), someone in Ravi's shoes might, when stimulated even if just by prankish curiosity, act impulsively to get sneakily what seems temptingly close by. And, like Jason, Ravi could have confused his actions with something heroic that would bring him fame because he was, at some level, acting in front of an imaginary, undefined, yet existent, virtual group of others who could approve his derring-do. His trophy would have been the scene depicted on a digital screen, similar to the shimmering Fleece of myth. Remarkably, in another parallel to the myth, Ravi had a female companion who enabled his theft—the dorm neighbor from whose computer they initiated the spying.

My point is not to assert that the unconscious dynamics of this particular myth necessarily were enacted in this tragic situation, because we do not know that they were. Rather, we might wonder if the adolescent dimension of the myth tells us something about stealing as it can sometimes occur among contemporary adolescents. In this way, technology becomes a vehicle—a projective screen, if you will—for acting out unconscious mythic themes with ease and even comfort because of the Internet's speed, seeming anonymity, lack of direct interpersonal feedback of a nonverbal kind, and its enabling commerce in the trading of personal information and secrets. Heroic inflation can occur when someone believes him- or herself to be a prime catalyst in this virtual world and arrogantly imagines that his or her viewers, followers, and "friends" are surging forth with admiration over the "hero's" ability to demonstrate that he or she can manipulate this medium. This state of affairs might lead us to speculate whether the social dimensions of our Internet-infused world create tendencies toward not only more primitive forms of expression, but also more archetypal ones that this medium frequently encourages by serving as a ready outlet for exhibitionistic and grandiose fantasies. In adolescence, both are susceptible to happening because of thinking that, in general, is less regulated by higher cortical processes of the brain, which are still developing. This is particularly crucial for the growing ability to exercise social judgment. Social media on the Internet now offer a relatively new performance arena for adolescents whose own vulnerabilities may tempt them to take advantage in primitive and archetypal ways of the same issues in others.

Implications of Technology-Enhanced Stealing

The three examples show various aspects of modern connective technology (mobile texting, social networking, webcam viewing) that can each facilitate a theft of private conversations, intimate activities, and secrets. Although these examples pertain primarily to adolescents, there is little reason to believe that it is confined to them. For example, as the mobile phone hacking scandal in the U.K. shows, adults can also justify stealing private information in the name of their work. This affair involved illegal access of mobile phone accounts by employees of News International, which publishes British newspapers, so they could steal confidential information for stories in their papers. A problematic byproduct of our newer forms of technology ironically stems from the very thing that these advances and innovations overcome, namely they reduce effort, barriers, and time—making commerce in personal data and information relatively easy to obtain and trade. Such information can now be widely disseminated at increased speed. Thus, we have many opportunities, if we want, to publicize what we believe to know or, conversely, to insure we stay "in the know" about whatever piece of gossip has the most perceived value.

David Rosenfeld, a contemporary psychoanalyst, writes about distortions of the mind that can result when someone becomes overly invested in virtual reality. In discussing psychotic addiction to video games, he mentions two specific kinds of psychological mechanisms that can impoverish such a person's psyche.[22] One is a type of autistic encapsulation in which external reality is neglected and made even inaccessible so that a person is walled off from environmental stimuli. The other is massive projective identification, which empties a person's mind of internal resources and valuable identifications—creating a loss of stable internal reality, essentially evacuating what's inside. Both mechanisms add greatly to the psychological risks of participating in any kind of virtual world, including not only video games but also other forms of connecting through modern technology. Whatever the medium—cell phone, computer, video gaming, social networking on the Internet—it can offer a potential screen for massive projection, leading to emptiness, isolation, and a loss of an interpersonal anchor. These devices and their services can exercise an addictive allure, as many of us know. That we now depend on them is a cliché, but when and how does that dependence turn into something darker? These virtual worlds are often highly impersonal, lack the reassuring presence of a face-to-face encounter, and mostly operate in a distorted loop absent much subtle emotional feedback. Emotions in these virtual environments do not contain the valuable information acquired from being in someone's physical presence, and they often get expressed through extremes of either hyperbole or vacuous sterility.

Jack and Ben each learned these lessons the hard way, whereas the Ravi-Clementi case illustrates both the potentially high collateral costs and the unanticipated dangers inherent in stealing someone's privacy. One possible difference in these examples is the parental roles: Jack and Ben had parents who could insist on therapeutic intervention, which from what we know of the Rutgers case does not seem to have happened. Seeing anything positive in the latter situation is very difficult because of its tragic outcome. We might consider in the first two examples, however, that some emotional learning was forced on each boy, in large part because they got psychotherapy, and painful as it was, these thefts actually helped them to better understand that certain boundaries have to be acknowledged and respected. Jack became more conscious of his choices in whom he dated and how he flirted with girls. He came to see that flirting too carelessly and too aggressively was not what he wanted to do anymore. Clinically, we might say that he understood better some of the narcissistic tendencies in himself that contributed to the ways he flirted. He came to value a new perspective on living with emotional stability, which he had disdained before because he equated it with being "boring, same ol', same ol'."

Ben began to see how he let himself repeatedly get into situations in which he inevitably felt persecuted and lonely. He realized that he had some willpower that he could exert in not allowing this to happen so often in his life. Interestingly, both boys at one point in their treatments decided on their own to close their social networking accounts. Jack felt he needed "a timeout" from this activity, whereas Ben said, "It's too much of a headache." Maturity is frequently hard won in later adolescence, and from that perspective, the first two examples contrast tellingly with the third one, which might just leave us wondering about our assumptions of what will constitute meaningful interpersonal connections in a world that increasingly depends on the Internet for entertainment and social networking. Rosenfeld's ideas warn us to be on guard for the psychological consequences of evacuation (too much projection) and isolation (too little real contact). In looking at the myth of the Golden Fleece, we can see a further warning about these technologies when they are used to enable theft. This kind of theft within a virtual world can assume archetypal proportions and appear, for example, to be done for vengeance, for glory, or for treasure. But such techno-theft, as I term it, exposes us to what can happen when an archetype consumes the psyche. Our hold on consciousness gets overwhelmed, and this situation can unleash primitive instincts, which although seemingly expressed in a virtual realm, nonetheless can have shattering real-world effects like depression, ostracism, and even death. The reader might recall that in Chapter 4 I discussed how some classics scholars have viewed Medea's monstrousness, which we can also think of as another archetypal aspect of the myth. In this chapter's adolescent case examples, some of that monstrousness is evident in what happened between Ben, Jack, and their girlfriends, and perhaps, too, in how the Clementi-Ravi tragedy escalated rapidly to a deadly conclusion. Monsters can act recklessly, unpredictably, and violently, but we might pause to consider that they often are created unconsciously out of very complex and uncontained situations. The virtual technologies provided by our computers and cell phones—including not just video gaming, but also social media and messaging through texts and email—are far less containing than we have yet to understand.

Notes

1 L. Alvarez, "With personal data in hand, thieves file early and often," *New York Times*, May 26, 2012. Alvarez notes that thieves steal social security numbers from a number of sources, including those who are dead, imprisoned, and in healthcare facilities.
2 "The Purloined Letter" was published in a collection of Poe's stories in 1845.
3 W. Shakespeare, *The Merry Wives of Windsor* (Modern Library Classics), eds J. Bate and R. Rasmussen, New York, Random House/Modern Library, 2011.
4 d. boyd and A. Marwick, "Social privacy in networked publics: Teens' attitudes, practices, and strategies," paper presented at Oxford Internet Institute's A Decade in Internet Time: Symposium on the Dynamics of the Internet and Society, September 21–24, 2011, in Oxford, UK.
5 A. Lenhart, K. Purcell, A. Smith, and K. Zickuhr, "Social media and young adults," Washington, DC, Pew Internet and American Life Project, 2010. This report can be accessed online at www.pewinternet.org/Reports/2010/Social-Media-and-Young-Adults.aspx as part of a larger study at www.pewresearch.org/millenials; it provides data about Internet and social media use among age groups 12–17 and 18–29. (Accessed May 1, 2013.)
6 boyd and Marwick, "Social privacy in networked publics," p. 10.
7 This figure is from the National Institute of Mental Health's website, for data as of 2007. In addition, the rate of male deaths by suicide is anywhere from five to six times

the number for female deaths in this age group. See HTTP: <www.nimh.nih.gov/health/publications/suicide-in-the-us-statistics-and-prevention/index.shtml#children> for data and additional context.

8 Robin Anderson has described this process in detail from a Kleinian perspective; he notes that the healthy part of the personality can be undermined by destructive and aggressive internal objects that overwhelm the young person's ability to cope with them. He asks, "Why is it that some people can bear these surges of primitive anxiety within themselves when others seem precipitated towards impulsive action?" See R. Anderson, "Suicidal behavior and its meaning in adolescence," in R. Anderson and A. Dartington (eds), *Facing It Out: Clinical Perspectives on Adolescent Disturbance*, pp. 65–78, New York, Routledge.

9 See A. Millicker and R. Kumar, "Timeline: Dharun Ravi's trial," *The Daily Targum*, March 19, 2012. Online, available HTTP: <www.dailytagum.com> (accessed April 10, 2013). *The Daily Targum* is the official student newspaper at Rutgers University.

10 I. Parker, 2012, "The story of a suicide," *The New Yorker*, February 6, 2012. Online, available HTTP: <www.newyorker.com/reporting/2012/02/06/120206fa_fact_parker> (accessed April 10, 2013). Parker reports that Clementi wrote in a text exchange with a friend "mom has basically completely rejected me," although he also indicated that his father was "very accepting."

11 Ibid.

12 This chain of events is largely taken from *The Daily Targum's* "Timeline" article. See Millicker and Kumar, "Timeline."

13 Parker describes Ravi as being adept at computer technology. During high school, he had developed programs that could take pictures of users unbeknownst to them and then upload these photos to a website. Parker notes, "He disguised the program as something else, and tried to get friends to install it . . . (Clementi, then, was apparently not the first subject of a webcam experiment.)" See Parker, "The story of a suicide."

14 Millicker and Kumar, "Timeline." Twitter describes itself as "a real-time information network that connects you to the latest stories, ideas, opinions and news." See <www.twitter.com/about>. Parker adds that Ravi had about 150 followers on Twitter. See Parker, "The story of a suicide."

15 Many believed that Clementi did feel bullied by Ravi's actions, and Clementi's death called much attention to the topic of gay suicide. See D. Sikorski, "Suicide brings LGBTQ, bullying concerns to forefront," *The Daily Targum*, May 2, 2011.

16 K. Zernike, "Jury find spying in Rutgers dorm was a hate crime," *The New York Times*, March 16, 2012. Zernike writes, "The case was a rare one in which none of the facts were in dispute." Further, she reports, "His lawyers said he simply did not believe he had committed a hate crime." See also A. Millicker, "Ravi found guilty on all 15 counts in webcam spying case," *The Daily Targum*, March 16, 2012.

17 K. Zernike, "Rutgers webcam-spying defendant is sentenced to 30-day jail term," *The New York Times*, May 21, 2012.

18 Ibid. Parker too notes, "Ravi is largely an unsympathetic character." I. Parker, "Dharun Ravi's contrition problem," *The New Yorker*, News Desk, May 21, 2012. Online, available HTTP: <www.newyorker.com/online/blogs/newsdesk> (accessed April 10, 2013).

19 R. Pérez-Peña, "Rutgers dorm spying trial begins with questions of motivation," *The New York Times*, February 24, 2012.

20 Zernike, "Jury find spying in Rutgers dorm was a hate crime."

21 Parker, "The story of a suicide."

22 D. Rosenfeld, "Psychotic addiction to video games," in *The Soul, The Mind, and The Psychoanalyst: The Creation of the Psychoanalytic Setting in Patients with Psychotic Aspects*, pp. 117–44, London, Karnac Books, 2006.

10

SOME INSTANCES OF STEALING IN THE CONSULTING ROOM

Perhaps one of the most unique aspects of psychotherapy and analysis is the welcoming invitation to a patient to bring any emotions or fantasies freely into the therapeutic endeavor. Patients frequently understand this to also include behaviors, although traditionally their appearance has fallen into the categories of "acting out" (or "acting in" when observed in the office) and, more recently, "enactment," by which I mean a mutual behavioral occurrence taking place in the analytic field. An increasingly common example of this, especially in working with adolescents and young adults, is the ringing of a mobile phone during a session. Often dismissed with "Oh, I forgot to turn it off," this ringing is nonetheless a kind of communication to a therapist too, albeit disguised. Such an occurrence often indicates an unconscious "ringing" about how a patient is feeling in regard to interruption, distraction, sustained interest, and so on. We might consider such instances as intersubjective phenomena that call our attention to reciprocal unconscious connections and influences appearing within a relational field.

Jung writes:

> For psychotherapy to be effective a close rapport is needed . . . The rapport consists . . . in the dialectical confrontation of two opposing psychic realities. If for some reason these mutual impressions do not impinge on each other, the psychotherapeutic process remains ineffective, and no change is produced. Unless both doctor and patient become a problem to each other, no solution is found.[1]

This remarkable statement emphasizes the particular relationship that develops between an analyst and a patient, and how crucial that connection is for growth and psychic development. Jung did not believe in a caricatured portrait of an analyst as someone aloof and withdrawn, hiding behind a cloak of medical and psychological authority. Instead, he saw it as absolutely necessary for the transference and countertransference to become "problematic" for any progress in a patient's understanding of him- or herself to emerge.

Michael Fordham notes:

> Jung went along with Freud in recognizing the incestuous, erotic and infantile characteristics of transference, as well as accepting its resistance phenomena. Where he went beyond psychoanalysis is his emphasis on the goal-seeking and therapeutic function of transference in which the real personality of the analyst became significant.[2]

Within the last 20 years, much of the entire psychoanalytic field has now moved in Jung's direction with the ascendancy of relational and intersubjective models of contemporary psychoanalysis. Fordham explains that the analyst's personality has to be a critical factor in a patient's individuation because otherwise the latter would occur in a type of psychological vacuum that precludes the internalizing of mutual understanding and reciprocity. He adds that individuation takes place within "an evolution" of transference that facilitates a patient's consciousness about his or her relational patterns in their full complexity of developmental and archetypal components. Fordham believes that "the most impressive feature of Jung's researches into transference is his consistent championing of the patient as a person in need of relationship."[3]

Nowadays, this position is fairly much assumed as a *sine qua non* across traditions of psychoanalytic psychotherapy. Looking at transference and counter-transference, Antonino Ferro writes of the "bi-personal field"; Betty Joseph of the "total situation"; Thomas Ogden of the difference between "holding and containing"; Judith Mitrani of "taking the transference"; and Patrick Casement of "analytic holding under pressure."[4] This theoretical shift becomes practically important for fostering a patient's various relational experiences and also for helping him or her to develop greater tolerance for illusion and ambiguity since these are critical for psychological depth. Stealing usually opposes this sort of development. Appreciation of illusion enhances a person's capacity to symbolize important aspects of his or her life, giving the person an ability to dream them in creative ways. On the other hand, stealing, in most cases, pulls a person into the concrete world of tangible things, where possession of an item is all important. Most thieving, therefore, is at odds with and impairs a person's internal resilience for exploring feelings, for relating truthfully, and for tolerating life's illusory aspects.

Transference is mostly based on illusion—this was Freud's great discovery. We are not ever a patient's parent, even when we might be perceived as if we are acting that way. Nor are we a lover, a spouse, an uncle, an aunt, a child, a teacher, a judge, a jailer, a thief, or so on, to a patient, even when he or she might imagine us in any of those roles, or experience us as being in them. Part of the excitement of analytic work is that the patient gets to do just that—fantasize about us as being like any of the possible multitude of people who live in his or her psyche. Holding onto this aspect of an analytic relationship is not without its challenges. We might think of illusion as being in service of transference exploration and discovery. Engaging in such a process helps to undergird a patient's ability to symbolize, which is usually a desired analytic outcome.

At the same time, there exists another potential for enactments, described earlier, which although initially unconscious, can present opportunities for an internal problem to become visible for observation and, with effort from the patient, for conscious understanding. At a different level altogether, we might encounter a patient's need to emotionally discharge a complex with us in a way that represents acting out, or acting in.[5] Such discharge frequently communicates intolerable states of emotional pain that are conveyed through projective identification. In this difficult place, which any of us can fall into, verbal terms that connote illusion—*like, as if, similar to, representing, dreamlike*—feel irrelevant because relief is felt to arrive mostly through emptying and evacuating from our minds the sources of distress.

When Emotional Discharge Raises the Prospect of Stealing

What happens when stealing enters this complex relational picture of transference and countertransference? A patient might, for example, wish she could steal something from her analyst, but then only plays with this idea and perhaps dreams about it. Phoebe (Chapter 7) wished she could steal private details about my life because a part of her believed she could only get what she wanted—especially when she experienced someone as acting like a depriving mother—by taking it. Another patient might, however, reverse the roles of thief and victim. For example, Marie (Chapter 8) felt stolen from because of our encounter in the jewelry store. At that time, she felt she had lost a sense of me as a man who was trustworthy and who found her appealing. On further examination, she became aware of why we got entangled in a way that was painful for her when she felt betrayed by me. Hypothetically, any patient might actually take something, and a therapist or analyst would be left to deal with an actual theft, as happened when Kyle stole (Chapter 5). For some patients, it is important to keep in mind that it might be a positive sign when they do show a desire to steal from their analyst—along the lines of trying to incorporate what they did not fairly get during their early development. For instance, I often felt if Noah (Chapter 6) had wanted to take more from me that this would have been important in a way that helped, not hindered, our relationship, even supposing that he had tried to take from me in a way that might have seemed like stealing.

A desire to steal can become activated in a transference relationship when a patient is struggling with what seems either unattainable or unreachable in his or her life. Transference itself signifies something about relating that is mostly impossible to ever realize. As such, it bears a commonality with the archetypal desires evoked by the Golden Fleece. Clinical examples of two dreams will demonstrate when unattainable desires are operative in the transference and bring forth impulses to steal from the analyst. Within desire, stealing can arise as a possibility and overwhelm us. This contributes to both uncertainty and the intensity of working through transferences imbued with Fleece-like dimensions.

One might ask, why even consider the myth of the Golden Fleece in this regard? Does it provide any useful insight into the dynamics of an analytic relationship that have not already been described elsewhere? (And without the added context of a very old story that remains mostly in popular media in significantly altered form?) I hope to illustrate that the story of Medea and Jason's actions toward the Fleece reveals something about how intense human feelings can override an appreciation of illusion. I am not going to discuss so-called delusional transferences in which any recognition of consensual reality is discarded, but rather intensely experienced ones that acquire insistence, a demanding tone, and an expectation that wishes come true. Although each analytic relationship may consist of various threads of similar feelings, I want to investigate what can happen when they appear to take over. The myth of the Golden Fleece tells us a story of two people chasing something that they imagine has to conform to a fixed idea about what it should really mean.

In this context, the Golden Fleece symbolizes pent-up longing, an irresistible wish, and a desirous ambition: none, however, intended to be actualized. This notion differs from a more classical Jungian one about quests that might see in the Fleece an end product (like the lapis, boon, or hard-won treasure) of an individuation process. Instead, I consider that the Fleece signals a different message about determining when to stop oneself, which can often be a painfully experienced insight. Many desires, even most, are not meant to be lived out: this could be because of human limitations, environmental obstacles, or even the wrong timing. A problem results when stealing looms as an appealing workaround to this condition. In analysis, limits are encountered emotionally in the transference, which is frequently dense with power and love, both of which patients might, at times, feel they would like to steal from their analyst. Analysts are trained to recognize clues of the transference relationship in a patient's conscious fantasies, in slips of the tongue, in the affective tone in the room, in dreams, in reactions to the therapeutic frame, and, perhaps most importantly, in the countertransference. The complexity of a transference relationship encompasses nearly everything that occurs in the analytic space.

In a good enough analysis, containment for strong emotions and their accompanying urges is available. The story of the Fleece can be understood as an allegory that helps to delineate those times in the transference when something particularly unattainable might have to be viewed, named, experienced by both participants, and never acted on. It is not just an experience of beholding something like the Fleece that has to be contained because the Fleece is a metaphorical screen, in the sense discussed here, for catching a patient's desires, projections, and hopes. It is also the stormy, unrelenting feelings that a patient might develop for his or her analyst that have to be held within a secure analytic relationship that functions as a container. If they are too similar to what Jason and Medea feel in the myth toward the Fleece, then such feelings press for locating a reality where wishes do come true, even when this includes stealing. Integration of these desires eventually takes place in an analysis when a patient becomes capable of resisting their allure so that he or she gains adequate perspective to think about them.

Clinical Examples

In both these cases, wishes to take something from me centered on some difficulties with the illusory nature of transference, and such complexities are fairly common. My patients' wishes were, I believe, positive and helped to move the clinical work in the right direction because they represented a subset of what I have earlier termed Promethean stealing. This type of stealing has a potential to advance a person's individuation by bringing consciousness to unrevealed parts of the self that are crying out for attention. A wish to steal can shed light on what has been hidden, unconscious, and stuck in the dark. The two examples are purposely selected to represent different entries into this theme of illusion and stealing within transference. One is from Marie, who we met in Chapter 8 and who was quite far along in her analytic process. The other comes from a male patient who presented an initial dream to me that conveyed a deep paternal longing that immediately colored his transference to me.

Erotic Transference

Marie reported this dream from later in her analysis, when she was discouraged about her prospects of meeting another man for a meaningfully intimate relationship:

> *You and I are driving in a car with two young people in the back. I'm at the wheel. One person in the back is a crazy woman and the other is one of my sons. The young woman really goes nuts, and you deal with it. We drive over some dead bodies buried under gravel, and I think it was the crazy woman who killed them. We stop down by a river. The young people are gone. Standing by the water, you and I kiss and hug one another. We have so much to talk about. It feels so intimate and right. Later, we drive back, and there is a sense we'll have to deal with how things have changed. You give me your phone number, and I'm going to write it on the front page of my newspaper, but I can't find it.*

Marie at first associated the crazy woman with a coworker who was overwhelming because she had poor boundaries. In reality, this person was not young—she was middle-aged. Marie said that the feeling about us in the dream was that she could be honest and forthright with me. She contrasted this feeling of being seen and heard with how she felt ignored and neglected by a man she recently had dated. I wondered aloud if Marie was idealizing me, but she thought not. She added that later in the dream she recognized "this is my therapist." Her not being able to write my phone number represented to her a worry that she could lose track of me as her inner therapist. She described her son in the dream as inexperienced in the world of adult relationships. The crazy woman's crimes in the dream—the bodies—were to Marie her own lost relationships that she felt guilty about.

When I heard this dream, I felt attentive to Marie's description of the natural quality of our intimacy. Several prior dreams about us occasionally had details of erotic encounters, although Marie frequently felt this image of our relationship as problematic. She sometimes became irritated or angry with me when exploring those dreams because she professed to be embarrassed by them. They made her worry she was dependent on me in an aching sort of way. My countertransference during many of those discussions picked up on an aspect of this conflict around dependence and intimacy because I often felt she wanted to take something from me, like stealing my affection. This dream, however, had a similar wish for physical intimacy, but also a commentary that it was improbable. For example, I wondered if Marie's not finding a newspaper to write down my phone number indicated a new appreciation that the activity between us in the dream was not intended for front-page publication—or, in other words, for realization. Perhaps this seeming obstacle to further contact now expressed an acceptable inner limit on a demand to steal some intimate contact from me.

Marie felt it was important to make a distinction between how she experienced me "live" in her analytic work and, alternatively, symbolized as an inner figure with whom she wanted to remain in communication. She thought that this was what our intimate embrace by the river symbolized. This inner figure of her analyst assisted her with crazy feelings (as represented by the coworker with poor boundaries), with loss (the bodies), and with inexperience in certain aspects of relating (her son). Marie seemed to find some enjoyment in creating this inner version of me, and although it arose from our work, she began to understand more about the unattainable quality of her wishes toward the "live" version. This change made them seem less demanding to me and less aching to her.

In subsequent sessions, Marie and I discussed her dream in more detail. She came to think that the trip implied by riding in the car was a reference to her work in therapy. In this context, the young woman in the backseat was Marie many years before, a younger Marie who felt crazy and struggled with staying emotionally present. She explained that the bodies represented the grieving that she had done with me. She had processed many losses: her mother, her father, and her divorce. The river reminded Marie of her increasing familiarity with the unconscious, as well as a growing confidence that she could trust what she was learning about intimacy. Along this line, she understood her intention to write down my phone number on the newspaper to mean that she needed to continue working at awareness of what she had learned—in other words, to publish it for her conscious mind where the documentation would remain available. She joked that the resulting imaginary newspaper articles would be called "The Intimacy Chronicles."

Marie's dream shows an evolution of an erotic transference wish that such a relationship could be attained with me into something quite different, thereby losing much of its insistence. Its attainment was based on an unconscious fantasy that would have required her stealing valuable things from me, such as my privacy, my ability to manage my own affections, my analytic attitude, including how I held the frame of our work, and my conviction about the ethics of our relationship. Because of her steady analytic work with me, this particular transference wish became less infused by an impulse that felt too quickly to tip into a kind of thieving demand. Her transference dream presented a contrast to the theft of the Golden Fleece. Whereas Jason and Medea were not able to withdraw their projections about the Fleece and had to steal it, Marie was able to transform certain idealized projections about a romantic relationship with me because she felt able to both contain and explore them as part of the transference relationship. She felt a less pressing need to take something from me, and her emotional insight diminished what I had sometimes previously felt to be the case, namely when it seemed as if she were presenting me with a claim that I owed her more than I could offer. Although there continued to be aspects of an erotic transference to me, it was held more as something unattainable—not an incitement for stealing—that indicated far greater tolerance for illusion within our relationship. I later found my countertransference also changed because I did not feel such pressure coming from her; in many ways, I then felt I could let myself experience more fully the natural affection I did feel toward Marie. This was a change she also noticed and liked.

An Initial Dream

Tom was a man in his thirties who lived with his spouse. This example highlights the importance of initial dreams as unconscious communications about the impending analytic work. Initial dreams have long interested analysts. Renaldo Maduro, writing from a Jungian perspective, comments, "The initial interview is the ambiguous stimulus in response to which an initial dream reflects an individual's psychic reality."[6] He highlights the valuable, though disguised, information contained in initial dreams that typically show "great affect" and tend to reflect the dreamer's core psychic issues as well as hints of their "potential resolution." Jung writes that "initial dreams are often amazingly lucid," but that with the passage of time, these dreams "tend to lose their clarity."[7]

Tom sought me out because of a confused relationship with his mother that he felt intruded too much into his psyche. He reported a complicated first dream, represented here in summary form:

> *I'm walking into the courtyard of an old castle. People are preparing a feast. I go into a large hall with my father where a banquet will occur but*

we've not been invited. A woman who is a tradeswoman might be following us to kick us out. We have to be careful of her.

We pass a guard. Now it's clearly you and me—we go into another room by walking right through a wall. We're not ghosts—how do we do it? We sit down in the middle of a treasure room. From our hearts, gemstones are coming out, and we're exchanging them. They are clear, transparent, and green. We keep doing this until there's quite a few. Yours are bigger than mine. It feels very special . . . .

At the end, I'm alone on a hill looking back at the castle and I feel sad.

After telling me this dream, Tom said, "The feelings were clear. I was younger and I felt anxious around the tradeswoman—that she might be pursuing us, threatening us. The dream feels like a wish for an ideal father—and for unconditional love from him. It's almost unbearable to talk about because it comes with such painful longing." Tom was upset as he told me this.

We spent many sessions talking about his dream, and it became a landmark for us in referring to how he felt when he first met me. When I first heard the dream, I wondered if it foreshadowed something about how things might unfold between Tom and me. It told of a joint exploration with hazards, a magical exchange, and then a lonely recognition of loss viewed from a distance. It also spoke about stealing his way into a private event. Components of this dream paralleled a quest for treasure that is like the tale of the Golden Fleece.

The transformation of Tom's father into me likely indicated the power of an immediate transference wish that I could help him escape an internal threat coming from an intrusive mother (that is, the threatening tradeswoman who we might interpret as trying to evict anyone else threatening her claim on his psyche). Tom's parents divorced when he was 3 years old, and after he had lived for a year with his father, he was then sent to live with his mother, who subsequently descended into a serious mental illness that lasted into Tom's adolescence. I found it heartbreaking that, although he still visited his father, Tom had not continued to live with him for his own wellbeing and stability. Unfortunately for the young Tom, this never materialized.

In Tom's dream, I appear to represent a father figure, although I'm not just his personal father, but also an archetypal one with extraordinary powers like a magician. A magician archetype often incorporates aspects of hero, healer, and trickster.[8] The boy Tom lost steady contact with his real father, an experience he referred to often as not only being abandoned but also, as he later came to see, "ripped off," "cheated," and "taken from." This loss of an apparently stolen father may have come to represent internally an unconscious longing to steal a father back in whatever way Tom could find. I suspect as a young boy Tom had to create an idealized father by reaching into an archetypal layer of the psyche as one way to cope with the wound of his father's abandonment. In that regard,

Tom's psyche was searching for a magical solution to a father problem somewhat like Jason, who endows the Fleece with a capacity to make up for what he also lost by his father's abandonment. In some of my first countertransference feelings, I was aware of the imposing burden of his idealization that made me anxious about missteps and mistakes I knew I would make. I wondered how Tom would handle these.

The question in Tom's dream, "How do we do it?" [walking through walls], pointed to a moment when the dreamer glimpsed the magic of an archetype at work in arranging an impossible outcome. To the dreaming Tom, it did not follow that we could walk through walls (although he did not later question our ability to produce gemstones from our hearts). His question within the dream was similar in a way to Marie's not being able to find a newspaper to write down my phone number. An observed inconsistency within the dream created a moment of self-reflection about the impossibility of what was occurring, perhaps opening the door a crack on the projected idealization of what he wished could happen. At the point of Tom's first telling me this dream, I was not at all sure what this question could have meant. I speculated then that his wondering about our walking through walls possibly referred to another question Tom might have had about how to feel substantial in a relationship with a man who to Tom was imbued with powerful and magical projections. I noticed that I stole his father's place and thought that Tom might have felt confused by his wishes for me.

The creation of the green gemstones in the dream involved material coming right from the heart. The dream's symbolism indicated to me that we had to find how to share precious parts of ourselves, parts that reflected treasured, though buried feelings that could lead to Tom's emotional growth, represented, I thought, by the green of the stones. As Tom's therapeutic process unfolded, I was very aware of how he idealized me. Importantly, this initial dream conveyed an "exchange" of a fatherly sort ("yours are bigger than mine"). The possibility of exchange contrasts almost as an opposite with an interaction like stealing. I began to think that Tom felt his father was stolen from him, an event that had overwhelmed him emotionally. Could he steal something of a father back? How was he to relate to an older man—or men in general—when strong desires appeared? Exchange implies a trade, one freely entered into, that includes a swap of valuable items for mutual satisfaction. Along those lines, the dream gave a hint of one direction for Tom's therapeutic work, namely, how does one exchange in relationships rather than face a choice of stealing or being ripped off? The gemstone section of Tom's dream made me think that we could process what I suspected would be an unavoidable deflation of an idealized father, if we could engage in a more basic form of emotional exchange.

A year into our work, a synchronicity occurred that seemed to call attention to this aspect of our relationship—how to understand a wish for an idealized, magical father who appears when needed? One day I happened to find a check on the sidewalk near my office. It was a check from Tom made out to me for his recent sessions. He had lost it on the way to see me. At first, he apologized for losing it, but then he saw that I actually had the check in hand. I didn't know what to say because the situation astonished me—that I had obtained the check through an unlikely coincidence. I seemed to have become an embodiment of a magical father, appearing exactly when Tom needed me to help him. This was much like the same magical, idealized father we had been deconstructing in the context of Tom's therapy; I had been encouraging him to view me in ways that were not idealized. In retrospect, however, I wonder if something about this incident did not show a shadow side of the idealized father, namely, that he could also be a sneaky father who appeared, at times, to steal from Tom.

In discussing his reaction to the missing check, Tom said that among his first thoughts was "What an *idiot* I am. How could this happen to me?" I noted that he blamed himself for what seemed to be an accident, and he began to cry. He continued, "Everything's my fault. I can't see a way around it." I thought his total self-recrimination probably included blaming himself for the "accident" of his father's disappearance early in his life. We know that children often blame themselves when parents separate. Tom spoke about how extraordinary this incident of the lost and found check had been. He described feeling "like you must have had magic, and you rescued me." He was able to say that this wish to be rescued felt familiar and probably dated to when his father left him. I noticed how Tom's idealizing me paralleled how he now persecuted himself with blame and guilt. It seemed as I loomed larger in his mind, both powerful and rescuing, he shrank internally and became more powerless and culpable.

Idealization usually has a flipside of persecution when an internal standard or expectation is not met. A superego attack often follows with either a form of punishment against the self for failing or an attempt to spoil what is externally available for seeming inadequate. We can see a bit of this first dynamic when Tom said, "what an idiot I am." I began to understand the idealizing aspect of our relationship as a way for Tom to remember what he felt he had lost with his father—and what I guessed he felt to have been stolen from him. After all, what 4-year-old boy does not sometimes wish that his father might secretly be a hero, or even a magician, with great skills? Among many other things, Tom lost that experience. In addition, our exploration of this topic brought up many of his memories of persecution, when he felt attacked by his mother and helpless to respond. This recognition gradually helped Tom to understand more about when he shifted between states of idealization and persecution in his important relationships.

Tom commented that sharing his feelings with another man felt new, difficult at times, and especially hard in face of negative emotions like hate and envy. Later in our work Tom reflected, "I've never had so many feelings that I was aware of." He became more confident in speaking up when he felt disappointed over what he observed as my mistakes, shortcomings, and idiosyncrasies. But he also talked affectionately about our work in ways that often moved me. I think he developed a more conscious attitude about what he wished for from an idealized father, who had appeared so quickly in his initial dream and whose central importance became unavoidably clear to both of us.

Dreaming Fleece-Like Aspects of Transference

Dreams tend to reveal which central conflicts and core complexes are active at given moments in our lives. Jung especially emphasized the dynamism inherent to dreams, whose contents are "true symbols" that ought not to be interpreted "semiotically."[9] He advocated openness about the meaning of a dream and to resist simplistic categorizations. He believed a dream's significance emerged in analysis as a mutual undertaking: "Understanding should therefore be understanding in the sense of an agreement which is the fruit of joint reflection."[10] This represents an intersubjective view of dreamwork that was far ahead of its time.

The clinical material from Marie and Tom supports a pivotal role of dream analysis for understanding when intense projections might infuse a transference relationship with unattainable qualities. The Golden Fleece signifies a charged and sacred object that offers an archetypal configuration for the tempting allure of such experience, which may be so desired as to evoke a wish to steal it. Transference dreaming could be regarded as an instance in analysis that opens the door to exploring Fleece-like aspects of a patient's projections onto his or her analyst. These can, for example, represent impossible wishes for sexual intimacy, emotional fulfillment, and power. The application of the myth to clinical material helps to illuminate what happens when a transference wish carries an aspect of demand that the wish come true. A patient's dream might then reveal what he or she wants to steal from the analyst. The myth also points out the considerable danger that accompanies such wishes, mainly in mobilizing destructive and self-destructive forces within the psyche. After stealing the Fleece, Jason and Medea leave betrayal, deception, and murder in their wake.

How can analysts assist their patients in tolerating inner forces that seem to collapse any room for illusion? Metaphorically put: can a patient resist an urge to steal the Fleece, whose theft enacts the discharge of an archetypal experience into the real world? Marie was in a unique place after several years of analytic work because she had developed an inner version of me to provide helpful *internal* containment. Her inner therapist helped her to reflect on her desires, the ways she chose to express them, and her reactions to the responses she received from men. Tom, by comparison, was close to the beginning of his analytic journey. We had to sort through ordinary disappointments that I had no special powers, yet it was still possible for him to feel that I was special to him. Over time we worked through that I was someone who could help him with a real-world corollary of exchanging the green gemstones from his dream, namely, bringing his feelings into the open, man-to-man—in a form of *external* containment through our relationship.

Both dreams have in common an element of the dreamer's questioning within the dream what is happening. Doubt, however it arises, is the beginning of considering that something might not or cannot happen. For instance, the missing newspaper in Marie's dream and the question "How do we do it?" in Tom's dream indicated what was not available in the transference relationship: a lover and a magical father. They were unattainable. To integrate this knowledge, Marie's and Tom's projected feelings of love and power had to find a place in our mutual waking awareness. Locating a Fleece archetype within a transference dream orients the analyst to the unspoken edges of the existing transference relationship. If the grip of a Fleece archetype is not carefully explored, nor the wish to steal something made more visible, then clinical problems can arise, such as defensive rigidity in both the patient and analyst, uncontained discharge of a complex into the analytic field, and relational impasse.

We might ask these questions about our attitudes toward transference in an analytic relationship:

- How much of a transference relationship do we interpret?
- How much of it might we instead hold quietly in an effort to contain?
- How can we respond when there is an archetypal activation of something unattainable that seeks fulfillment?

These are difficult questions that, of course, cannot be reduced to simple answers, for they vary from one analytic endeavor to the next, as well as within it. In my early work with Marie and Tom, I seldom interpreted much about the transference, especially in the classical sense of making a developmentally based or otherwise dense interpretation that referred to their outer relationships. Instead, I focused on how they perceived me and what feelings that brought up. I think transference interpretations early in a treatment, owing to their emotional complexity, can sometimes undermine a developing analytic relationship, or at least burden it more than necessary. They probably work best only when offered as invitations to be curious. Emotionally and cognitively, welcoming doubt supports awareness of illusion.

At the beginning of an analysis, therapeutic work unfolds through a process of sustaining tensions, noting them as possible subjects for exploration, and averting conclusions about relational patterns that could seem to a patient to be coming too soon in the process. Later, we hope to say more about those patterns. Pressure on an analyst to respond verbally to a desire—to comment on it, to limit it, to discourage it subtly, to label it—can be immense, particularly when an archetypal layer of the psyche fuels too much energy or libido into a wish (perhaps every wish has an archetypal component). Study of myth is certainly not intended to predetermine or encumber what we do with our patients. We might recall the theoretical richness that Freud found in extrapolating the myths of Oedipus and Narcissus, and the tremendous creative impulse that Jung found in the great myths of death and rebirth. The story of the Golden Fleece provides a unique window into unconscious forces that can push a psyche toward demanding, acting, taking, stealing, and possessing. In some sense, if something unattainable does not become part of an analytic discourse, we might wonder why not. If there is not a demand, wish or urge to take something from the analyst, for example, his or her love, then perhaps something elemental is being missed.

In the myth of the Golden Fleece, there are no helpful parents. The older generation is corrupt (Pelias), abandoning (Aison), and wrathful (Aietes). Absent a transmission across generations, no dialogue occurs between those swept up in a quest and those who have power. Thinking of this gap, we might then imagine that an analyst seeing an impossible demand or unattainable wish must use a form of gentle analytic strength, not overt power, to weather the effects of a tumultuous exploration. In an archetypal application of the myth of the Golden Fleece to the consulting room, we might hope that an understanding of transference wishes leads a patient to where she can see the Fleece, does not run away in fear from the dragon guarding it, and also experiences that it will not be taken from its spot in the tree. If this can happen, then a patient might consciously integrate what she wants to steal from her analyst and why it tempts her in an illusory way.

Therapeutic containment is achieved, in part, when transference dreams, such as the two presented here, are discussed, amplified, and explored. During this process, they lose some of the purity of their psychic content. Made more conscious, various characters can then meet—dreamer, analyst in the dream, and their waking personalities. Perceptions about reality and imagination confront one another in their own mix of analytic soup. This also includes an analyst's countertransference, which helps to evaluate what sort of containing function might be required at any given moment. Containment is supported in an analytic relationship that can securely reflect whatever feels unattainable, yet allow it to be seen and named. Sometimes, this might mean not commenting directly on a transference wish to take or steal. At other times, a gentle interpretation is necessary, not so much for intellectual insight, but rather to enlist a patient's conscious effort in developing his or her own containing capacity.

This discussion applies mainly to a subset of transference dreams—those in which a Fleece-like quality of transference can be identified. Studying how frequently such dreams occur would be helpful, as would knowing how often they demonstrate forms of self-reflection, that is, doubts and questions. I suggest that the Fleece as an archetype can help in understanding certain kinds of transference, especially around desires to steal something from the analyst, and that, in many cases, the core of what is "unattainable" often shows up in transference dreaming. With closer examination, what is behind an unconscious impulse to steal can then become more evident.

Real Theft

Sometimes analysts and psychotherapists have tangible, valued things stolen from them. Stealing can, for example, occur when children take a toy from the office, and it frequently serves to bring attention to issues of deprivation, envy, and secrecy. Often, the child in these situations wants to be caught in a type of Promethean stealing, so his or her development can begin to process something unconscious and unnoticed that has gone awry. Like with Kyle (Chapter 5), these situations can be both poignant and amusing incidents that most child analysts and psychotherapists have experienced in their practices. On the other hand, there are occasions when adults steal, and one of the more common ways in which this occurs is when they refuse to pay their bill. Most, and maybe nearly all, of us have stories about some patient whom we might have felt especially ripped off by—that is, stolen from—or who took advantage of us in a troubling manner. I offer an example here to illustrate my own blind spot in being caught in a projective identification that baffled me at the time.

I saw a 13-year-old girl in my practice for nearly a year. Her parents had gone through a contentious divorce. Mother was a professional, and father (Mr. Y) was a manager in a department responsible for protecting a company's trademarks. I initially felt them both to be honest and engaging. Their daughter was an articulate, precocious child, who spent many sessions talking with me about her voracious reading of fantasy books with themes of magic, vampires, and alternate worlds. Her mother and father insisted on seeing me separately because of their discord, but they each presented as concerned parents fully supportive of their daughter's therapy. They agreed on how to split the costs for her therapy.

This girl seemed to benefit a lot from therapy. She became less depressed and more outspoken at home and in school, a change that boded well, so I thought. She expressed torn loyalties between her parents. Months passed, and only her mother paid me her share of the bill. I contacted her father, who first told me that he was swamped, this was his mistake, and a check would go out that day. The mother downplayed anything being amiss about his delaying payment.

The father's check never arrived and I felt irritated. I wondered if I had not been firm enough in my communications with him. I suggested meeting with him, and he agreed. He began by apologizing and told me that he forgot his checkbook. He promised to send me a check when he got home. I felt uneasy but couldn't identify why, perhaps not wanting to see myself as gullible. Thinking about his job responsibilities, I made excuses for him. I was telling myself, Surely he can be trusted. Six months into his daughter's therapy, however, he had not paid me.

After a vacation break, I phoned the father and said that in order for me to keep seeing his daughter, he and I had to discuss why he was not paying me. He blustered through a list of excuses—that he had just changed banks, that he was short on cash because of his daughter's school bill, that he was distracted because of a conference, and that he would take care of the bill later that week. I commented that now I felt unsure because his inattention to this indicated that he had some conflict around paying for his daughter's therapy. He laughed and replied, "We all have conflicts, right?" He gave me his word that he would take care of the bill.

We could understand Mr. Y's behavior as an attack on the therapeutic frame. This kind of assault has been well described by Langs, who views such aggression as undermining and possibly malicious.[11] In this case, I began to view it in a similar way. My countertransference feeling that I had not been firm enough suggested to me that I had been minimizing the intensity of Mr. Y's assault on his daughter's treatment. My communications had been clear; what was infirm was my conscious appreciation of how hostile Mr. Y felt toward his daughter. Much like her preferences for reading fantasy books, I had gotten caught in an alternate world where parents should not behave as he did. I addressed with him two aspects of what I understood to be his agreement with me. One was the importance of his daughter continuing to receive therapy, and two was that in order for this to occur, he would have to decide about whether he wanted to provide this for her. He acknowledged visible improvements in his daughter and expressed a wish for her treatment to continue. Mother also tried to persuade him to pay up but to no avail.

As time continued to pass with no payment from him, I felt angry and a bit stupid. I started asking myself, How had I let this drag on?—although I had made attempts to find a remedy. It seemed clear that I was unconscious of something, and I felt the best way to understand it was to speak again with Mr. Y. I phoned him, and I began by noting that I imagined he might know the purpose of my call. He said, "Oh, the bill. Damn, I keep forgetting." He turned the discussion to his daughter, and after I answered a few questions, I remarked that we had gotten off track from why I was calling him. He replied that he was writing the check then as we spoke, and that when he got off the phone, he would have his assistant put it in the mail to me. I didn't believe him, and for a few seconds, a tense silence hung between us.

He broke this silence, asking, "Are you still there?" I replied that I was. Then I said that I no longer felt I could believe him. He laughed and repeated condescendingly that he was taking care of it. After another pause, I responded that I hoped he was, but that now I really wondered if some part of him did not want his daughter to be getting help. He said angrily that if he was paying me, then "you belong in my pocket! You should be on my side." He suggested that my neutrality between him and his ex-wife was unacceptable because in his view she was clearly the source of his daughter's difficulties.

In retrospect, I think I did not understand a projective identification at that time about a fantasy my patient had that he was a good father who fully supported her. I unconsciously identified with her wanting to view him this way. She and I both were inhabiting this alternate world in which good fathers naturally paid for what their daughters needed. As a result, I did not quite see how disturbed his relationship with her was. He was ambivalent about being a good father to her because she reminded him of the ill will he felt toward her mother.

I believe that his expressing his anger in terms of whose side I might be on allowed him to defend (through splitting) against the aggression he felt toward his own daughter. He seemed to have a narcissistic attitude about relationships in which people could be either be bought, sold, and kept in his "pockets"—or stolen from.

This kind of theft is destructive. It was likely intended as an attack to impoverish me, perhaps as part of a fantasy about control and owning me. For a while, this tack worked since I kept pursuing him. Eventually, his daughter began to see him as untruthful. She said in one of her last sessions with me, "My father should have been an actor. You don't know how many people he fools. Even me sometimes."

Theoretical Considerations about Illusion and Stealing

In the cases of Marie and Tom, it was therapeutically important to accept their feelings of wanting to take something from me. Most analytic traditions would support this openness as part of an analytic attitude. Referencing Bion, Mitrani's notion of "taking the transference," by which she means accepting "realistic projective identifications," could easily include bringing into the analytic field a representation of someone stolen from or someone who steals:

> I find that when I can be with the patient while he/she is experiencing me as either "bad" or "good," then I may have the opportunity to provide him/her with an experience of a containing object for each of these situations.[12]

Bion and others who have elaborated his theory would view this as a necessary containing function for a patient's projective identifications. This allows for the patient's experience to be taken in, processed by the analyst, and then re-introjected later by the patient as something more acceptable, metabolized, and in line with promoting the development of a basic psychological transformation that Bion referred to as alpha function. In the sense discussed here, "taking the transference," therefore, embraces a willingness to remain open to fantasies of when a patient might either want to steal from his or her analyst or, conversely, see the analyst as a thief.

What might stop many a thief from acting on his or her impulse is recognition of the illusory aspects of what the thief believes the theft will provide. In his seminal article on transitional objects, Winnicott theorized about how we develop a capacity for illusion:

> The intermediate area to which I am referring is the area that is allowed to the infant between primary creativity and objective perception based on reality testing. The transitional phenomena represent the early stages of the use of illusion, without which there is no meaning for the human

> being in the idea of a relationship with an object that is perceived by others as external to that being.[13]

Winnicott stakes a claim here for the developmental importance of illusion in human relations. He finds illusion is necessary so we can see one another as separate beings yet also think about one another without doing anything. Illusion creates an imaginal space for entertaining doubts and alternatives. In this imaginary realm, we can simply dream about possibilities. Stealing is mostly antithetical to this experience because it is typically an action that shuts down our openness to illusions.[14] Instead, theft almost inevitably draws us into the world of tangible things. When stealing appears analytically, we have to be especially careful because there is an elevated risk that the analytic field might collapse when theft happens in a way that violates this relationship. Such theft, for example, derails a therapy by undermining what we offer in terms of illusion within a containing relationship. Of the types of stealing discussed in this book, perhaps Promethean stealing is among the easiest to address analytically because, as I suggest, it occurs in order to reach for something hidden away in the unconscious.

An ability to enter into an illusory space is not always simple or without struggle. Jung writes:

> Nobody who finds himself on the road to wholeness can escape that characteristic suspension which is the meaning of crucifixion. For he will infallibly run into things that thwart and "cross" him: first, the thing he has no wish to be (the shadow); second, the thing he is not (the "other", the individual reality of the "You"); and third, his psychic non-ego (the collective unconscious).[15]

Jung means that analysis is hard, painful work. That image of being crossed (crucified) is an apt one for depicting the steps in an analytic process leading to individuation. These arduous steps all involve repeated encounters with illusion. I find the symbol of a cross useful in thinking about stealing because theft does cross boundaries and, in a way, can penetrate to the core of whatever illusion the stolen thing might have once represented. Sometimes, this happens so a person can reach for something that has been beyond her or his grasp, but that the person needs, or believes she or he needs, in order to get on with life. Marie and Tom each used their analytic relationships with me to express positive aspects of a wish to steal—to cross me and then to cross what this meant to them. Their experiences of wanting to take from me seemed to assist them in retaking something stolen from them in their unconscious. Crossing me helped to bring that into consciousness. At other times in a psychotherapy, we might encounter stealing that is negative and damaging because it takes us from the light and into the dark—that is what my third example in this chapter shows, a kind of crossing that rips instead of connects.

Notes

1 C. G. Jung, *Memories, Dreams, Reflections*, ed. A. Jaffé, New York, Vintage Books/Random House, 1965, p. 143.
2 M. Fordham, "Jung's conception of transference," in S. Shamdasani (ed.) *Analyst-Patient Interaction, Collected Papers on Technique*, London, Routledge, 1974/1996, pp. 112–38. Quote is from p. 118.
3 Ibid., p. 133.
4 A. Ferro, *The Bi-Personal Field*, London, Routledge, 1999; Ferro presents a reinterpretation and expansion of a seminal paper by the Barangers (M. Baranger and W. Baranger, "The analytic situation as a dynamic field," *International Journal of Psychoanalysis*, 2008, vol. 89, 795–826, in what is a reprint of their earlier work from 1961–62). He emphasizes Bion's contributions, especially those related to projective identifications that have a tremendous impact on the analytic field. B. Joseph, "Transference: The total situation," in M. Feldman. and E. Bott Spillius (eds), *Psychic Equilibrium and Psychic Change*, pp. 156–67, London and New York, Routledge, 1989; Joseph discusses the totality of transference from a Kleinian perspective. T. H. Ogden, "On holding and containing, being and dreaming," *International Journal of Psychoanalysis*, 2004, vol. 85, 1349–64; Ogden is a prolific writer and creative theorist who has advanced our thinking about dreams and dreaming within the analytic session. "On holding and containing, being and dreaming" is but one sample of his work in which he discusses the different accents given to transference and countertransference by Bion and Winnicott. J. L. Mitrani, "'Taking the transference': Some technical implications in three papers by Bion," *International Journal of Psychoanalysis*, 2001, vol. 82, 1085–1104; Mitrani develops Bion's work on projective processes into her formulation of "taking the transference," which she writes "is a necessary and indispensable step on the way towards the interpretation of the transference, especially when dealing with primitive mental states" (p. 1092). Her discussion brings into focus Bion's notion of "realistic projective identification" that communicates extremely difficult unconscious emotional states in need of metabolizing. P. Casement, *Learning from the Patient*, New York, Guilford Publications, 1991; Casement writes about a particularly taxing case of trauma during infancy that was enacted within the patient's analysis. He eloquently comments on the pressures created by the patient, pressures that likely would have foreclosed important discoveries had he responded to them too acceptingly.
5 W. B. Goodheart, "*The Listening Process* (Langs); *The Therapeutic Environment* (Langs); *Technique in Transition* (Langs); *Intrapsychic and Interpersonal Dimensions of Treatment: A Clinical Dialogue* (Langs and Searles); *Collected Papers on Schizophrenia and Related Subjects* (Searles); *Countertransference and Related Subjects: Selected Papers* (Searles). Works by Robert Langs; Robert Langs and Harold F. Searles; and Harold F. Searles," *The San Francisco Jung Institute Library Journal*, Summer 1980, vol. 1, no. 4, pp. 2–39.
6 R. Maduro, "The initial dream and analysability in beginning analysis," *Journal of Analytical Psychology*, 1987, vol. 32, 199–226.
7 C. G. Jung, "The practical use of dream-analysis," in *The Practical Use of Psychotherapy*, *CW* 16, 1934, pp. 139–61. Quote from p. 145, ¶313.
8 Jung, C. G., "A study in the process of individuation," *The Archetypes and the Collective Unconscious*, *CW* 9i, 1959, p. 311, ¶553.
9 Ibid., p. 156 ¶339.
10 Ibid., p. 146, ¶314.
11 See R. Langs, *Psychotherapy: A Basic Text*, New York, Jason Aronson, 1977; and *The Technique of Psychoanalytic Psychotherapy* (2 volumes), New York, Jason Aronson,

1989. Langs believes the therapeutic frame to be necessarily regarded as inviolable, and that attacks on it must be confronted and rigorously addressed.

12 Mitrani, "Taking the transference," p. 1099.

13 D. W. Winnicott, "Transitional objects and transitional phenomena," *International Journal of Psychoanalysis*, 1953, vol. 34, 89–97, p. 95.

14 At the conclusion of his original article, Winnicott writes, "Pseudologia and thieving can be described in terms of an individual's unconscious urge to bridge a gap in continuity of experience in respect of a transitional object." Ibid., p. 97.

15 C. G. Jung, *The Psychology of the Transference*, *CW* 16, 1966, pp. 163–323, p. 262, ¶470.

11

IS STEALING NECESSARY FOR ECONOMIC REASONS?

Consumer Reports is a widely read, North American, monthly magazine that annually evaluates thousands of products, stores, and consumer services. Its evaluations produce ratings in various categories of interest, such as durability, quality, and price, for potential buyers. This publication often contains warnings for consumers about predatory and deceptive marketing practices that can lead to cheating, overpaying, and stealing. A 2012 issue of *Consumer Reports* lists 21 ways in which an unaware consumer could be cheated or stolen from.[1] A reader could easily get an impression that such cheating and theft are common and expectable. Further, in the wake of the Madoff scandal, in which Bernard "Bernie" Madoff stole billions through operating a Ponzi scheme, more media attention has also been given to what is called *affinity fraud*. In affinity fraud, a particular interest group of individuals—like a social club, professional organization, or religious congregation—is targeted for economic exploitation by gaining its trust and goodwill so its members will invest in complex, shady financial schemes. Such scams, in which funds are subsequently stolen from members of various groups, are estimated to run into the billions of dollars.[2] Without a doubt, cheating and stealing are endemic to our economy, but are they mere byproducts—scattered symptoms—of those who illicitly seek economic advantage, or might they instead be more essential to how our economy operates as a whole? Perhaps we need thieves in ways that are challenging to appreciate.

The myth of the Golden Fleece is partly a story about stealing a lost treasure that Jason feels entitled to take because of its relevance to his extended family—it belonged to the ram that saved Jason's cousins Phrixos and Hellé from their mad stepmother Ino. Recall, too, that the Fleece is a rare treasure imbued with many meanings. Mythically, it symbolizes glory, power, kingship, and vanity, as well as rescue, divine salvation, and an intersection of heaven and earth (symbolized by a flying ram). Economically speaking, treasure is generally defined as a limited resource with a very high price that results from scarce supply and incredible demand. Politically, treasure has caused many wars, violent conflicts, and miseries throughout human history. Treasure is inevitably related to stealing because its ownership evokes much envy and the need to protect it leads to open and covert struggles regarding power and status. The desire for treasure can produce hoarding among those who possess it, a condition that exacerbates competition and deprivation. We have seen, too, that something treasured can also result in a positive form of stealing, particularly when a valued object has to be reclaimed because it has been stolen by one's own unconscious complexes.

Rarity is a treasure's defining feature. Thus, treasure now includes, for example, certain scarce minerals necessary for modern manufacturing, relatively limited natural resources like oil, and intellectual property. The latter is seemingly guarded by patents, copyrights, and trademarks, but the annual value of intellectual property stolen from companies has recently been estimated at $300 billion in the United States.[3] A successful man in his fifties came to see me because he was feeling depressed and worried about his career. He was the co-founder of a company and had helped with certain discoveries that were being patented so the company could use them to manufacture its products. Mr. O told me a story of intrigue, deception, and ultimately loss, all arising from a situation in which his business partner successfully managed to isolate him and steal his rights to the patents. Mr. O felt blindsided because he and his partner had worked together over a period of many years, during which they realized their research could become quite profitable.

Mr. O was an articulate, highly intelligent, and well-educated man, who had been devoted to his work. Over the course of a year, as the patent applications were being prepared, legally vetted, and submitted, Mr. O was shocked to learn that his name was not included on key documents pertaining to ownership rights, although his partner's name was, as was the company's. His partner outmaneuvered him to diminish the weight of Mr. O's contributions and downgraded his standing within the company. Mr. O had trusted his partner in the role of CEO. Not until it was too late did he realize that this other man had essentially cast him into an organizational hinterland, where Mr. O was marginalized professionally and financially.

Mr. O spent much of his time in therapy lamenting that this had happened to him, grieving the loss and betrayal, and wanting desperately to understand how it had occurred. He wondered what he had missed, and soon I found myself wondering the same thing. As he told me his story, he overwhelmed me with facts about the people in the company, the legal complexities of intellectual property rights, and the bureaucracy involved in obtaining a patent. I felt that he was showing me how his mind worked, a mind that juggled so many facts and theoretical connections that it was hard to see any feelings. His ruminations conveyed a quality of someone trying to locate something that was lost, missing, or stolen. It was as if he was frantically trying to find something.

I soon felt that Mr. O, although talkative and extraverted, could not connect emotionally with others—however, he was trying to do this with me. Because his feelings were hidden in his unconscious, he struggled to relate interpersonally in a meaningful way. It seemed he could not comprehend how someone was responding emotionally to him. He was not "mind blind" along the lines of an autism spectrum disorder.[4] Rather, Mr. O communicated a vague hint that there could be more to him, but he was not going to offer access to his emotions. I began to feel that in his interpersonal communications he showed me an encrypted treasure map of where his emotional life resided, but it was up to me to decode it. I wondered if, instead of engaging in that pursuit, his friends and colleagues might not end up feeling a bit cheated in their interactions with Mr. O because his unrevealed feelings were too hard to find. I suspected they were likewise hidden—or stolen—from him and lying in his unconscious. We might speculate that there was a thief not only in Mr. O's external life, but also in his internal world.

Thieving among friends, relatives, and colleagues is certainly nothing new. Some of it can even, at times, help to dislodge obstacles in relationships and let people become more open to opportunities for righting imbalances, injustices, and one-sidedness that show up in relationships. Mr. O's example, however, illustrates a ruthless side to thieving in contemporary life when ideas are taken to assert a claim for power, status, and wealth. As Mr. O once said, "I was robbed in the boardroom, not held up in a parking lot." Mr. O's example is hardly uncommon. Many films revolve around such tales, for instance, the 2010 production *The Social Network*.[5] Stealing seems to be ubiquitous in the economic dynamic of our free market system, although aspects of modern thieving might appear more obscure because of the sophisticated technology, disputes about who owns an idea, and the financial wizardry that requires an advanced math degree.

The myth of the Golden Fleece probably emerged during the late Bronze Age—but its lessons seem as applicable to the twenty-first century when it comes to a desire to obtain treasure by any means possible. Perhaps, a contributing factor to Communism's failure as an alternative economic system was because it did not operate to create enough economically desired treasures that its citizens might have wanted to steal (although, granted, in those countries living under Communist regimes basic consumer goods frequently substituted for treasure). The free market systems that we see today in most Western societies function in a competitive way to guarantee that wealth accumulates for some and to create a demand for treasure, which appears "golden" both metaphorically and literally. The myth of the Fleece suggests that when there is treasure, there will be theft. More hypothetically, a free market might require some stealing in order to function as it does. Later in this chapter, I explore how it might be impossible to eliminate stealing as an economic activity in its own right.

Plagiarism

The word *plagiarize* derives from the Latin *plagium*, which means a kidnapping, that is, of a child or a slave.[6] This word, therefore, incorporates the notion of stealing someone else's offspring (or, in the case of a slave, historically someone who was regarded as property). Now plagiarism has come to mean the stealing of someone else's ideas in an attempt to pass it off as one's own instead. Another person's mental "offspring" is kidnapped. Plagiarism can be viewed as both positive and negative, and that it is so widespread helps us to see that pressures for achievement, public attention, and admiration can, on occasion, drive us to steal, especially when the alternative means more work, more effort, and more energy to create something of our own. The origin of the word *plagiarize* underscores that our individual creations can feel like our "babies," and when copied, we might also feel that our "baby" has been kidnapped by a thief.

Plagiarism often results from cutting corners because what is desired—like the Fleece—seems close but not attainable. The folk wisdom behind the colloquial saying "imitation is the sincerest form of flattery" refers to one motive for plagiarism since the theft is often unconsciously intended as a compliment for what someone has achieved. Plagiarism can be driven by a need for recognition that one feels is deserved but has not yet been properly bestowed. That can border on entitlement. For a plagiarist, treasure is perceived to lie in the accolades that he or she believes will be received for a certain achievement. The prevalence of plagiarism is not in dispute. *The Economist*, for example, notes one survey that reports 56 percent of students in the United States who were studying for a master's degree in business administration (MBA) admitted to cheating during the previous year.[7] In addition, *The New York Times* in 2012 highlighted a cheating scandal at Harvard University involving "nearly half of the more than 250 students" in a course on government.[8] In both reports, the students are among those we would characterize as belonging to an elite educational class in the United States, and the numbers of those cheating implies a high level of social acceptance for this behavior.

A colleague confirmed for me this dark side of stealing within academic settings. He sat on a student's dissertation committee and discovered that when he was reading this student's final work submitted for his doctoral degree, he was surprised at several paragraphs that sounded too familiar. He reread these passages many times until it dawned on him with eerie clarity that they were his own words, taken without quotation or citation from one of his own published papers. He confronted the student and brought it to the attention of the committee chair, and what followed was an attempt to remediate the dishonesty without being punitive. The student apologized, and he changed the offending sections of his dissertation to correctly attribute the stolen sections to their true author. However, my colleague was left wondering whether this student had ever understood the seriousness of what he had done.

Faking research results constitutes another form of plagiarism that steals the time, integrity, trust, and reputation of publishers, collaborators, and colleagues (as opposed to copying another person's published work directly). It is forgery—a copy of what should be the real thing. A flagrant example is the case of Diederik Stapel from Tilburg University in the Netherlands, who repeatedly disseminated "phony social psychology data."[9] In 2011, three whistleblowers reported his misconduct to the head of his department, and an investigation was launched.[10] Stapel apparently manufactured datasets for social psychology studies. He specialized in publicity-grabbing titles that popular media would latch on to, for example, "Coping with Chaos: How Disordered Contexts Promote Stereotyping and Discrimination," which appeared in *Science* but was later retracted.[11] This study purported to link garbage on the streets and other environmental debris with an associated increase in prejudicial behaviors.

Initially, Stapel cooperated with the investigation and admitted that he "failed as a scientist."[12] The investigation by his university noted that the majority of the doctoral theses that Stapel had supervised were corrupted by his inventing data to positively confirm the hypotheses that were being tested. In addition, the chair for the investigative committee stated, "We have some thirty papers in peer-reviewed journals where we are actually sure that they are fake."[13] Amazingly, during their peer review processes, none of the academic journals questioned some of the potential statistical problems that might have appeared evident in much of Stapel's work, for example, that his reported effects were often sizeable; there were few outliers in the data; and his hypotheses were usually confirmed. Ewen Callaway writes, "Journals publishing Stapel's papers did not question the omission of details about where the data came from."[14] In other words, scarcely anyone thought to check whether his subjects' identities could be verified and, further, to ask if they could be contacted for retesting. Nor did anyone apparently ask why there was not more observed variance in their responses, or inquire why Stapel was outwardly so secretive about the subjects participating in his studies. He was adept at hiding, like a thief, and covering whatever suspicions he might have aroused.

Christopher Shea writes about the institutional and social pressures many academics feel to publish eye-catching findings in order to promote their careers. Commenting on Stapel, he summarizes, "The now-suspended professor . . . served up a diet of snappy, contrarian results that reporters lapped up."[15] A desire for publicity with a wider audience might have led Stapel to design studies that he intuited would capture media attention. Shea cites another researcher who believes that the field of psychology may have become "addicted" to findings that appear to fly in the face of reason and common sense as one way to get publicity (and perhaps then funding).[16] This phenomenon of committing fraud in order to steal some limelight, therefore, takes on some of the golden glow of the Fleece, which rested in public view but was guarded by a dragon. The dragon in this case might be analogous to occupational limits that are defined and set by professional standards, hard work, and the possibility of documenting a failure instead of a success. Putting that guardian dragon to sleep usually turns out badly.

In this case, the sleeping dragon allowed academic theft that included fraud, deceiving collaborators, who were frequently students themselves, and disrupting a kind of faith in scientific truth that is a basis for sharing research findings in peer-reviewed academic journals. The part of this complicated situation that involved stealing seems outside the bounds of what we could regard as Promethean, in which something hidden is uncovered to advance consciousness. Instead, we might speculate that deception of those who evaluated Stapel academically and professionally could have been motivated by a wish for status and power, and that he struggled to integrate his limitations, whatever those were, in doing what it would take to reach these accomplishments without making up data. We might recall here that Jason was reckless in grabbing for the Fleece, through which he sought to claim a kingship and took advantage of others. To an observer, behavior like this can appear opportunistic, but in this discussion I can only offer an analogy to the myth that speaks to some aspects of thieving in academic settings. Stapel's actions, for example, might show us that a drive and ambition to be "king" or "lord of the data" were great enough to override professional ethics and standards for research.[17] The details of what I have presented here are based on secondary published reports of others about Stapel's misconduct. I cannot say for sure what motivated him and that remains something of a mystery.

A different kind of plagiarism can be seen through much of the history of art, when artists copy one another, often to great effect. Sometimes, one artist stumbles on a technique that others then imitate, leading to the genesis of a particular trend or school. If the latter continues to spread in influence, then a movement is born, and other artists begin to copy the aesthetic qualities and visual or musical characteristics that define it. This kind of plagiarism contrasts with what we have just examined in the case of academic fraud and theft because, in these circumstances, the creative drive is not only to imitate someone else's work, but also to explore new aspects of a technique and to disperse the discovery into the broader world of art and beyond. Used like this, copying and stealing another's artistic work can be viewed—at times—as more akin to what I have called Promethean stealing, in that it opens an enlightened attitude about a new perspective and transmits the relevant ideas to adherents for experimentation on their own. This is a theft in service of Promethean creativity.

An example of this positive stealing—often euphemized as "borrowing from a master"—can be seen in Édouard Manet's revolutionary painting *Luncheon on the Grass* (*Le Déjeuner sur l'Herbe*) from 1863. H. W. Janson, in a discussion about originality in his textbook on the history of art, describes how Manet used earlier work by Raphael (who likely used an even earlier work for his own drawing) to paint what was then considered a scandalous piece with two clothed men and a nude woman in the foreground of an outdoor scene (also a partially undressed woman is bathing in the background). Janson notes, "A relationship as close as this between two works of art is not as rare as one might think," and he elaborates further, "Manet did not *copy* or *represent* the Raphael composition—he merely *borrowed* its main outlines while translating the figures into modern terms."[18] In a way, this is similar to my motivations in "borrowing" from the myth of the Golden Fleece to reinterpret it for our contemporary world. Janson distinguishes a somewhat fine line between outright copying or plagiarizing and what he instead labels "borrowing." The former more clearly could be regarded as a form of theft, whereas the latter euphemizes a bit about an artist's motives.

This observation brings to mind a question, namely, what would our artistic traditions look like if artists did not steal or take from another? It is difficult for us to begin to imagine the burden this would impose on novelty and creativity. Janson notes that Manet was "indebted" to Raphael for his composition of *Luncheon on the Grass*, yet he explains this as a debt satisfied by Manet's "bringing the old composition back to life."[19] He then adds, "All works of art anywhere . . . are part of similar chains that link them to their predecessors."[20] Janson argues that this interlinking process is what establishes artistic traditions that define periods or epochs within art history. Manet's *Luncheon* was revolutionary in the world of painting because Manet provocatively claimed artistic freedom over color, composition, and brush stroke and advocated "pure painting" as fundamental to an artist's "primary reality."[21] Manet may have been copying, lifting, or borrowing the contents of Raphael's work, but his reinterpretation of it helped to launch an entirely new artistic movement called Impressionism. *The Luncheon* was rejected by the official art establishment, called the Salon, in 1863, but its very rejection led to an alternative exhibition that created a sensation within the art world.[22] Here, we glimpse an aspect of the rebellious Prometheus, who stole to enlighten, at work in Manet's taking from Raphael in order to rebel against the strictures of an encrusted art officialdom. Manet's innovation, as depicted in *The Luncheon*, therefore, copied or borrowed something old to break through a boundary and usher in something new that took painting in a different direction. James Elkins, in an alchemical exploration of painting, calls this a moment when art itself became more openly incestuous—by which he means that it took up its own medium in self-referencing ways. "It is not possible to imagine an interesting work that does not in some measure speak about itself. Paintings have routinely referred to paintings since Manet."[23] He sees this as a creative—and potentially maddening—force that is represented, in part, by the alchemical image of the hermaphrodite, through which opposites are brought together. Manet could be viewed as acting like a mythical Prometheus, who challenged a ruling order and visually lit up a way for a radical break with that hierarchy. His theft, if we allow ourselves to part from the euphemistic "borrowing," was indeed one we can be thankful for because it created many new treasures for us to admire and collectively enjoy.

Economic Evidence for Stealing and Irrational Outcomes

Of course, treasure, including art, is frequently, and perhaps usually, not collectively available and instead is hoarded and kept secret in vaults, banks, impenetrable offshore accounts, blind trusts, and obscure financial derivatives. Secrecy and treasure almost seem to go hand in hand, an observation that might even define, for example, the basis of Swiss banking. Evidence for hoarding treasure, some of which has been stolen, might be behind data that document how prevalent inequality is within market-based economies. For example, a University of California at Berkeley economist, Emmanuel Saez, has tracked where national income in the United States goes and found that the current disparities in income distribution approach levels last recorded during the 1920s. As of 2007, the top 10 percent of wage earners took home 46 percent of the nation's total salaries.[24] Further, between 1993 and 2010, over half of the gains in real income went to those in the top 1 percent.[25] Updating his most recent numbers to account for contractionary effects from the Great Recession, Saez still finds that income growth overwhelmingly went to the top 1 percent. As Steven Rattner writes in *The New York Times*,

> [t]he top 1 percent has done progressively better in each economic recovery of the past two decades. In the Clinton era expansion, 45 percent of the total income gains went to the top 1 percent; in the Bush recovery, the figure was 65 percent; now it is 93 percent.[26]

Who are the 1 percent? An article in *The Economist* poses this question and finds that their average household income in 2008 (data for the United States) was $1.2 million, of which a quarter is earned from interest, dividends, capital gains, and rents.[27] Almost 14 percent work in the financial sector, 16 percent in health care, and 8 percent in the legal profession.[28] Symbolically, the 1 percent represent something akin to an aristocracy, underscoring a point Bion made decades ago about social institutions when he wrote his seminal work about basic assumption groups, which obstruct the abilities of people to come together and work productively.[29] Bion believed that a collective fantasy about aristocratic breeding underpinned utopian ideals and satisfied a group anxiety about wanting to be led rather than working at leading ourselves. In some sense, today's focus on the 1 percent reflects Bion's assertion that as a society we, because of deep needs in our group psychology, are inclined to desire and find a kind of security in social stratification—although we may also rebel against it—because it expresses group longings and allays our associated anxieties. For better or worse, we may be somewhat conditioned at a primitive unconscious level—Bion considered many of our group emotions to operate at this level—to desire a 1 percent so our irrational hopes about an idealized future can be socially represented and embodied.

In the United States, inequality is frequently explained away and justified as an inevitable outcome of a free market that must be left relatively unfettered to permit economic growth and expansion. Whenever shadow aspects of this market-based argument are exposed and criticized, often the counterresponse is an outcry mixing platitudes about freedom, the inherent desirability of markets, and personal responsibility. That a free market approach can produce irrational outcomes, including stealing, is not something that makes its way into mainstream thinking much. For example, if the 1 percent accumulates a portion of its wealth by stealing in various ways from others, then the resulting inequality reflects a tolerance for theft as well as for its social and economic consequences. This circumstance presents a question, namely, just how much wealth would any society want its elite to accumulate? That is a question about fairness, power, and equality of outcomes and opportunities. Statistics from the Organisation for

Economic Co-operation and Development (OECD) for 2010 ranked the United States 27th out of 30 countries on a standard economic measure of inequality for wealthier countries, a number that means greater inequality is much more common in the United States than in most other rich nations.[30]

Adam Smith published his insights into the mechanisms undergirding a capitalist free market-based economy in 1776 in a work entitled *The Wealth of Nations*. Smith saw and described "an invisible hand" that guided "the private interests and passions of men" and steered them "in the direction 'which is most agreeable to the interest of the whole society.'"[31] The force behind the hand is competition, which should, therefore, result in a self-regulating market where no one hand dominates all the interactions. Our modern markets, however, are creatures with enormous hands, no longer invisible, and frequently active in colluding and distorting supply, demand, and prices. Smith did not foresee massive market manipulations that reinforce inequality, stealing, and hoarding of treasure. Competition has given way to large corporate conglomerates, banking behemoths, resource cartels, and, by necessity, various kinds of big government intervention. In the nearly two-and-a-half centuries since Smith published *The Wealth of Nations*, dimensions of scale have come to override his quainter notion of individual competition governing the state of any market in a way that could be construed as an aggregate of rational interests coming together for everyone's benefit.

If anything, the irrationality and precariousness of allegedly free markets, especially those encompassing oversized participants, appear relatively clear when we consider some of the causes of the recent banking crisis. To see this, it might help to take a short detour into some modern economic understanding that competition within free markets does not always result in optimal social benefit. A classic example of this finding is what is known as the *prisoner's dilemma*, in which two thieves are separately offered sentencing deals if one testifies against the other. If each thief pursues his own self-interest, they both end up worse off in jail time than if they had cooperated. Andrew Schotter describes this result as demonstrating "the self-defeating aspects of rational competition."[32] Thus, "the invisible hand" produces, in this case, a suboptimal overall result that is not rational from a market standpoint. Schotter explains that the prisoner's dilemma is not just an academic exercise based on game theory, but rather, as he elaborates, it relates to economic stealing in various forms that affect us all. He cites the vicissitudes of paying for a society's public goods, which can include everything from its parks, transport hubs, and roads, to its hospitals, schools, zoos, and museums. Many of these items are funded through taxes, government fees, and entrance charges. Yet it is, economically speaking, difficult to ascertain the actual cost of use for many public goods and, as a result, something called a *free rider phenomenon* occurs. As in the prisoner's dilemma, pursuit of individual self-interest can create a less desirable social outcome in which some look for a free ride (that is, steal) in order to use what others are willing to pay for. Jason exhibits many behaviors during the Argonauts' expedition that show him to be a bit of a free rider, such as repeatedly expecting others to act on his behalf and bear the costs for his mistakes.

When these irrational and distinctly paradoxical effects of free markets are not taken into consideration, then an incomplete justification for a free market system as a whole can readily overlook its many problems, such as the creation of lop-sided inequality. A simplistic way to understand inequality is that it falls largely on the shoulders of those who cannot compete. Schotter notes that reflexive devotion to a free market approach fails to account effectively for what are called "corner solutions," namely items of labor or capital for which the price is zero.[33] An example is unemployed and unskilled workers whom no one wants to hire. In such a situation, stealing is actually an economic explanation for their predicament because they have no other "rational" options for obtaining income or goods—in this case, stealing would be considered a "rational" choice. No small wonder that economics is often referred to as "the dismal science."

As an example of how these shortcomings in an unfettered free market can result in theft, consider the 2007–8 subprime mortgage debacle that has resulted in the worst recession since the Great Depression. Carmen M. Reinhart and Kenneth Rogoff note that this crisis was perhaps foreseeable because of the manic rise in real estate valuations that were fueled overwhelmingly by domestic and foreign debt.[34] Arrogance by many senior banking and government leaders accompanied declarations that "improvements in financial engineering and monetary policy had done much to tame the business cycle and limit the risk of financial contagion."[35] The real estate bubble that ensued became Fleece-like, both in its illusory glory and in its seeming to offer an attainable reality for anyone willing to take a gamble. As Reinhart and Rogoff find,

> Since 1891, when the price series [for housing] began, no housing price boom has been comparable in terms of sheer magnitude and duration to that recorded in the years culminating in the 2007 subprime mortgage fiasco. *Between 1996 and 2006 (the year prices peaked), the cumulative real price increase was about 92 percent—more than three times the 27 percent cumulative increase from 1890 to 1996!*[36]

Many of those subprime mortgages resulted, as we now know, from shady banking practices that sold them at too-good-to-be-true terms and subsequently bundled them into packages for investors who did not realize the crumbling foundation that lay beneath. We can think of this process as a collective stealing that twisted snake-like from poorer home-buyers to real estate firms to banks to investors. Many were innocent and unsuspecting in this process. Yet many were also thinking they could pull off a heist and not get caught. That is an essential Fleece comparison—like Jason, those individuals believed they could grab the money and run away with it.

Ironically, the many government bailouts of the involved banks forestalled a larger and deeper crisis, yet also implicitly rewarded many of those same banks for their fleecing of others (for instance, their customers, borrowers, and investors). Reinhart and Rogoff explain it this way:

> In the run-up to the recent crisis, in the case of rich countries one of the main this-time-is-different syndromes had to do with a belief in the invincibility of modern monetary institutions . . . Market investors, in turn, relied on the central banks to bail them out in the event of any trouble . . . Thus, markets believed, the Federal Reserve provided investors with a one-way bet.[37]

Although that certainly rings true enough as a parallel to the mythical Jason, who grabbed the Fleece in the mistaken conclusion that he had nothing at all to lose, their comment about an illusory market belief in guaranteed one-way bets also shows how pervasive an attitude toward fleecing others may be in our economic system. Reading Reinhart and Rogoff's conclusions, I suggest that the psychology behind a manic conviction that "this-time-is-different" for making easy money includes an archetype for the power and temptation of what appears available like the Golden Fleece.

The Fable of the Bees

The tale of the Golden Fleece tells us quite a lot about a generalized human tendency to steal. This propensity contributes to why our economic system tolerates theft and even creates circumstances that promote it, especially pertaining to what is widely regarded as treasure. A companion piece to the Fleece myth is *The Fable of the Bees*, a somewhat more modern interpretation of why an economy might actually require vices, such as stealing, in order to function and prosper. Written in the early eighteenth century by Bernard Mandeville, a physician and philosopher, the fable describes a hive of bees in satirical form, a hive that thrives on each member's numerous vices because the sum of all their activities creates a busy and prosperous nest.[38] When vices are eliminated, the hive deteriorates to the point of virtual collapse. E. J. Hundert, in his introduction explaining Mandeville's point of view, writes, "Contemporary society is an aggregation of self-interested individuals necessarily bound to one another neither by their shared civic commitments nor their moral rectitude, but, paradoxically, by the tenuous bonds of envy, competition and exploitation."[39] Implicit in that statement is that stealing is part and parcel of what binds us together economically and socially. Mandeville provided later eighteenth-century thinkers with "a map" of social processes and interactions that seemingly contradict one another but, as a whole, explain how societies operate. He pointed out that a ruling class might like to view itself as virtuous, unsullied, and patriotic, but this presentation is mainly to hide its own selfishness and greed.

Mandeville's metaphor of the beehive symbolized "morally unbridled economic activity."[40] He was, in many ways, an antecedent to later psychologists who would understand human behavior as instinctual. Hundert notes that Mandeville laid a "foundation of a science of socialized man" that became a topic of great interest for many Enlightenment philosophers and thinkers.[41] What happens within Mandeville's beehive? Mandeville explains that what one sees there are man's "vilest and most hateful qualities," which taken together build "the most necessary accomplishment to fit him for . . . the most flourishing societies."[42] Mandeville's opinion is that if the preachings of moral rectitude were implemented, we could no longer live in prosperity.

The main text of *The Fable* is a kind of doggerel approximately 12 pages in length. Mandeville begins it, "A Spacious Hive well stockt with Bees,/ That liv'd in Luxury and Ease" and notes "Millions endeavoring to supply/ Each other's Lust and Vanity."[43] He calls attention to the essential paradox of this hive: "All Trades and Places knew some Cheat/ No Calling was without Deceit" and further, "Thus every Part was full of Vice,/ Yet the whole Mass a Paradise;/. . . Their Crimes conspir'd to make them Great."[44] Although stealing persists in this prosperous environment, the inhabitants profess to be appalled by this state of sin and crime. Mandeville cannily describes a psychological process of projection in which "every one cry'd, *Damn the Cheats*/ And would, tho' conscious of his own,/ In others barb'rously bear none."[45]

Mandeville's beehive represents a social commentary that was breathtaking for its time, and yet, one that still commands relevance—because our free market economies today do seem to require a modicum of stealing to function as they do. Mandeville explains that the existence of stealing gives rise to entire occupations and industries, which for us today would include different kinds of insurance we might buy to protect our homes and property, alarm systems to fend off thieves, private security personnel hired by stores and the wealthy, and financial hedges against questionable investments. We might also consider in the same light the highly profitable and dangerous trade in illegal substances supported by extensive drug dealing and its affiliated underground activities. Further, the inequality that we accept as a social condition may be partly offset by an associated tolerance that theft is acceptable in certain socioeconomic circumstances (that is, stealing as a safety valve when it seems a "rational" choice). Mandeville goes, however, one step further by postulating what happens to the imaginary beehive when crime and vice are eliminated. His simple answer is that prosperity and commerce collapse, "it [the hive] deteriorates and decays . . . Fools only strive/ to make a Great an Honest Hive."[46] A wave of moral and legal enforcement thus backfires, much like what an individual would suffer in terms of depression, inhibition, and loss of vitality when under the internal influence of a punishing and constricting superego.

In a short text that perhaps business schools should make required reading, Mandeville has given us a sobering reflection about human nature. More importantly, he reminds us that stealing and cheating are necessary parts of free enterprise. From his standpoint in the early eighteenth century, this is largely because we are ruled by "various passions" that drive us to seek a path of least resistance, unless we are capable of thinking and weighing alternatives that frequently require more time and effort—more work. Perhaps, we might find Mandeville to be pessimistic about human nature. Another view would be that he is entirely too realistic. He does not see his beehive as morally bad—rather, he finds those who moralize about its lack of virtue are problematic, although he wryly takes note that they, too, depend on their work by reason of vice's prevalence. Mandeville finds that envy is a potent force that drives us "to grieve and pine at what we conceive to be a happiness in others."[47] Interestingly, he sees envy as born of unresolved grief over a felt loss at what we cannot have. For him, envy erodes how we see ourselves and contributes then to cheating and stealing from others. Although we might see other motivations behind theft, as I do, Mandeville makes a compelling argument, 300 years old, for theft's role as an essential part of our socioeconomic system:

> I never said, nor imagined, that man could not be virtuous as well in a rich and mighty kingdom, as in the most pitiful commonwealth. But I own it is my sense that no society can be raised into such a rich and mighty kingdom, or so raised, subsist in their wealth and power for any considerable time, without the vices of man.[48]

If the myth of the Golden Fleece offers us a glimpse into an archetypal layer of stealing, Mandeville's *Fable of the Bees* provides a penetrating social commentary for considering that stealing might actually be basic to what keeps much of our economic hives humming along.

Notes

1 "Scamnation! Fraud is on the rise. Protect yourself from the latest tricks," *Consumer Reports*, October 2012, pp. 22–27.
2 "Affinity fraud: Fleecing the flock," *The Economist*, January 28, 2012, pp. 63–64.
3 "Intellectual property: Can you keep a secret?" *The Economist*, March 16, 2013, p. 67.
4 F. Happé, *Autism: An Introduction to Psychological Theory*, Cambridge, MA, Harvard University Press, 1998.
5 *The Social Network,* screenplay by Aaron Sorkin, adapted from Ben Mezrich, *The Accidental Billionaires: The Founding of Facebook, A Story of Sex, Money, Genius, and Betrayal*, New York, Doubleday, 2009, directed David Fincher, Columbia Pictures, 2010.
6 *Oxford English Dictionary*, Third Edition, 2006. Online, available HTTP: <www.oed.com>.
7 "Schumpeter: A tissue of lies: A social psychologist looks at why people lie and cheat and what it means for business," *The Economist*, June 9, 2012, p. 75. The author discusses a new book by D. Ariely titled *The (Honest) Truth about Dishonesty*, in which Ariely "contends that the vast majority of people are prone to cheating." (p. 75.)
8 R. Pérez-Peña and J. Bidgood, "Harvard says 125 students may have cheated on a final exam," *The New York Times*, September 1, 2012; and R. Pérez-Peña, "Harvard students in cheating scandal say collaboration was accepted," *The New York Times*,

September 1, 2012. As the reporter notes in the second article, however, "Instructions on the final exam said, 'students may not discuss the exam with others'" (p. A16).

9 S. J. Breckler, "Faking it," *Monitor on Psychology*, September 2012, p. 56. See also J. Achenbach, "Diederik Stapel: The lying Dutchman," *The Washington Post*, November 1, 2011. Online, available HTTP: <www.washingtonpost.com/blogs/achenblog/post/diederik-stapel-the-lying-dutchman/2011/11/01/gIQA86XOdM_blog.html>.

10 T. Bartlett, "The fraud who fooled (almost) everyone," *The Chronicle of Higher Education*, November 3, 2011. Online, available HTTP: <www.chronicle.com/blogs/percolator/the-fraud-who-fooled-almost-everyone/>.

11 D. A. Stapel and S. Lindenberg, "Coping with chaos: How disordered contexts promote stereotyping and discrimination," *Science*, 2011, vol. 332, pp. 251–53. Online, available HTTP: <www.sciencemag.org/content/332/6026/251>. Seven months later, the editors printed "an expression of editorial concern" and the article was soon retracted. See B. Alberts, "Editorial expression of concern," *Science*, 2011, vol. 334, p. 760. Online, available HTTP: <www.sciencemag.org/content/334/6057/760.1>. The latter piece states "the extent of the fraud by Stapel is substantial."

12 G. Vogel, October 31, 2011, "Report: Dutch 'lord of the data' forged dozens of studies (update)," *ScienceInsider*, October 31, 2011. Online, available HTTP: <news.sciencemag.org/scienceinsider/2011/10/report-dutch-lord-of-the-data-fo.html>. This article further notes, "When Stapel did conduct actual experiments, the committee found evidence that he manipulated the results."

13 E. Callaway, "Report finds massive fraud at Dutch universities," *Nature*, November 1, 2011, vol. 479, no. 15. Online, available HTTP: <www.nature.com/news/2011/111101/full/479015a.html>.

14 Ibid.

15 C. Shea, "Fraud scandal fuels debate over practices of social psychology," *The Chronicle of Higher Education*, November 13, 2011, Online, available HTTP: <www.chronicle.com/article/As-Dutch-Research-Scandal/129746/>.

16 Ibid.

17 Vogel, "Report: Dutch 'lord of the data' forged dozens of studies."

18 H. W. Janson, *History of Art: A Survey of the Major Visual Arts from the Dawn of History to the Present Day*, Second edition, New York and Englewood Cliffs, NJ, Harry N. Abrams, Inc., and Prentice Hall, 1977, pp. 15–16. This text has been continually updated by his son Anthony, another art historian, since Janson's death in 1982.

19 Ibid., p. 17.

20 Ibid.

21 Ibid., p. 608.

22 R. Rey, *Manet*, New York, Crown Publishers, 1977, p. 54.

23 J. Elkins, *What Painting Is: How to Think about Oil Painting, Using the Language of Alchemy*, New York & London, Routledge, 2000, p. 153.

24 "Inequality: The gap widens, again," *The Economist*, March 10, 2012, pp. 40–41.

25 Ibid.

26 S. Rattner, "The rich get even richer," *The New York Times*, March 25, 2012.

27 "Income inequality: Who exactly are the 1%?," *The Economist*, January 21, 2012, pp. 31–32.

28 Ibid.

29 W. R. Bion, *Experiences in Groups*, New York, Routledge, 1961/1991.

30 Organisation for Economic Co-operation and Development, "Quality of life, income inequality and poverty, and income inequality," *OECD Factbook 2010: Economic, Environmental and Social Statistics*, OECD Publishing, doi: 10.1787/

factbook-2010-en. Online, available HTTP: <www.oecd-ilibrary.org/economics/oecd-factbook-2010_factbook-2010-en>. The OECD numbered 30 countries until 2010; more members have since joined. The relevant statistic is referred to as the *Gini coefficient*, named for its developer. It is a measure of frequencies of dispersion of various income levels. A score of 0 would translate as perfect equality in which every person has the same income. A score of 1 would indicate maximal inequality in which one person has all a nation's income. In 2010, the U.S. score was 0.38.

31 R. L. Heilbroner, *The Worldly Philosophers: The Lives, Times and Idea of the Great Economic Thinkers*, New York, Simon & Schuster, 1986, p. 54.

32 Ibid., p. 47.

33 Ibid., p. 66.

34 C. M. Reinhard and K. S. Rogoff, *This Time is Different: Eight Centuries of Financial Folly*, Princeton, Princeton University Press, 2009. The title of their book is based on an anecdote in which a trader said, "More money has been lost because of four words than at the point of a gun. Those words are 'This time is different'" (p. xxxvii).

35 Ibid., p. 199.

36 Ibid., p. 207.

37 Ibid., p. 291.

38 B. Mandeville, *The Fable of the Bees and Other Writings*, ed. E. J. Hundert, Indianapolis, IN, Hackett Publishing Company. Mandeville lived from 1670–1733 and wrote versions of the fable in 1705, 1714, and again in 1723, when it was anonymously published as social satire.

39 Ibid., "Introduction," p. x.

40 Ibid., p. xxii.

41 Ibid., p. xxxi.

42 Ibid., "The Preface," p. 19.

43 Ibid., "The Grumbling Hive," p. 23 and p. 24.

44 Ibid., p. 25 and p. 27.

45 Ibid., p. 29.

46 Ibid., p.34.

47 Ibid., p.80.

48 Ibid., p. 101.

12

OUR INTERNAL THIEVES

For Better and for Worse

Jung was much concerned with how we reconcile opposing tensions within our psyches, as he saw this shaping what becomes available for consciousness and what remains unconscious: "There is no consciousness without discrimination of opposites."[1] Jung viewed this resulting tension of opposites as giving emotional valence to our inner life. Without it, he inferred, we would have less depth, probably less conflict, but assuredly less curiosity. He termed these pairings of opposites as a form of "conjunction" within the psyche (preferring, as was his habit, the Latin *coniunctio* to any other modern words that might have denoted meaningful connection, implicit relationship, and contextual affinity). He observed that the opposites face off "either confronting one another in enmity or attracting one another in love."[2] Such basic polarity creates both confusion and opportunity because out of it new perspectives and symbols can emerge, if a psyche is willing.

Jung sometimes defined these opposites as sparking a kind of energetic conduit between consciousness and unconsciousness. For example, he writes, "There is no energy unless there is a tension of opposites; hence it is necessary to discover the opposite to the attitude of the conscious mind."[3] He saw a benefit in exploring the unconscious to fathom how an individual deals with these opposites and the problems they bring about, which include avoidance of ambiguity, a preoccupation with certainty, one-sidedness, and a lack of perspective on relationships and a person's own self:

> The conscious mind is the top, the shadow underneath, and just as high always longs for low and hot for cold, so all consciousness, perhaps without being aware of it, seeks its unconscious opposite, lacking which it is doomed to stagnation, congestion, and ossification. Life is born of the spark of opposites.[4]

As an example of how this principle can affect behaviors in paradoxical ways, we might think of a renowned moral crusader who has fallen on the sword of his or her own vices, frequently the very ones he or she rails against, or conversely, the appeal we often find in many dramatic portrayals of criminals who inexplicably show compassion and justice to someone vulnerable and weak.

Along these lines, perhaps we are all thieves in different ways, at least internally, and grapple with our own internal urges for what our thief might want us to steal or take. This observation is not at all an excuse or rationalization for actual stealing, but rather leads to a hypothesis about its universality within the psyche. In the myth of the Golden Fleece, Jason, as noted earlier (in Chapter 4), is often understood to be *amechanos*, a Greek word that, depending on context, can signify being without means or resources, incapable, and helpless. Medea, on the other hand, is considered *sophe*, which could mean, among other things, wise, clever, and crafty. In these tales, she is a fox to Jason's donkey. We can easily imagine that a character like Jason would need a character like Medea if he is to succeed at gaining what he desires. Their pairing in the myth is not accidental, suggesting certain personified opposites that operate to some extent in all of us, if we believe that myth tells us something important about the collective unconscious. Who has not, when caught in a helpless bind, at times wished for an easy fix that might cut moral, ethical, and legal corners? This psychological perspective underscores why this myth has power to fascinate us even today. Peter Green comments that we are never quite sure why the Fleece is so important in the story and that we are left to wonder what it really means.[5] Interestingly, the object of desire becomes less important to the plot arc than the actual deed of stealing it.

From a psychological standpoint, the Fleece could represent a kind of projective screen for what we wish to steal. For example, it mirrors our projected and unmet desires, gathering them into a state of being hypercharged, and then compelling us to grab what we want, even when we do not understand why we are taking it. The Fleece reflects only one side of an internal bind, and this onesidedness prevents us from containing competing opposites in our own minds. It represents an incomprehensible object full of overdetermined meanings that are mostly unconscious and, therefore, make us act without awareness. In the myth, some of these meanings include not only power, status, entitlement, birthright, wealth, and dominion, but also something sacred, which was divinely granted to rescue helpless children, a numinous gift hovering between heaven and earth. This latter connotation invokes partly why the Fleece itself seems inscrutable—it is something that symbolically transcends our projections when we are able to recognize that it is more than just a projective screen. The myth eventually alludes to this kind of evanescence, for instance, when we consider that the Fleece practically disappears from the story after it is used as a marriage bed for Jason and Medea. Ultimately, it is the stealing that matters to the plot. In the language of contemporary analytic thinking, we might hypothesize that the Fleece represents what could optimally function as an emergent object, a third thing that potentially spans opposites however they might appear, for example, within relationships as well as within an individual psyche.

When this function degrades, however, then like in the myth the Fleece is a mere psychic screen for capturing one side of an intolerable polarity. In this case, theft might appear a ready outlet for easing anxiety or emotional pain. The unbearable polarity that cannot be contained within the psyche might encompass longing and gratification—or absence and possession, foreclosure and ownership, stealing and earning, taking and offering. One need not be impulsive to admit to a temptation to act it out. It resides in all of us. Whenever we experience the pain of not having, of missing, of losing, and of lacking, something of this polarity becomes active. Our individual histories and development guide how we deal with this particular tension of opposites represented by gain and loss, as I believe the various case examples show. The clinical material addressed the great variance we find in what motivates theft. To what extent is theft shaped by episodes of deprivation and developmental trauma? By frustration at seeing our human limitations? Or by insatiable envy? And is theft sometimes helpful and positive in bringing hidden stories and buried pains up to consciousness? Behind these questions, that polarity of loss and gain lurks in the unconscious part of our minds, and the tale of the Golden Fleece offers us a lesson on how it might actually play out.

Stealing for Better

Little in the story of the Golden Fleece or Euripides's drama about Medea supports a positive type of stealing. I instead elaborated on this by referring to the myth of Prometheus stealing fire from the gods and giving it to humankind. Prometheus was not the only thieving Titan or god in Greek myth. Hermes also had a reputation for stealing. Rafael López-Pedraza writes about Hermes's misdeeds from an archetypal Jungian perspective.[6] He reminds us that Hermes was the god of commerce who showed "elements of silence, cheating and thieving."[7] He develops his ideas about Hermes based on Hesiod's *Homeric Hymn to Hermes*, a tale about Hermes stealing cattle from his brother Apollo's herd. López-Pedraza believes that this agricultural theft symbolizes psychological thieving because of the sibling relationship. He writes, "One has to be close enough to thieve psychologically, for one psyche to thieve from another."[8] He later expands this idea to include a dimension of the analytic process in which he believes thieving of the analysand from the analyst to be a promising development.

Are Hermetic stealing and Promethean stealing equivalent? The short answer is no, because López-Pedraza views Hermes as performing a reparation for his theft, whereas he sees Prometheus as being sacrilegious. Prometheus's protest and rebellion against the established divine order disqualify him, in López-Pedraza's opinion, from representing a positive type of stealing. López-Pedraza's insights into Hermetic stealing are intriguing, especially in regard to his interpretation of theft between brothers as a symbolic closeness that indicates the psychological proximity required to cross a boundary in a relationship. Nonetheless, I find Prometheus's rebelliousness against a hierarchy makes him more appealing for carrying this torch—which he did mythically—for a positive type of stealing. Not only did he bring light into humanity's darkness, but also Prometheus questioned authority in the name of creativity. Both motivations seem fitting attributes for stealing when it is necessary to circumvent an established order. Importantly, Promethean stealing challenges rigidity and closed systems that may require defiance to create new alternatives.

When a person's development is stuck or stalled, Promethean stealing can be a signal to the environment that help is desired and needed. For example, Kyle (Chapter 5) stole cosmetics as a way to help us see that his psyche could not find a pretty mother within, namely a maternal object that would not threaten his very existence. We came to find his thieving as something we could even laugh about because it became apparent that he wanted to be caught and that he liked the contact that ensued afterward. In those moments, he was able to face compassionate teachers and therapists who did not punish or overtly persecute him. In his mind, he might have, of course, felt persecuted, but his repeated stealing seemed to help in repairing considerable damage that his real mother had done to his internal world. Kyle latched on to these newer supportive figures in a dependent way and with an obvious maternal transference. His stealing showed an unconscious wish to enlist his environment in rectifying harmful parts of his internal world.

Likewise, Phoebe (Chapter 7) stole partly so she could be found out as a girl who felt emotionally deprived by a starving parent. She expressed that she felt ripped off by how her family had to deal continually with her mother's severe anorexia. For her, shoplifting became a way to show how oppressive this family system, itself an established and oppressive order, had become. Her theft from the family she babysat for was also motivated by her envy of how those children were cared for, how emotionally well supplied they seemed to her, and how she wished she could trade places with one of them.

Within the transference relationship, both Marie and Tom wanted, at times, to steal something from me. I think López-Pedraza has it right that such thieving moments can be powerful indicators of desiring to cross a line in the name of forward development, not regression. I would add that the transference relationship at these junctures becomes like the Golden Fleece, imbued with many confusing projections, inviting the patient to take something from the analyst. Indeed, within many transference relationships, a core is often found in which childhood incidents of feeling stolen from result in lingering and even aching desires about whether one can steal back what was felt to have been originally taken. For Marie (Chapter 8), some of this experience centered on the intentions of an envious mother, who seemed to have wanted to steal much of her own daughter's femininity. Her mother may have viewed Marie more as a competitor, whose advantages she sought to minimize, rather than as a daughter whose development and appeal she might promote and contribute to. Marie may have also felt, at times, that the only way to get a man's affection was by believing she had to steal it.

For Tom (Chapter 10), his boyhood experience of losing contact with his father spun off an unconscious wish to find a magical substitute. In his treatment, that created an opportunity for a projective identification onto me of an idealized paternal role, though of a kind of father who seemed to be able to provide and get what he wanted magically. Magic can sometimes appear like theft, fooling us with its trickery and taking away our common sense. "Now you see it, now you don't" could as well be a thief's motto as a magician's. Tom's father's abandonment robbed him of an experience that occurs almost naturally in most children's development. There is an early period, typically, when parents are wholeheartedly and enthusiastically idealized and believed to have special powers that a boy or girl aspires to get one day for him- or herself. This idealization stimulates a psychologically important process of internalization. Although children eventually let go of most of these idealized projections, it seems critical that an opportunity for more extensive idealization occurs because this developmental experience later comes to influence our abilities to learn emotionally and intellectually from elders, mentors, teachers, supervisors, doctors, and even psychotherapists.

Stealing for Worse

Frequently, the appearance of a wish to steal in a therapeutic relationship is a positive sign. Negative types of stealing, however, usually point to some avoidance of facing loss. Loss takes many forms, including the real losses of a relationship like in death, separation from someone dear, perceived lack of enough of a desirable quality in ourselves, absence of meaning or purpose, and sentimental longing for what cannot be. As we grow older, we also lose time, which moves in only one direction, at least until physicists can tell us otherwise.

Freud wrote a short and beautiful essay on the topic of how we experience time called "On Transience."[9] In it, he describes a walk with two companions, one of whom was a poet who could recognize but not enjoy the beauty of the day or the surrounding landscape because these "seemed to him to be shorn of its [their] worth by the transience which was its doom."[10] Freud notes two common reactions to awareness of transience—one being to despair of it, the other being to protest it. He defines transience as "scarcity value in time." After attempting in vain to convince his companions that this should only add to their appreciation of the moment, he concludes, "What spoilt their enjoyment of beauty must have been a revolt in their minds against mourning."[11] In other words, they believed the estimated pain of mourning was too much to offset any enjoyment of (that is, attachment to) what they would gain by appreciating something that would eventually pass. Freud's observation is consistent with the findings of loss aversion that I discussed in Chapter 3, for example, that we are more hedonically sensitive to the costs of losing something than to the pleasure of gaining something of equal value. (Recall the garage sale dilemma where used items might not only be priced according to economic value, but also include an irrational premium to account for personal emotional value.) Freud notes that we "cling" to lost objects even in the face of suitable replacements that are readily accessible.[12] Threat of loss or disappearance of what we already have, possess, and own would seem to drive our psyches in paradoxical and pervasive ways that operate unconsciously, automatically, and often to our detriment. This threat also speaks to what is partly at the heart of the myth of the Golden Fleece around the polarity of loss as opposed to gain.

Stealing may play a greater role in our preference for avoiding loss than is generally recognized. Losses can be real, anticipated, or imaginary. Real loss confronts us with a task of mourning whether or not we choose to take it up. Anticipated loss creates states of anxiety and vigilance about whether we are capable enough to get through what we forecast as a decrease in our resources (for example, of time, money, energy, health, relationships). Imaginary loss wreaks havoc on our minds by our repeating "what if" scenarios of supposedly missed opportunities. Transience is salient to each of these kinds of loss because it reminds us of risks to our mortality, the passage of time, and death. Stealing may on occasion help to divert our awareness of transience and the losses it implies.

Why does loss create intense emotional pain? Answers to this question probably seem self-evident. In the context of this book, losses almost always evoke an experience of having something taken away. This psychological reality is not so far from that of feeling stolen from. Chronic situations of real losses often lead to feelings of deprivation. They also usually take a traumatic toll on the psyche, as in the cases of Kyle, TJ, Sally, and Noah. Each of us has an internal thief, part of whose function it is to compensate for loss as we encounter it throughout our lives. Sometimes, this thieving aspect of our psyche might help us to grow, especially when we have experienced situations of deprivation and trauma, but, at other times, it undermines and reinforces in us an unconscious cycle of loss avoidance. Then, awareness of real, anticipated, or imagined losses is felt to threaten our psychic equilibrium too much.

An inability to mourn and accept life's transient features does not always lead to stealing. But it almost always results in some difficulty in maintaining interpersonal relationships and, consequently, a person's mental health. Stealing behaviors can resemble addictive processes with parallels in secrecy supported by hiding and lying, crossing boundaries, courting danger, and a kind of false self adaptation that attempts to deny emotional pain. One slight difference might be that addiction tends to both isolate us and unravel our grip on reality, whereas stealing entangles us with others, their affairs, and personal effects. Negative types of stealing cut deeply inside accepted interpersonal boundaries and violate tacit agreements about trust, responsibility, and mutuality. Medea reacts violently in large part because she feels Jason has betrayed these same aspects of their relationship after they have stolen the Fleece and are eventually settled in Corinth.

Problems in mourning and grieving losses figure prominently in the cases presented in this book. Sally (Chapter 1) never grieved her cruel and abusive upbringing in a chaotic family. Instead, her internal thief seemed to spoil her finding someone in the world who would not emotionally rip her off. Conversely, this character gave her license to cheat others and embezzle from the bank where she worked. Likewise, in Chapter 5, TJ's parents' incessant fighting inflicted a great deal of emotional damage on him. He came to identify strongly with a thieving part of his psyche as one way to cope with this turmoil, the kind of negative identity described in Erik Erikson's work.[13] Perhaps because his emotional losses were so overwhelming, TJ scoffed at suggestions that he might ever be sad. Instead, he behaved like a sadistic and brutal type of thief, more thug than cat burglar.

Kyle was a pilferer, whose stealing was a nonverbal communication and a projective identification about his search for a good enough mother. His internal thief sought the salvation that a different environment might offer from the traumatic one he knew. Maternal loss long pervaded his psyche, and his fascination with *Knight Rider* well into his teenage years, spoke to his attempts to symbolize this. Fortunately, he thrived within an intensive therapeutic milieu that supported his healing and provided necessary containment for a very gradual mourning to occur over many years.

Noah (Chapter 6), on the other hand, lived through profound traumas with both his abandoning father and his murderous mother. Neither ordeal was meaningfully processed nor therapeutically addressed when he was younger, which meant that he suffered for years while his internal thief grew more destructive and more powerful. This figure eventually began to steal more outlandishly from him, first undermining his academic achievements and later leading to shadowy sexual behaviors that threatened his physical health. Noah's losses were devastating, and they flooded him early with despair beyond his years. His experiences in psychotherapy helped him to grieve many of these awful events and slowly to gain some counterbalance to the frenzied piracy of his internal thief.

Phoebe's losses seemed to have accumulated as a result of years of being mothered by someone who suffered from severe anorexia and herself was starving. Phoebe was appropriately enraged by what she regarded as her mother's definition of hunger as "normal." But this anger could hotly turn into manic self-righteousness that somehow justified her shoplifting—her believing she could take whatever she felt she deserved. Phoebe struggled to mourn her recognition of not having a "normal" mother. This absence in her life became more intolerable when she entered her own adolescence, when she might have hoped for someone other than a starving mother to identify with and to rebel against. Parental impairments often constitute a kind of lost experience for many children when they begin to realize that there are what look to be better alternatives than what they have known.

Similarly, an overpowering parent can crowd a child's psychic development and impose a loss of vitality and individuality. Overpowering parents likely do not see (or agree) that they are depriving their children of anything. However, they can colonize too much psychological space in their children and steal from them liveliness, independence, and spontaneity. Antonino Ferro makes this point when he describes the many difficulties of having a parent who looms giant-like within a child's psyche.[14] A parent's oversized representation in a child's mind can impair the development of alpha function, which Bion theorizes helps us to process raw, undigested emotional elements (called beta elements) and turn them into something more useful.[15] These parents are sometimes felt by a child to be intruding into their minds and distorting their own emotional processing. Such colossal-seeming parents steal space from a child's internal house, which that child hopes to furnish on his own as he grows. Children in this situation frequently manifest extreme states of anxiety almost as if their own minds have become claustrophobic to them.

To some extent, Tom, like Phoebe, had to struggle as a young child with an experience of a psychologically disturbed parent. Because of his parents' divorce, however, the family dynamics differed considerably, especially because he initially lived with his father, who was not impaired. His subsequent dislocation to his mother's home represented a real loss of his father and became a depressing, life-shaping event for Tom. His psychotherapy helped him to distinguish and articulate his experiences of loss with each parent. With his mother, this meant, in particular, a loss of boundaries, for which she had a more compromised emotional understanding. With his father, this meant a loss of the chance to fully idealize a parent as special in all the ways that a boy—or girl—might hope and want. Unconsciously, his internal thief led Tom to question whether any trusted figure might eventually try to steal from him.

Marie also lost something precious because of an overpowering parent, who, in her case, was her mother. Marie's mother seemed to envy the potential of her lovely and intelligent daughter to rival and displace her. In Marie's early dream image of a woman with no organs in her pelvic cavity, the toll of this loss felt apparent to her and made her worry it was irreparable. Her mother seemed to steal from Marie a good enough internal feminine self-image, taking a resource that Marie could have used throughout her childhood and adolescence. Marie grieved that her mother had not offered her something hopeful instead. She missed a mother who could dote on and admire a young girl's femininity. Through exploring childhood and adolescent memories, Marie found that she was able to integrate her experiences with other girls and women in meaningful ways that compensated for some of what she felt she had lost with her own mother. In Marie's analysis, it became important that she could openly express and consider instances of feeling cheated in our relationship. At times, Marie's internal thief appeared to want to sneak into my private life, stealing my secrets and my affections for those I loved. Two sides of this identity complex showed up at various times—not only stealing as part of an envious attack, but also a positive (Promethean) type of stealing to take what she felt rightly belonged to her. In the work with Marie, Tom, Phoebe, and Kyle (whose case I mostly supervised), I often felt optimistic when I sensed their wanting to take something from their psychotherapist in this latter way because I believed it would help them grow psychologically by bringing attention to what was missed—and perhaps felt to be stolen—in the context of their developmental histories. This affirmative countertransference experience contrasts with other times when I would have reacted differently to a patient's urge to steal, for instance, when the underlying motives seemed instead to be fueled by some mix of envy, impulsivity, greed, and domination.

When we avoid facing the emotions brought up by mourning a loss, we also lose something important about knowing what goes on in both our inner world and our relationships with those we are close to. Bion wrote about an ability to know emotional truth through what he termed a "K link" that allows for a reciprocal interaction conducive to emotional learning.[16] *K* stands for *knowing*, and an example is when two people talk meaningfully and honestly about how they feel toward one another. Bion believed that when we interact openly in this way, we can learn about another person as well as about ourselves. Open interaction is more difficult to do than it sounds because so many of our daily social conventions are geared toward disguise and conformity. The reverse of such a K link would be another kind of interaction, a –K (minus K) situation, in which relationships are depleted or "denuded" and "approximate to inanimate objects."[17] We might consider that when a person refuses to mourn situations of loss, he or she is at risk of adopting a –K attitude toward relating with him- or herself and others. Bion is clear that –K is highly unfavorable for a psyche and impedes psychological development. Continuous preference for –K results in what he calls "nameless dread."[18] An example of –K is when we choose to communicate through lying during which we explicitly hide from another and by extension hide from ourselves.

Why would a theoretical construct like –K matter for a discussion about stealing? I think it adds to our understanding because most types of negative thieving—which are driven by avoidance of painful affects (that is, not the positive type of Promethean stealing)—reinforce denial of truth about some kind of experienced loss, including transience. Stealing, aside from the positive type, is, in general, an activity supporting –K that overrides a feeling of loss by substituting a stolen gain. Bion writes that –K interactions lead to internalizing objects that are empty, or as he put it, defined by "without-ness," "an internal object without an exterior," and denuded "of all good."[19] By translating Bion's abstraction about the effects of –K to stealing, we might further theorize that theft operates primarily within a world where objects (people as well as things) are taken to be simply concrete and not symbolized. Their actual meanings, if any, are so obscured as to seem unmediated and even blank. To a thief, such objects are probably devoid of any real emotional substance even after the thief takes them. In terms of Jung's work on alchemy, much of which shows how we unconsciously come to symbolize aspects of our internal world and our dreams, a –K condition would be like an alembic without any sulfur, lead, or mercury—a vacant flask without any vital interactive elements and no promise of gold.[20] In that sense, what is stolen, even if golden like the Fleece, may not be available for any psychologically transformative process until the unconscious purpose behind the theft is revealed.

Bion, speaking in a seminar close to the end of his life, remarked, "Our capacity to speak the truth dies through the lies we tell other people."[21] Lying fails regularly as a psychological solution to our life's problems because it hollows us out—especially when we try to deceive ourselves by shirking the emotional pain of our losses. Jung emphasized that we must take on our shadow in order to individuate because our shadow is a necessary part of what makes us whole. Negative types of stealing deprive us of this chance and tend, instead, to reinforce self-deception—lying to ourselves. We all live with a thieving aspect of our psyche that can be useful when we are conscious of it. However, when our internal thief unconsciously prompts us to act in ways that foreclose our abilities to accept the pains of losing what we love, want, desire, and envy, this character puts us in a relationship to ourselves and the people around us that is dominated by a lack of emotional truth (–K, in other words). More significantly, such an internal thief takes away—steals—our ability to communicate with ourselves. A fundamental paradox here is that we have to make room in our consciousness for this thief, not aim to evict him or her. If repressed or abandoned in the unconscious, our internal thief's power to influence our actions can grow. To understand stealing, we probably have to acknowledge our thieving tendencies as they live in us, and we have to attempt to give them meaning (as, for example, through Bion's K links, or alternatively, through Jung's holding onto opposites to allow for something else to emerge from this tension). Just as charity and generosity are virtues that potentially belong to any of us, the thief in all his or her guises belongs to us as well.

The Usefulness of an Internal Thief

This universal aspect of thieving has formed a cornerstone to many myths and great stories. Shakespeare used thieves to stage for us our greediness, our love of money, and our vulnerability to betraying those to whom we proclaim our loyalties. His later play *Timon of Athens* dramatizes many of these issues during an historical time when the word "use" was often associated with *usury*, which was practiced then but also socially disdained.[22] Usury refers to moneylending at exorbitant interest rates, a kind of "highway robbery" from someone typically in pressing circumstances. *Timon* appeared in the 1623 First Folio of Shakespeare's plays and was probably written between 1605 and 1610, when James I was king and spending with profligacy.[23] The play shows the travails of the main character, Timon, a wealthy citizen who is overly generous to the point of bankrupting himself. (The historical Timon lived during the fifth century BCE.) His so-called friends then become his creditors and show him no leniency after having previously taken advantage of him themselves. Thus, their "use" (and usury) contrasts with Timon's naiveté. Timon withdraws into nature and there discovers gold, which he gives in support of an outcast military captain, who subsequently besieges Athens and overruns it. Timon, meanwhile, apparently kills himself to die a misanthrope.

At first, Timon is gullible about the intentions of his entourage and blithely believes himself to be in the embrace of good fortune. When his resources are depleted, he can scarcely believe it. He rails, "How goes the world that I am thus encountered/ With clamorous demands of debt . . . Against my honor?"[24] It is as if he let himself be stolen from by repressing the good sense that an internal thief might have represented by warning him against what comes from a reckless generosity. Timon's steward instead represents this devalued sensibility and tries in vain to persuade Timon to see the truth about how his followers have used him: "Who would not wish to be from wealth exempt/ Since riches point to misery and contempt?"[25] I think the steward symbolizes, here in projected form, a valuable aspect of an internal thief who can help us to be mindful of the risks of interpersonal motivations that center on greed, duplicity, and falseness.

Unfortunately, Timon suffers complete despair at humanity and only bitterly recognizes that thieving is part of our condition. When he encounters a band of thieves who want some of his newly discovered gold, Timon retorts, "Yet thanks I must con/ That you are thieves professed, that you work not/ In holier shapes, for there is boundless theft/ In limited professions."[26] Timon condemns humankind for its own thieving, but he cannot see his own unconscious role that enabled this activity in those close to him. He presents as an unsympathetic victim, professing to the end that his naiveté excuses him from knowing about interpersonal underhandedness and the shadow in human nature. In this context, we might consider that part of the function of an internal thief is to alert us to the hazards of our own gullibility.

In a fit filled with irony, Timon protests that thieving is everywhere, even in nature: "I'll example with thievery./ The sun's a thief and with great attraction robs the sea," and after indicting the moon, the sea, and the earth, he concludes, "Each thing's a thief."[27] His social withdrawal, hate of humankind, and suicide thus show his inability to come to terms with what essentially is true for him too—that in him is a thief.

The character of Timon offers a startling example of what can happen to us through blanket repression of our internal thief: we can get duped into foolish choices, can engage in masochistic self-negation, and, ultimately, can fall into a state of ingratitude and hate. Consciousness about what our internal thief has to offer could counter any of those outcomes by providing us with some of the thief's resourcefulness: a good dose of shrewd cleverness, a healthy respect for selfishness, and an appreciation that thieving is everywhere—even part of nature as Timon complains. This is not to say that our internal thief should give any of us permission to steal, but rather that this figure can protect us from being taken advantage of and being stolen from because it shows us how easily this could happen to anyone. And how easily we could also do the same things ourselves.

As counterintuitive as this might sound, I believe our internal thief has a place in safeguarding our capacity for gratitude. Timon ends up in a loathsome state of ingratitude because he disowned his internal thief, saw only an infantile possibility of abundance—good breasts flowing with sweet milk—and unwisely clung to a denial of greediness, hunger, envy, and loss of resources. Klein believed that gratitude helps us to resolve many of the demands of envy. Segal, discussing Klein's theory of envy, writes, "The ideal breast, introjected with love, gratification and gratitude, becomes part of the ego, the ego is more full of goodness itself."[28] When, as very young children, we internalize idealized parental objects, their goodness comes to be felt inside us as a source of our own goodness. As a result, we obtain comfort in being thankful for what we have and, seeing that, more able to tolerate what we do not have. A capacity to experience gratitude later in development tames much of the primitive wildness of envy for what we want, and because we do not just internalize an ideal breast but also its negative companion, we need this. Timon, not perceiving these limits, allows himself to be fed upon by envious followers. If the devalued sensibility of his steward had been something Timon could listen to, then Timon might have been able to acknowledge the existence of his own internal thief (that is, as part of himself). On the contrary, the steward represents this split off and projected aspect of Timon.

Ingratitude surely results from many factors. But when it arises from situations in which we might well end up feeling ripped off, cheated, and stolen from, then an internal thief could keep us on our toes and conscious of what happens when people steal. Part of this recognition rests on seeing that we could do the same. An internal thief can, in a healthy way, prevent us from falling prey to other thieves we might encounter, and he or she can also help us to avoid painful thefts that could usher us into a state of ingratitude characterized by depletion and despair.

I have been discussing this figure of the internal thief as if he or she resides somewhat personified with our psyche. That is a bit of a conceptual device because truly we cannot know exactly how such a concept is shaped in the unconscious. I suggest as a further explanation that our internal thief is more like an emergent unconscious tendency that eventually takes some form based on familial (that is, maternal, paternal, sibling, and so on) identifications, as I hope many of the examples throughout this book have illustrated. How families navigate situations of deprivation, power differentials, entitlement, envy, and adolescent escapades of crossing boundaries—all of these can create moments when thieving might be acted out and become a developmental event for something indelible and potent to take hold within our psyche. Whatever personal identifications we might develop around stealing are, I would add, further influenced through an archetypal layer of the unconscious. Exploration of the myth of the Golden Fleece shows how this part of the psyche, the collective unconscious, expresses many facets of stealing. The universality of stealing throughout human history and across cultures attests to this archetypal underpinning.

I have spoken of our internal thief, in part, to conceptualize an intersection of an archetypal process with our internal object relations that arise from our individual developmental histories. This approach is intended to help us understand what happens when our thieving impulses gain the upper hand in us. How do we get something intensely desired—treasured—that does not belong to us? How do we gain back what we've once lost? How might we obtain what is beyond our means? As long as these and similar questions about possession, title, and ownership remain central to human exchange, stealing will continue to be both a material fact and a piece of psychic reality.

Notes

1 C. G. Jung, "Psychological aspects of the mother archetype," *The Archetypes and the Collective Unconscious*, *CW* 9i, 1954, p. 96, ¶178.
2 C. G. Jung, *Mysterium coniunctionis*, *CW* 14, 1954/1963, p. 3, ¶1.
3 C. G. Jung, 1953, "On the psychology of the unconscious," *Two Essays on Analytical Psychology*, *CW* 7, 1953, p. 53, ¶78.
4 Ibid., p. 54, ¶78.
5 P. Green, *The Argonautika: The Story of Jason and the Quest for the Golden Fleece (Apollonios Rhodios)*, Berkeley, CA, University of California Press, 1997, p. 40.
6 R. López-Pedraza, *Hermes and His Children*, Einsiedeln, Switzerland, Daimon Verlag, 2010.
7 Ibid., p. 14.
8 Ibid., p. 58.
9 S. Freud, "On transience," SE 14, 1915, 303–7.
10 Ibid., p. 305.
11 Ibid., pp. 305–6.
12 Ibid., pp. 306–7.
13 Erik H. Erikson, 1963, *Childhood and Society*, New York, W.W. Norton, 1963; and *Identity and the Life Cycle*, New York, W.W. Norton, 1980.
14 Antonino Ferro, *The Bi-Personal Field*, London, Routledge, 1999.
15 W. R. Bion, 1962, *Learning from Experience*, Oxford, UK, Jason Aronson, 1962.
16 Ibid. See pp. 89–94.
17 Ibid., p. 90.
18 Ibid., p. 96.
19 Ibid., p. 97.
20 C. G. Jung, *Psychology and Alchemy*, *CW* 12, 1953, *Alchemical Studies*, *CW* 13, and *Mysterium coniunctionis*, *CW* 14, 1963.
21 W. R. Bion, *The Italian Seminars*, trans. P. Slotkin, London, Karnac Books, 2005, p. 98.
22 C. Kahn, "Timon of Athens: A modern perspective," in B. A. Mowat and P. Werstine (eds.), *Timon of Athens, Folger Shakespeare Library*, New York, Washington Square Press, 1987/2001, pp. 217–28.
23 Ibid., p. 222.
24 W. Shakespeare, *Timon of Athens, Folger Shakespeare Library*, eds B. A. Mowat and P. Werstine, New York, Washington Square Press, 1987/2001, p. 57, Act 2, Scene 2, lines 47–50.
25 Ibid., p. 119, Act 4, Scene 2, lines 36–79.
26 Ibid., p. 151, Act 4, Scene 3, lines 477–80.
27 Ibid., p. 153, Act 4, Scene 3, lines 488–95.
28 H. Segal, *Introduction to the Work of Melanie Klein*, New York, Basic Books, 1964, p. 52.

INDEX

For Product Safety Concerns and Information please contact our EU representative GPSR@taylorandfrancis.com
Taylor & Francis Verlag GmbH, Kaufingerstraße 24, 80331 München, Germany

www.ingramcontent.com/pod-product-compliance
Lightning Source LLC
LaVergne TN
LVHW021128300926
849160LV00010B/916
9780415830898